GOD, ETERNITY, AND TIME

'God is eternal' is a standard belief of all theistic religions. But what does it mean? If, on the one hand, 'eternal' means timeless, how can God hear the prayers of the faithful at some point of time? And how can a timeless God act in order to answer the prayers? If God knows what I will do tomorrow from all eternity, how can I be free to choose what to do? If, on the other hand, 'eternal' means everlasting, does that not jeopardize divine majesty? How can everlastingness be reconciled with the traditional doctrines of divine simplicity and perfection?

An outstanding group of American, UK, German, Austrian, and Swiss philosophers and theologians discusses the problem of God's relation to time. Their contributions range from analyzing and defending classical conceptions of eternity (Boethius's and Aquinas's) to vindicating everlastingness accounts, and from the foreknowledge problem to Einstein's Special Theory of Relativity.

This book tackles philosophical questions that are of utmost importance for Systematic Theology. Its highest aim is to deepen our understanding of religious faith by surveying its relations to one of the most fundamental aspects of reality: time.

God, Eternity, and Time

Edited by

CHRISTIAN TAPP
Ruhr-Universität Bochum, Bochum, Germany

and

EDMUND RUNGGALDIER
Universität Innsbruck, Innsbruck, Austria

ASHGATE

Published by
Ashgate Publishing Limited
Wye Court East
Union Road
Farnham
Surrey, GU9 7PT
England

Ashgate Publishing Company
Suite 420
101 Cherry Street
Burlington
VT 05401-4405
USA

www.ashgate.com

British Library Cataloguing in Publication Data
God, eternity and time.
　　1. God (Christianity) – Eternity. 2. Time – Religious aspects – Christianity.
　　I. Tapp, Christian. II. Runggaldier, Edmund.
　　231.7–dc22

Library of Congress Cataloging-in-Publication Data
God, eternity, and time / Christian Tapp and Edmund Runggaldier.
　　　　p. cm.
　　Includes bibliographical references and index.
　　ISBN 978-1-4094-2391-1 (hardcover : alk. paper) – ISBN 978-1-4094-2392-8
(ebook) 1. Time—Religious aspects—Christianity. 2. God
(Christianity)—Eternity.
I. Tapp, Christian. II. Runggaldier, Edmund.
　　BT78.G58 2010
　　231'.4–dc22

2010040803

ISBN 9781409423911 (hbk)
ISBN 9781409423928 (ebk)

Printed and bound in Great Britain by
TJ International Ltd, Padstow, Cornwall.

Contents

Part IV. In Defence of Divine Temporalism, or: In Debate With Science

Notes on the Contributors

Reinhold **Bernhardt**, born 1957, earned a doctorate from the Theological Faculty at Heidelberg University in 1989 and was director of studies at the Oecumenical Institute and head of the hall of residence (*Studentenwohnheim*) from 1991 to 1996. In 1996–1998 he earned his postdoctoral qualification (*Habilitation*) from Heidelberg University as a fellow of the *Deutsche Forschungsgemeinschaft* (German Research Foundation). He spent the autumn of 1997 as a visiting lecturer at Vanderbilt University in Nashville, Tennessee. He served as a protestant minister, and University lecturer. Since 2001 he has been full professor of Systematic Theology at Basel University, Switzerland. In 2004 he became editor of the *Theologische Zeitschrift*.

William Lane **Craig** is Research Professor of Philosophy at Talbot School of Theology in La Mirada, California. Born in 1949, Craig pursued his undergraduate studies at Wheaton College (B.A. 1971) and graduate studies at Trinity Evangelical Divinity School (M.A. 1974; M.A. 1975), the University of Birmingham (England) (Ph.D. 1977), and the University of Munich (Germany) (D. Theol. 1984). From 1980 to 1986 he taught Philosophy of Religion at Trinity. In 1987 Craig moved to Brussels, Belgium, where he pursued research at the University of Louvain until assuming his position at Talbot School of Theology in 1994.

Christoph **Jäger** did graduate work at Münster, Hamburg, and Oxford. He has been an Assistant Professor at Leipzig University (1994–2003), a Visiting Assistant Professor at Georgetown University, Washington (2001), and the James Collins Visiting Professor at Saint Louis University (2007). Since 2005 he has been Lecturer in Philosophy at Aberdeen University (currently on leave). Christoph Jäger was awarded a Heisenberg Research Fellowship by the *Deutsche Forschungsgemeinschaft* (German Research Foundation), and in 2008 he took up the position of University Professor (fixed term) at the Department of Philosophy in the Theological Faculty at Innsbruck University. His areas of specialization are: epistemology, metaphysics, philosophy of religion, and philosophy of mind (self-knowledge, emotions).

Hans **Kraml**, born 1950, studied philosophy and theology in Munich and Innsbruck. In his dissertation he applied methods from the philosophy of language to the talk about God. Since his *Habilitation* he is a well-known expert in medieval philosophy and theology. His areas of interest comprise: philosophy of language, theory of action and culture, edition of medieval philosophical and theological texts. Since 1989 he has been *Akademischer Oberrat* (Senior Researcher equivalent) at the Institute for Christian Philosophy and has taught philosophy at both, the Catholic Theology and the Humanities Department of Innsbruck University (Austria).

Alan G. **Padgett** is a United Methodist minister, philosopher and theologian currently serving as Professor of Systematic Theology at Luther Seminary in Saint Paul, Minnesota (USA). He studied history and social science at Vanguard University in Southern California (B.A. 1977), theology at Drew University (M.Div. 1981), and philosophy and theology at Oxford University (D.Phil. 1990). Formerly he was professor of theology and philosophy of science at Azusa Pacific University in California (1992–2001). His work and research interest moves between theology and biblical studies, philosophy, and the theology-and-science dialog.

Robert **Pasnau** works mainly in the areas of mind and knowledge. His research has run from the Presocratics all the way to contemporary thought, but at present is focused mainly on the late scholastic and early modern era. Pasnau is editor of the *Hackett Aquinas*, and the *Cambridge History of Medieval Philosophy* (2010). An earlier book, *Thomas Aquinas on Human Nature*, won the APA Book Prize in 2005. Pasnau is professor of philosophy at the University of Colorado at Boulder (USA).

Edmund **Runggaldier**, SJ, studied philosophy at the Jesuit Faculty in Pullach, near Munich (Germany, 1968–1970), and Theology at Innsbruck University (Austria, 1970–1973). In 1977 he received his Ph.D. from Oxford University, his thesis having been supervised by Alfred J. Ayer. He started his career the same year as a *Universitätsassistent* at Innsbruck University's Institute for Christian Philosophy, where he has been professor since his *Habilitation* in 1983. He was a Visiting Scholar at Notre Dame and Loyola University, Chicago, USA. From 2000 to 2006 he was President of the Austrian Ludwig Wittgenstein Society and from 2003 to 2007 *Professore titolare di ontologia analitica* at the *Università Cattolica di Milano* (Italy). From 2007 to 2009 he held the Romano Guardini Chair at the Protestant Theological Faculty at Humboldt Universität Berlin (Germany).

Thomas **Schärtl**, born 1969, did his graduate studies in Regensburg and Munich, where he earned a degree in Catholic Theology and an M.A. in Philosophy, both with honors. He started his career as a research assistant (*Wissenschaftlicher Mitarbeiter*) in Regensburg and Paderborn while he earned a doctorate in Catholic Theology at Tübingen University. From 2003 to 2006 he worked as a research assistant and teaching fellow at Münster University. In 2007 he got his *Habilitation* from the Jesuit School of Philosophy in Munich. From 2006 to 2009 he was Assistant Professor of Systematic Theology at the School of Theology and Religious Studies at the Catholic University of America in Washington, D.C. In 2009 he became tenured Professor of Philosophy at the Catholic Theology Department of Augsburg University.

Eleonore **Stump** earned a B.A. from Grinnell College (Classical Languages), in 1969 and graduated with an M.A. from Harvard University (Biblical Studies,

New Testament) in 1971 and an M.A. from Cornell University (Medieval Studies, Medieval Philosophy) in 1973. In 1975 she received her Ph.D. from Cornell University (Medieval Studies, Medieval Philosophy). She began her academic career as a teaching assistant in 1972 at Cornell University. From 1974 to 1975 she was an instructor at Oberlin College and Cornell College. In 1978–80 she worked as an Assistant Professor at Virginia Polytechnic Institute & State University, where she also became an Associate Professor from 1980 to 1984 and a Professor from 1984 to 1991. During 1988–89 she was also a Visiting Fellow at the University of Notre Dame, where she also became Professor (1991–92). Since 1992 she has held the Robert J. Henle Chair of Philosophy at Saint Louis University. She is past President of the American Philosophical Association (Central Division), past President of the Society of Christian Philosophers, and past President of the American Catholic Philosophical Association. Her areas of specialization include medieval philosophy, the philosophy of religion, and metaphysics.

Christian **Tapp**, born 1975, studied catholic theology, philosophy, and mathematics in Bonn, Münster, Freiburg, and Munich. He graduated from Münster University as a *Diplom-Mathematiker* (M.Sc. in mathematics equivalent 1999) and *Lizentiat der Theologie* (S.T.L./M.Div. equivalent 2002). He earned two doctoral degrees from Munich University, one in the history of science (Dr. rer. nat. 2004) and one in philosophy (Dr. phil. 2007). He was a *Wissenschaftlicher Mitarbeiter* at Munich and Göttingen, and a postdoctoral research fellow at CMU Pittsburgh and at the Institute for Christian Philosophy of Innsbruck University (Austria). Since August 2008 he has been *Juniorprofessor* (assistant professor equivalent) for Interdisciplinary Questions of Philosophy and Theology, and head of the research group "Infinitas Dei" (Emmy Noether Program of the DFG) at the Faculty for Catholic Theology of Bochum University (Germany). In 2009 he became a member of the *Junges Kolleg* of the *Nordrhein-Westfälische Akademie der Wissenschaften*.

Linda **Zagzebski** earned a B.A. in Philosophy from Stanford University in 1968 and graduated with an M.A. in Philosophy from the University of California, Berkeley, in 1969. In 1979 she received her Ph.D. from the University of California, Los Angeles. She started her career at Loyola Marymount University in Los Angeles where she taught for 20 years and chaired the department from 1996–1999. Since 1999 she has held the Kingfisher College Chair of the Philosophy of Religion and Ethics at the University of Oklahoma and has been appointed George Lynn Cross Research Professor at that institution. She is past President of the American Catholic Philosophical Association and is past President of the Society of Christian Philosophers. She has received grants or fellowships from the National Endowment for the Humanities, the Templeton Foundation, the Pew Scholars Program, and the Center for Philosophy of Religion at Notre Dame.

Introduction

Is God in time? If he is, how can he be a perfect being that has created time? If he is not, how can he relate to a temporal creation? These seem highly theoretical questions, of interest only to a small group of philosophers of religion. But in fact, they are closely related to topics that feature widely in theology, metaphysics, and anthropology. Can a timeless God understand our prayers, can he be compassionate with his suffering creatures, can he act in any way in time, and can he be present to creatures – as the biblical image of God has it? Can the knowledge of an infallible, omniscient being change over time? If not, would not the existence of an infallible, omniscient, temporal being preclude human freedom? If God knows now that I shall do *p* tomorrow, am I really free not to do *p* tomorrow?

This volume presents contributions from scholars of world-wide reputation who tackle various aspects of these complex questions. The contributions have been presented and intensely discussed during a conference on *God, Eternity, and Time* held in Berlin September 28–30, 2008.

The **First Part** of this book contains three papers devoted to the analysis and defence of a classical conception of divine timelessness. In his paper, *On Existing All at Once* (pp. 11ff.), Robert Pasnau argues that with respect to traditional conceptions of eternity, one should distinguish carefully between two aspects of timelessness: being "outside of time" (atemporality) and having no temporal parts ('holochronicity', Pasnau's neologism). Atemporality implies holochronicity (what is outside of time cannot have temporal parts), while it is not clear that holochronicity implies atemporality. Pasnau then considers Boethius' traditional definition of eternity as *interminabilis vitae tota simul et perfecta possessio* (the complete possession all at once of illimitable life). Pasnau takes it for granted that eternity requires holochronicity (which seems to be a perfection), and he asks whether it also requires atemporality. According to Pasnau, Boethius' statement that God is not in time is open to other interpretations than the atemporality of God. If it is understood in the sense of holochronicity, it denies the temporal locatability of changing, merechronic (that is, non-holochronic) entities. This view was, Pasnau points out, evident to Anselm of Canterbury who advocates the thesis that God is in time, but in a holochronic sort of way that makes God immune to temporal change. Pasnau argues that, given that holochronic but temporal existence is possible, this would be a mode of existence much more likely to be a perfection than is holochronicity possessed in virtue of atemporal existence. Moreover, he shows that the contemporary debate about 3- vs. 4-dimensionalism has a striking parallel in medieval times. When medieval philosophers and theologians distinguished between successive and permanent entities, they did not necessarily mean that God is the only permanent entity while all of creation is successive (which would have approximated modern 4-dimensionalism). Instead, for instance, Nicole Oresme proposed that creatures are not merechronic *simpliciter*, but merechronic *in a certain respect*: a temporal being's life has successive parts while its essence remains permanent during the succession of the events of its life. Pasnau draws an interesting parallel between the medieval distinction of existence and essence and the modern distinction between perduring through time and enduring (in the sense of a thing's existing wholly at each moment of its existence). Pasnau advocates an Oresme-inspired view that 'the mode of existence manifested by divine eternity is simply the perfect instantiation of a phenomenon displayed by ordinary substances all around us'.

For ELEONORE STUMP it is beyond dispute that timelessness is a divine perfection. In her paper, *Eternity, Simplicity, and Presence* (pp. 29ff.), she examines arguments for the thesis that the classical doctrines of eternity and simplicity preclude God from being present to human beings and from being known in the ways biblical scriptures presuppose. Those arguments have led some philosophers and theologians to reject the classical doctrines in favour of what they take to be a biblical view. Stump wants to show that this rejection is groundless. To this end, she analyzes what it means for persons to be present to one another. Then she shows that such presence is not ruled out by classical conceptions of eternity like that of Thomas Aquinas. In accord with Aquinas, she rejects arguments based on the principle that to be present to temporal beings requires being temporal oneself. Stump's main reason for rejecting this principle is that the generalization of it (presence generally presupposes a shared mode of being) is completely implausible, even though the affirmation of the generalization seems to be the only reason for accepting the principle with respect to time.

As for the unknowability of God as allegedly implied by the doctrine of divine simplicity, Stump presents several reasons for doubting such an implication. She holds Aquinas to be correct in saying that we cannot know what God is. The impossibility of knowing the *quid est* (a technical term of medieval logic) of God does not rule out every form of positive knowledge about God, for even Aquinas, when explaining divine simplicity in negative terms, relies on several positive claims about God.

If, contrary to her reasoning, divine simplicity did make propositional knowledge of God impossible, then there would still be, Stump says, another kind of knowledge whereby God *could* be known by human beings: the knowledge of persons. While the sentence 'Aquinas knew that God exists' expresses *knowledge that*, the sentence 'Aquinas knew God' expresses *knowledge of persons*. According to Stump's account of knowledge, these two sentences are neither equivalent nor can the second be reduced to the first. Knowledge of persons, Stump says, is a prerequisite for shared attention and, thereby, a precondition for the presence of one person to another. Hence, it is presupposed in biblical stories about God's presence to human beings, but it is in no way affected by divine simplicity. Thus, Stump arrives at her central thesis that the doctrines of divine eternity and simplicity do not imply that God can be neither present to nor known by human beings in the way the biblical stories presume.

THOMAS SCHÄRTL presents an overtly theological argument for divine timelessness in his paper *Why we Need God's Eternity* (pp. 47ff.). Most systematic theologians today are, according to Schärtl, in favour of a temporal conception of God, for eternity as timelessness seems to be incompatible with the interactiveness of the Christian God. Schärtl follows Robert Jenson in his diagnosis that there is also a deeper Christological problem at issue: the intimate relation between Jesus Christ, a temporal person living in Palestine some 2000 years ago, and the *Logos* or Son in the sense of the second person of the Trinity. If God is a non-temporal entity, how can such an identification be possible?

Jenson drew the conclusion that we must conceive of the Trinitarian God in a radically temporal way. He tied the Holy Spirit to the future and read Karl Rahner's famous axiom, that the 'economic' Trinity is the 'immanent' Trinity, as an identity claim. But then, Schärtl complains, we face a modal problem, since the Father is necessarily the Father, but the *Logos* is not necessarily the Word Incarnate, Jesus Christ. Furthermore, Jenson's account leads to paradox, for it implies that Jesus Christ had once been a future entity for a God whose second person is identical to Jesus Christ. Jenson can solve this problem only by what Schärtl calls 'futurizing' God, making him a future entity. But then is God still a 'temporal' God? Can he be said to be present at any moment of history at all?

Schärtl tries to follow Jenson's incentive to focus on the "Christological frame of reference" while avoiding such *aporias*. He thinks the only way to keep the immediate reference of the Trinitarian *Logos* to Jesus Christ in a stable way is to hold onto a strong concept of co-presence between God and Jesus Christ. This is possible only, Schärtl argues, by employing a concept like Stump and Kretzman's ET-simultaneity (a concept of simultaneity according to which temporally separated events can both be simultaneous to something eternal) and, in consequence, by holding onto the classical doctrine of an eternal God.

Schärtl finds his conclusion especially pressing in case temporal presentism (the thesis that something temporally exists if and only if it is temporally present) is right in that the predicate 'exists' can only be truthfully attributed to present entities. In this case, the possibility of referring to past events may require a mind which is aware of them. This "job" could only be done by an eternal entity which can be termed 'super-present', that is, co-present with all past and future events in the sense of ET-simultaneity. As a result, for Schärtl, the possibility of temporal presentism presses us towards accepting the traditional concept of divine timelessness. This is especially remarkable, as many philosophers have argued that temporal presentism is incompatible with the conception of an atemporal God.

While the First Part of this book is devoted to divine timelessness as conceived by its defenders, the **Second Part** supplements it with two papers devoted to the relation of divine omniscience and human freedom. Both papers show that this important topic in the philosophy of religion is intimately connected with the question of Divine timelessness.

In *Eternity and Fatalism* (pp. 65ff.), LINDA ZAGZEBSKI examines three kinds of fatalist argument – logical, theological, and causal – and the attempt to escape the dilemma of theological fatalism by appeal to divine timelessness. A fatalist argument is one to the effect that we have no control over future events, and therefore, 'since the past used to be future', over any events whatsoever. Zagzebski finds that all fatalist arguments have certain features in common (like the use of the Transfer of Lack of Control Principle, which transfers having no control over the past to having no control over the future). Zagzebski's primary interest in her paper is in theological fatalism, as sharply distinguished from logical fatalism. Both forms of fatalism argue that we have no control over the future. Logical fatalism says that this is so because the truth values of propositions cannot change. Theological fatalism reaches the same conclusion via the infallibility of God's past beliefs about the future.

Theological fatalism seems to be resolvable by assuming divine timelessness, in that God does not know propositions at certain times and therefore *a fortiori* not in the past. Zagzebski argues that the timelessness move can survive recent objections that do not clearly distinguish logical and theological fatalism, but it falls prey to a parallel fatalist dilemma that does not make use of temporal relations as the standard arguments do. In the end, her conclusion is that although there may be many reasons for Christian philosophers to adhere to divine timelessness, finding a solution to fatalism is not one of them. The crucial point of her argument is that timeless eternity may be outside our control just as the past is. If this is true, one could formulate a dilemma similar to theological fatalism. And although this dilemma presumes the 'necessity of eternity' (its being outside our control), which has a weaker hold in our intuitions than the necessity of the past, the dilemma is worse than theological fatalism in that the 'fall-back position' of qualifying divine omniscience in order to "save" human free will is of no help.

In his *Molina on Foreknowledge and Transfer of Necessities* (pp. 81ff.), CHRISTOPH JÄGER discusses one of Luis de Molina's (attempted) refutations of the view that divine omniscience and human freedom are incompatible. Theological incompatibilists essentially rely on a certain modal principle, but this principle, Molina argues, is false. Whether this verdict is correct depends on what exactly the principle is. In Jäger's reconstruction, it has the general structure: $Np \land \Box(p \rightarrow q) \vdash Nq$, where $\Box$ stands for metaphysical necessity while there are several candidates for N. N cannot reasonably be taken as logical or metaphysical necessity, Jäger argues, for then it could not be applied to the argument Molina wishes to refute (for instance, Molina takes p as the metaphysically contingent proposition 'God knows eternally that Peter will deny Christ the night before crucifixion'). Nor can N be taken as 'accidental necessity', i. e., as a kind of necessity that pertains to states of affairs that are already past (a reading suggested by Alfred Freddoso). For then, Jäger says, the principle would be true. Given Molina's great logical sophistication, an interpretation in terms of accidental necessity would thus be rather unconvincing. Moreover, Jäger argues, such an interpretation would be in strong tension with the general Molinist conception of God as an extratemporal being.

Jäger concludes that N should be taken as what he calls 'causal impact (= CI-) necessity', in the sense that a state of affairs p is 'CI-necessary' for S at t iff S is not able at t to 'contribute causally to something that constitutes, or grounds, a necessary or sufficient condition for p'. As an agent performs an action freely only if it is not CI-necessary for him, this reading provides the most charitable reconstruction of the argument that divine omniscience is incompatible with human free will – the argument Molina sets out to refute. Jäger presents two versions of such an argument, one regarding God's 'free knowledge' (which He can have only postvolitionally, i. e., after having decided to actualize a certain possible world) and one regarding God's 'middle knowledge' (a hypothetical kind of knowledge which He is supposed to have (logically) independent of any creative act). However, Molina can rightly reject both versions of the argument, says Jäger. For both versions rely on the aforementioned closure or transfer principle regarding CI-necessity. But, according to Jäger, CI-necessity is indeed not closed under entailment, which is shown by counterexamples in which some state of affairs is causally overdetermined. Jäger concludes his article by drawing a parallel between the closure of accidental, but not CI-necessity, under metaphysically necessary implication on the one hand, and the closure of knowledge, but not belief, under known entailment on the other hand.

Most of the authors in the First Part of this book argue strongly in favour of divine timelessness. The **Third Part** differs in this regard. It consists of three papers that deal to a lesser or greater extent with the question of a "third way" besides purely temporal and purely atemporal accounts of God.

In the first paper of this part, CHRISTIAN TAPP examines the relationship between the concepts of *Eternity and Infinity* (pp. 99ff.). He distinguishes three senses of infinity (quantitative, comparative, metaphysical) and shows in which sense sempiternalism (the thesis that God is everlasting and not timeless) makes use of quantitative infinity. Then he discusses the comparative use of infinity in the traditional doctrine of God when God is called 'infinitely good' or 'infinitely powerful'. He raises some doubts about whether infinity is needed for the purposes of the threefold traditional way of enunciating divine predicates by *via positiva, negativa et eminentiae*. In order to clarify the third, metaphysical, concept of infinity, he examines Thomas Aquinas's doctrine of divine infinity and divine eternity in some detail. He shows that sometimes Aquinas talks about 'eternity' in the sense of sempiternalism, while at the core of his doctrine of God, eternity is used in the Boethian sense of the complete and perfect possession of illimitable life.

Although Tapp stresses the differences of a quantitative concept of infinity as used in mathematics and the metaphysical concepts, he defends an analogy between mathematical and metaphysical infinity: in mathematics, a set is infinite iff it is equivalent to a proper subset; in the traditional doctrine of God, God is the only entity whose essence coincides with its existence. He concludes his paper with a section which he himself characterizes as 'a little experimental in character'. In this section he critically examines the widely held position that God could either be temporal or timeless but not both. Tapp, however, thinks that 'before' and 'after' refer to an ordering relation which could, for instance, be time extended by an "infinitely distant" point. By this move, motivated by Christian Eschatology, he also tries to make sense of a statement by Boethius that most contemporary philosophers and theologians think is senseless, namely, that the Trinitarian God existed with His interpersonal relations even 'before creation' ('*ante mundi constitutionem*'). While Tapp considers his closing considerations 'experimental', the next author is well known for a fully worked-out account of relative timelessness.

Under the title *The Difference Creation makes: Relative Timelessness Reconsidered* (pp. 117ff.) ALAN G. PADGETT presents a review of his conception of relative time-lessness, which he has modified to some extent. Relative timelessness attempts to combine the advantages of both the timelessness account and the temporal account of God. The key point is that although God is timeless relative to our space-time world, He is in some way temporal.

According to Padgett, God is timeless in that His infinite dimension of time cannot be measured by our earthly space-time coordinates and He is never subject to the negative effects of time's passage. He is immutable with respect to his essential properties, while in his relations with the world God can change. For Padgett, change and duration are conceptually connected, and so he comes to the conclusion that if God is capable of change (as he must have been when creation came into existence) he must be in some way temporal. In the end, Padgett's position is: before creation and all change God was relatively timeless, i.e., changeless and free of temporal measures. After creation God is omnitemporal, which means that God's time or eternity transcends physical time by being infinite and immeasurable. He is, then, immutable with respect to his essence, but enters into relative change with us, being in some way temporal yet never being bound by time.

In the following chapter *Timeless Action? – Temporality and/or Eternity in God's Being and Acting* (pp. 127ff.), REINHOLD BERNHARDT presents a genuinely theo-logical perspective on this debate. According to him, it is a datum of Christian faith that God acts: in continuously creating and sustaining the world, in walking with his people as the biblical narratives tell us, and in individual situations of history. Bernhardt takes for granted that a rigid conception of divine timelessness, conceiving of eternity as completely opposed to time, is not compatible with these basic convictions of Christian faith. On the other hand, he is not convinced that temporalists do better – their main danger is to build temporality into their con-ception of God's nature, losing sight of his transcendence over time. So Bernhardt set out to develop an alternative: God, he says, is not temporal in the sense of creatures which are spatio-temporal entities, but he is also not completely timeless. Instead, God is non-temporal, but intimately related to time as its ground, creator, and encompassing whole.

From a theological point of view, Bernhardt presents a threefold concept of eter-nity, parallel to the doctrine of the Trinity. He then develops a model of divine action that avoids the shortcomings of the traditional models taken from human action or from natural causality, but that aims at integrating their various advantages. To this end, he introduces the notion of a spiritual force-field that influences human actors. God in the third Trinitarian person of the Holy Spirit acts in this way through the action of creatures (as in Aquinas's model of the prime cause). The spiritual force-field is not identical to God. It is a mode of His acting. By this move, Bernhardt avoids the lurking danger of pantheism and aims at integrating the concepts of action, as well as causation into one model, which he calls the model of 'operative presence'. In his final reflections on the 'power of weakness' in God's spiritual self-representation, he eventually hints at an answer to the problem of evil.

The **Fourth Part** of this book is devoted to the defence of temporal conceptions of God. The papers of the Third Part opted for a "third way" besides divine timelessness and temporality, mainly for the reason that while they realize the convenience of the traditional timelessness account (as exemplified by the arguments in Part I of this book), they also see the advantages of a temporal picture of God, especially with respect to the biblical stories and the beliefs of "ordinary believers". Not everyone finds this temporal picture compatible with the traditional timelessness account, as, for example, do Eleonore Stump in following Aquinas or Brian Leftow in following Anselm. Therefore, some hold that a Christian position should develop a convincing temporal conception of God as, for example, the influential British philosopher of religion Richard Swinburne does. This is what the Fourth and last Part is devoted to. It could also be termed 'dialogue with natural science', for the two papers of this section stand in intimate relation to positions advocated by many natural scientists.

In his paper *Divine Eternity and Einstein's Special Theory of Relativity* (pp. 145ff.), WILLIAM LANE CRAIG deals with an argument to the effect that the Special Theory of Relativity (STR) conflicts with a temporal conception of God. For if STR is correct in its description of time then, allegedly, there is no absolute time but only time relative to inertial frames. But it is impossible to choose a particular inertial frame as God's frame or to associate God with all the times of all the frames. So it seems to be impossible that God be temporal if STR is correct. Craig assesses this argument by focusing on two of its premises: (1) that STR's description of time is correct and (2) that if its description is correct, then God could be temporal only if associated with a particular inertial frame or a set of inertial frames. Concerning (2) Craig argues that while STR is a limited theory, the General Theory of Relativity (GTR) has shown how a 'cosmic time' can be defined by a preferred slicing (in the model) of the universe. So even if STR is correct within its limits, it does not require us to associate God with the times of inertial frames. Concerning (1) Craig provides a fascinating analysis going back to Newton's absolute time. Craig charges that Einstein's rejection of Newton's absolute conceptions and, in fact, all of STR relies on a verificationist theory of meaning. And as verificationism has been proven untenable, an Einsteinian rejection of Newtonian absolute time has no sound foundation but is based upon mere stipulation. Craig is keen not to take sides with Newtonian absolute time or a temporal conception of God. He nevertheless refutes an argument against both, trying to keep open the possibility of maintaining a Lorentzian interpretation of the relativistic nature of space and time, according to which a temporal God would determine the existence of a preferred reference frame of absolute time.

The paper of HANS KRAML, *Eternity in Process Philosophies* (pp. 157ff.), deals
with philosophical ontologies which are especially popular among natural scientists. Kraml strongly opts in favour of an ontological pluralism. According to
his analysis, we use different ontologies in our everyday lives, depending on the
purposes pursued in concrete situations. For an analysis of time, he considers process ontologies to be best suited, but he also claims, a little surprisingly perhaps, that
they are largely compatible with an Aristotelian account of time. In this perspective,
time is something that beings which act in the world abstract from processes in cor-
relating their activities with their plans. Then God's eternity becomes the actuality
of processes – an idea which fits much better with the scholastic idea of God as *actus
purus* than the static concept of a *nunc stans*. Moreover, Kraml presents *en passant*
some arguments against scientific reductionism. According to him, the language
of science and even the metalanguage of philosophy are meaningful only because
of their connections to our everyday language – one more argument for taking our
everyday ontological pluralism seriously.

What, then, is time, what is eternity, and how do they relate to each other? This
book shows that philosophy has in a sense proceeded much farther than where it
stood in the times of St Augustine, who coined the famous words: 'What then is
time? If no one asks me, I know, if I want to explain it to someone who asks, I do
not know' (*Confessions* XI). While Augustine's statement is surely true for many of
us in our everyday lives, philosophical and theological deliberation has advanced
since his time. New insights shed more light on the nature of time, even if they may
not combine to a full explanation of what time is.

When Ludwig Wittgenstein commented on the above statement of St Augustine
in his *Philosophical Investigations*, he wrote: 'Something that we know when no
one asks us, but no longer know when we are supposed to give an account of it, is
something that we need to remind ourselves of' (Aphorism 89). The modest aim of
this book is to serve as such a philosophical reminding.

Christian Tapp

Part I

In Defence of Divine Timelessness

Chapter 1

On Existing All at Once

Robert Pasnau

The nature of divine eternality is obscure in both historical and modern discussions. In a way its obscurity is no surprise, given that the nature of time is so mysterious. But the obscurity is still notable relative to the other traditional divine attributes, which are comparatively much better understood. Our perplexities regarding eternality are compounded, I will argue here, by a failure to recognize the full range of conceptual possibilities concerning divine eternality. Modern discussions have been ignoring what is not only an intrinsically plausible conception of eternality, but what might also be regarded as its most historically prominent construal.

1.1 Two Conceptions of Timelessness

Discussions of divine eternality ought to distinguish between the sort of complete timelessness – God's being outside of time – that is sometimes associated with the concept, and a different sort of timelessness, also frequently associated with eternity, that involves lacking temporal parts, and so existing "all at once". The main thesis of this chapter is that a plausible case can be made for all-at-once existence, rather than complete timelessness, as the best understanding of what eternality is.

To be clear about exactly what these different notions involve, I need some precisely defined terminology:

> A *temporal* entity, as I will use the term here, exists at one or more times and, unless it exists for just an instant, exists through time. It coexists – that is, exists simultaneously – with other entities existing at the same time.
>
> An *atemporal* entity, on my usage, is one that is not temporal. It does not exist in time, in the sense that it does not exist at any time and so, *a fortiori*, does not exist through time. It cannot be said to exist simultaneously with, or before, or after any other entity.
>
> A *merechronic* entity partly exists at some instant in time, but also existed or will exist at other times, and does not wholly exist at any one time.
>
> A *holochronic* entity is one that is not merechronic. It exists as a whole, all at once, for all of its existence, and does not partly exist at different times.

To make this last distinction, I might have appealed instead to the standard scholastic terminology of 'successive' and 'permanent' entities, or to the modern terminology of 'perduring' and 'enduring' entities. As will become clear, I think all these terms aim at a similar distinction. This is, however, a conclusion I want to derive from the discussion, rather than build it into my terminology from the start. Hence it will be safer for now to employ these neologisms, so that we can talk directly about the notion of all-at-once existence, without entangling it with various other issues.

Under any name, the notions of merechronicity and holochronicity are seriously obscure. To see what they involve, begin with an ordinary physical event, like kicking a football. The event takes place over time, and we can distinguish between parts of the event, such as the motion of the foot before contact and the motion of the foot after contact. Now try to extend this same idea to a substance that changes over time, like a growing boy. Just as we talked about parts of an event, it seems that we might talk about the six-year-old part of the boy and the seven-year-old part of the boy. Inasmuch as the boy is something that exists through time, it seems possible to conceive of him as having parts, temporal parts, just as he has spatial parts such as his right half and his left half. To have temporal parts in this way is to be a merechronic entity. If it is right to conceive of temporal stages of existence as parts, then anything that changes, at least if it changes intrinsically, must have such parts, and so must be merechronic. But now consider an entity that does not change intrinsically in any way. If such a being is possible, then it cannot be merechronic, because merechronicity itself is a kind of intrinsic change, a part-by-part traversal of a complete life. A wholly unchanging being would therefore have to be holochronic.

As I have defined these terms, atemporality and holochronicity are compatible. Indeed, atemporality entails holochronicity. Since an atemporal entity does not exist through time, there can be no question of its lacking some past or future part of itself. Holochronicity, in contrast, does not entail atemporality. An entity can exist through time, and so be temporal in my sense, and yet not have the sorts of temporal parts associated with ordinary temporal existence. Such a being would wholly exist at one moment and then wholly exist at the next moment, such that no part of it gets left behind. One might want to argue that in fact this apparent possibility is illusory, and that whatever exists through time must have temporal parts. In that case, holochronic existence would entail atemporal existence. This is, however, very far from obvious, and one might even argue to the contrary that ordinary material substances are themselves holochronically temporal entities.

The notion of holochronicity has a venerable pedigree. Skipping over its various antecedents in Greek thought, it appears among Christian philosophers in Augustine:

> Why, my soul, do you perversely follow your flesh? It would follow you, if you   1
> turned away. Whatever you sense through it is partial. You are unaware of the whole
> of which these are the parts, and yet these parts delight you. But if the sense of your   3
> flesh were suited to comprehend the whole, and were not, in punishment, justly
> confined to a part of the universe, you would wish to pass over whatever exists in   5
> the present, so that the whole would provide you with more pleasure. For so it is that

you hear, with the same sense of the flesh, the words we speak, and you certainly do 7
not want to stop at the syllables, but to pass on so that other syllables may come and
you may hear the whole. So it always is when all of what makes up some one thing 9
does not all exist at once (*omnia simul*): if it could all be sensed, it would be more
enjoyable than it would individually. But far better than these is he who made all 11
things, our God. He does not pass away, because nothing succeeds him.[1]

It also seems to appear in Boethius's famous discussion of eternity:

Eternity is the complete possession all at once of illimitable life. This becomes clearer 1
by comparison with temporal things. For whatever lives in time, as present, proceeds
from the past into the future, and there is nothing located in time that can embrace 3
the whole extent of its life equally. On the contrary, it does not yet grasp tomorrow
even though it has already lost yesterday, and even in your life today you live no 5
more fully than in a mobile, transitory moment. Therefore whatever undergoes the
condition of time, even if (as Aristotle held about the world) it never began or ceases 7
to exist, and even if its life is extended with the infinity of time, still it is not such as
is rightly judged to be eternal. For although the extent of its life is infinite, it does 9
not encompass and embrace it all at once; instead it does not now have the future
that has not yet arrived. Therefore whatever encompasses and possesses the whole 11
fullness of illimitable life equally and is such that nothing future is absent from it and
nothing past has flowed away, this is rightly judged to be eternal.[2] 13

There can be hardly any doubt that both of these authors are describing the merechronic character of the created world. For Augustine, we sense the present parts of things, 'unaware of the whole' (line 2). For Boethius, 'there is nothing located in time that can embrace the whole extent of its life equally' (lines 3–4). Each author is taking the familiar spatial notion of a whole and its parts, and applying that to temporal extension, conceiving of a thing's existence in a moment of time as a part of its existence, and then imagining how God might exist wholly, entirely lacking in such parts. This is the famous Boethian notion of the '*interminabilis vitae tota simul et perfecta possessio*' (line 1).

So far, I do not think that I have said anything controversial. I am, however, right on the brink of various controversial questions. One such question is whether this Boethian conception of eternality as holochronicity might best be captured without removing God from time entirely. Rather than make any bold assertions, I will frame this as a query:

Query 1: Is eternality just illimitable, temporally extended, holochronic existence?

A start toward answering Query 1 in the affirmative would be to observe that holochronicity appears to be a plausible candidate for a perfection. Certainly, at any rate, merechronicity looks like an imperfection. Beings that are only fragmentarily realized at an instant look quite imperfect, and it looks to be quite an improvement to exist holochronically. Indeed – given that the two options are exhaustive – it seems plausible that a perfect being would have to exist holochronically. I thus take

---

[1] *Confessiones*, IV.11.17. Throughout, all translations are my own.
[2] *Consolation of Philosophy*, bk. V, prose 6

it to be uncontroversial that holochronicity is at least part of what it is to be eternal. The crucial question then becomes whether atemporality is also required.

Here it is important to be very clear about the notion of timelessness. Although it is commonly agreed that eternality requires timelessness, there are different ways of being timeless.[3] Particularly relevant for present purposes is that one can be timeless by being either atemporal or by being holochronic. It seems to me that the messy interconnections between these three concepts – timelessness, atemporality, holochronicity – have led to much confusion regarding eternality. Boethius, in the famous passage above, is committed not just to holochronicity but also to time-lessness, when he remarks that 'there is nothing located in time that can embrace the whole extent of its life equally' (lines 3–4). From this we can safely infer that God is not 'located in time'. It is certainly not unreasonable to suppose, then, that Boethius is committed to God's atemporality. On this reading of the passage, one would have a ready explanation of why he talks about holochronicity, since holochronicity follows trivially from atemporality. But there is another way to read the passage. Mere holochronicity itself might be considered a kind of timelessness. Since such a being is entirely changeless, without even a distinct past or future, it fails to be located in time in the usual way. Hence it might be argued that Boethius's denial of God's being located in time should be understood merely as the denial of God's merechronicity, not as the claim that God is entirely outside of time. I am not taking a position on whether this is the most plausible reading – we would need to look at more texts – only that we should be alert to the conceptual room here for different sorts of timelessness, including illimitable holochronicity, rather than atemporality.[4]

Why suppose that, in addition to illimitable holochronicity, eternality also re-quires atemporality? One reason, as noted already, would be that atemporality is the only way to achieve holochronicity. Suppose for now, however, that this is not so, and that there is nothing logically impossible about the notion of existing holo-chronically through time. Why, then, insist on adding atemporality? One reason to doubt whether atemporality should be added is that, in a sense, it diminishes

---

[3]   As LEFTOW remarks, 'Discussions of God's eternality often proceed as if there were just two options, that God is temporal and that he is not. But there is in fact a continuum of possible views of God's relation to time – as it were, of just how temporal God is' (*The Eternal Present* [2002], p. 23). Although Leftow does not here or elsewhere usually consider holochronically temporal existence, he does offer a brief, seemingly supportive discussion of the view in his *Parts, Wholes, and Eternity* [2001].

[4]   Many recent discussions seem to leave no room for even the conceptual possibility of temporally holochronic existence. CRAIG, for instance, remarks at the start of *God, Time, and Eternity* [2001] that 'God is temporal if His duration has phases which are related to each other as earlier and later' (p. 3), thus associating temporality with what I call merechronicity, and atemporality with holochronicity. But on the next page 'atemporality' is taken to mean 'wholly outside of time': 'if, then, God exists timelessly, He does not exist at any moment of time'. The conjunction of these claims leaves no room for holochronically temporal existence.

the perfection of holochronicity. Although an atemporal being is, strictly speaking, holochronic, it satisfies the definition vacuously, inasmuch as an atemporal being does not exist through time in such a way as even possibly to have temporal parts. *Anything* that might exist outside of time – the number 9, a Platonic form, a solitary, immutable rock – would be holochronic in this sense. It is only when holochronicity is manifested in time that it appears to be a positive perfection, because we then have the picture of a being existing wholly at one time, possessing its whole life, and also existing wholly at the next time, still possessing its whole life, and so without any gain or loss between the two times. Supposing such holochronicity is a possible mode of existence, it surely looks like a great-making feature. An atemporal being, in contrast, is holochronic only trivially, by default, in virtue of being unable to pass from time to time. Hence there is a real sense in which those who wish to associate eternality with atemporality are turning their back on the perfection of holochronicity. They are, to be sure, avoiding the clear imperfection of merechronicity. But they are doing so in a way that debars them from capturing what appears to be the great-making feature of being holochronic.

Of course, this would be a serious objection to atemporality only if there are no countervailing advantages in adding atemporality to the notion of holochronicity. It is a familiar idea that some great-making features have to drop out of the concept of a perfect being because they do not fit within the overall package of the divine attributes. So the real issue behind Query 1 is whether we have good reasons for thinking that atemporality, once distinguished from holochronicity, must be a feature of a perfect being. Here then is a second query, directly flowing from the first:

Query 2: Is atemporality a perfection?

Once atemporality is distinguished from holochronicity, it seems far from clear that it is a perfection. Abstract objects, such as numbers, are supposed to be atemporal, supposing they exist at all. They do not, however, seem obviously more perfect for that reason than concrete entities. Suppose, to switch examples, that God is atemporal and that God creates two and only two things: an ordinary rock that exists in time and a rather unusual rock that does not exist in time. I cannot see that the second rock is impossible. Perhaps that rock would have to be utterly changeless, perhaps it would be wrong to call it a 'rock', but still it seems to me that if anything can exist outside of time, a rock-like entity might do so. My question then, of course, is whether the second rock is any more perfect than the first, simply in virtue of existing out of time. It is not clear to me that it is.

It may be that atemporality is not a perfection, but simply a concomitant divine attribute entailed by some other perfection. Yet once we distinguish atemporality from holochronicity, it is unclear whether this is so. Both immutability and simplicity entail holochronicity, but it is not clear that they entail atemporality. Another idea would be that atemporality, while not strictly implied by any other attribute, is nevertheless extremely useful to explain various problematic features of God's nature and God's relationship with creation. Obvious candidates here are divine foreknowledge of contingent events and the tension between divine omniscience and immutability. This large issue deserves a separate query:

Query 3: Does atemporality play a crucial theological role that temporally extended holochronicity cannot play?

Of course, this is far too vast a question even to begin discussing here, since it requires coming to grips both with whether atemporality does any work at all in explaining divine foreknowledge or anything else, *and* with whether holochronicity might do just as well.[5] Here I will content myself with wondering whether part of the reason that holochronicity and atemporality have sometimes been conflated is that the first looks like a perfection we should ascribe to a perfect being, but that the second has seemed useful in solving the various paradoxes involved in a changeless, provident God's activity in the world. In any event, holochronicity and atemporality are quite different notions, and it is important to be clear about which, if either, belongs in the concept of a perfect being.

1.2 Presence in Time

God either exists through time or does not, and if God exists through time, then He does so either merechronically or holochronically. I am supposing, for purposes of this chapter, that we can rule out merechronic existence. That is to say, I am working within the Anselmian tradition of perfect-being theology that takes God to be simple and immutable. Suppose, then, that we decide atemporality is not a perfection, and that we want to conceive of God's existing through time, holochronically. What does it mean to locate God in time in this way? We should, at least initially, leave open the question of whether God would exist through our time or through some other distinct time of His own. One might of course wonder what it means to distinguish between 'our' time and some other time. I do not have a good answer to such questions, but I nevertheless think this has to be registered as a possibility – at least an epistemic possibility from our limited vantage point. Even so, I think there is an argument to be made to exclude the obscure notion of God's existing through His own, distinct time. The argument is that if we decide to locate God in any time at all, then we should decide to locate God in all times. This seems to follow from divine perfection: If God is a temporal being, then why would we limit His existence to only some times? This is not a demonstrative argument, to be

---

[5]   To be even a candidate for helping with the problem of divine foreknowledge, holochronically temporal eternality would presumably need to yield the familiar lemma that there is no 'fore' in God's knowledge. Whether it can get this lemma would seem to depend on whether it can get the prior result that, as ANSELM puts it, 'in the eternal present all time is encompassed at once, as well as whatever occurs at any time' (*De concordia* [1968], 5). It is unclear to me whether this is a legitimate result, on any account of eternality, because it is unclear what the meaning of 'encompassed at once' (*simul*) would be, in a non-temporal context. This is a crucial issue for any discussion of eternality and foreknowledge, but is much too large a problem to be taken up here.

sure, but I think it plausible enough that we should concentrate our attention on the two scenarios on which I have implicitly been concentrating: the scenario in which God is wholly atemporal, and the scenario in which God exists through the whole temporal extent of our universe.

In restricting my focus in this way, I mean to leave open the possibility that God came to exist in our time only when He created the world and only for as long as He sustains it, and that He is otherwise not in time at all, or perhaps only in some other time.[6] Reaching a conclusion about these various possibilities would require a discussion of the nature of time that goes beyond the scope of this chapter. In order to remain neutral on this issue, then, I will focus only on the question of whether, for the period in which there is a spatiotemporal universe, God should be said to be in it.

When our topic is so restricted, several possible ways of talking about eternality are excluded, and purposely so. First, it is traditional to speak of eternality as a kind of duration.[7] It does not seem to me (as it has to others) that this need be a contradiction in terms, but I think it more confusing than helpful to depict God as having duration in a way that is wholly outside of time (and so atemporal in my sense of the term). The concept of duration, if it has any meaning at all, must be linked with time in some sense of the term. This may be some wholly distinct temporal (or spatiotemporal) framework, and it may be holochronic rather than merechronic, but I do not think we should tolerate a notion of duration that is wholly atemporal. I therefore think we must choose between describing God as atemporal, and so as not having any duration, and describing God as being in time, and so persisting through time.[8] Second, it seems to me similarly unhelpful to speak of God's being co-existent with or present with creatures, and at the same time to insist on atemporality. To be sure, an atemporal being may be epistemically aware of all creatures, for all time, and may be causally active on all creatures at all times. Such epistemic and causal facts certainly license the claim that, in some sense, an atemporal God might be present to us. But although this would be a very robust and significant form of presence, it would also be a wholly equivocal use of the term. It is crucial that discussions of eternity distinguish between the sort of presence that comes from epistemic and

---

[6]   For this sort of view, see CRAIG, *God, Time, and Eternity* [2001]. For further considerations, see ZIMMERMAN, *God Inside Time* [2002].

[7]   See, e. g., the opening sentences of SUÁREZ's discussion of eternity: 'First and principally duration is divided into created and uncreated. Uncreated duration is eternity spoken of unconditionally, or essentially. Created duration is every duration that is not true eternity' (*Disputationes* [1866], 50.3.1).

[8]   STUMP AND KRETZMANN, *Eternity* [1981], p. 432 hold that 'the life of an eternal entity is characterized by beginningless, endless, infinite duration', but then go on to speak of such existence as 'atemporal' (p. 433). PADGETT remarks that 'Stump and Kretzmann have chosen the wrong word. The word 'duration' means an interval of time, namely that interval of time through which something endures. The notion of an atemporal duration is, therefore, a contradiction in terms' (*God, Eternity, and the Nature of Time* [1992], p. 67).

causal ties, and the literal sense of presence at issue in the question of whether God is in time.[9]

I wish to focus exclusively on presence of the most literal sort. Such presence might be thought to require both temporal and spatial presence – that is, God's being located in both time and space. I do not want to presuppose that these questions have to be dealt with in conjunction. Although one might argue that a being can be in time only if it is in space, and vice versa, these issues are murky enough that it is reasonable to treat them separately. Still, the spatial case is worth discussing, if only briefly, because it can help illuminate the temporal case. Just as holochronicity was defined as a kind of temporal all-at-onceness, we might similarly define a kind of spatial all-at-onceness:

> A *meremeric* entity partly exists at some location in space, but also partly exists at some other location in space. It is an extended entity, having part outside of part.
> A *holenmeric* entity is one that is not meremeric. It exists as a whole, altogether, wherever it exists, and so lacks extended parts.[10]

One way of being holenmeric is to exist outside of space. But just as with holochronic existence, a thing might exist holenmerically through space, so long as it wholly exists in every place where it exists. This is how philosophers from Plotinus through Descartes standardly understood the human soul's existence within the human body: whole in the whole, and whole in each part.[11]

Just as holochronic existence counts as a kind of temporal existence, so holenmeric existence counts as a kind of extension, although not the usual, meremeric

---

[9]   Compare STUMP AND KRETZMANN, *Eternity* [1981], p. 441: '[T]he entire life of any eternal entity is co-existent with any temporal entity at any time ... From the standpoint of eternity, every time is present, co-occurrent with the whole of infinite, atemporal duration.' Although their work sometimes gives the impression that God will be literally present to creatures in time, they expressly deny this in various places, e. g.: 'Of course, if simultaneity must be understood as occurrence or existence at the same time, then clearly the concept of eternal-temporal relationships is incoherent and nothing eternal can be simultaneous with anything else, eternal or temporal' (*Eternity, Awareness, and Action* [1992], p. 474). In place of literal presence, they define God's co-existent presence in terms of cognitive and causal connections. I am hardly alone in wanting to distinguish literal presence from other senses of the term. See, e. g., HELM, *Eternal God* [1988], p. 29: '[S]omething being present to His [God's] mind has not to be confused with God being temporally present with anything.'

[10]   The term 'holenmerism' was coined by MORE, the seventeenth-century Cambridge Platonist, in his *Enchiridion Metaphysicum* [1671]. See ROZEMOND, *Descartes* [2003] and the discussion in Ch. 16 of my *Metaphysical Themes* [2011].

[11]   See, e. g., PLOTINUS, *Enneades* [1951], IV.2.1; AUGUSTINE, *De trinitate* [1968], VI.6.8; JOHN DAMASCENE, *De fide orthodoxa* [1955], 13.3; AQUINAS, *Summa theologiae* [1888], I, q. 76, a. 8; DESCARTES, *Oeuvres* [1897], *Passions de l'âme* I.30.

sort of extension. (Descartes calls the latter 'true extension', and it is this extension that he describes as the principal attribute of body.[12])

Although it is now commonly supposed that God exists outside of space, this was not the standard conception among earlier theologians. Medieval Christian authors, despite being generally misread on this point, are in complete agreement that God is literally present, spatially, throughout the universe. One simply does not find anyone wanting to remove God from space, all the way through to the end of the seventeenth century.[13] Of course, no one wanted to say that God has spatial, integral parts. So the universally accepted view was that God exists holenmerically throughout space, wholly existing at each place in the universe. It does not immediately follow that God is also located holochronically throughout time, but of course the two views form a neat package. God can be said to exist everywhere, and at every time, and to exist wholly wherever and whenever he exists.

I am less confident about whether medieval Christian theologians universally held the analogous claim that is my focus here: that God exists wholly (that is, holochronically) at every time. This was, however, certainly a common view. It is, for instance, very clearly Anselm's view in the *Monologion* [1968]. There he quite quickly arrives at the view that God's constant causal role in the universe requires God to be 'everywhere, and throughout all things, and in all things' (Ch. 14). But he returns to this issue later in the same work, in a brilliant discussion that runs continuously through Chapters 20–24. He begins by recalling his earlier conclusion and then describing 'a little voice within of contradiction, which compels me to inquire more carefully into where and when that Being exists' (Ch. 20). He then sketches the argument for God's being located in all places and times. God is either in none, some, or all places and time. The finite middle ground – *some* place and time – is untenable given God's perfection. But the no-location view is even worse, and he makes two quick arguments against it:

- 'what would seem more contradictory than that what exists most truly and supremely exists nowhere and never?'

---

[12]   See Descartes's correspondence with More, DESCARTES, *Oeuvres* [1897], V. 270 and V. 342.

[13]   The *locus classicus* for discussions of God's 'immensity' is LOMBARD, *Sententiae* [1971], I.37. The consensus in this area is noted by SUÁREZ: 'God is intimately present to this corporeal universe, not just by presence (that is, cognitively) and by power or action, but also by His essence or substance, just as all the theologians teach, as certain to the faith, on account of divine immensity' (*Disputationes* [1866], 51.2.8). There was no unanimity among Muslim authors. AVERROES, for instance, regards literal omnipresence as a 'puerile' doctrine (*Destructio* [1961], 14, p. 375).

HASKER is typical of the modern conviction that God must be outside space: 'Few points in the theistic metaphysics are as clear as that God is not simply a very large object occupying huge amounts of space or even all of it. God must, somehow, *transcend* space.' (*God, Time, and Knowledge* [1989], p. 178) Of course, God is not "simply" a very large object, but that he is a very large object, existing throughout space, was the unchallenged consensus for most of the history of Christian theology.

- 'since there is no good nor anything at all without that Being, if it exists nowhere or never then nowhere or never is there any good, and nowhere and never is there anything at all' (Ch. 20).

Despite these quick arguments, Anselm's next chapter reconsiders the matter anew, offering a line of argument for the conclusion that God cannot be in either space or time. That chapter begins by distinguishing the two options we have already been considering: existing merechronically and meremerically, or else existing holochronically and holenmerically. In Anselm's terms:

> How does it exist as a whole, everywhere and always? For either it is to be understood that it exists as a whole at once, in all places or times, and by parts in individual places and times; or that it exists as a whole, even in individual places and times. (Ch. 21)

The first option gets rejected out of hand, on the grounds that God does not have parts (something that Anselm takes himself to have shown back in Ch. 17). Consideration of the second option leads Anselm into a lengthy discussion of 'the nature (*ratio*) of place and the nature of time' (Ch. 21). What both of these natures require, he argues, is part-by-part existence. Nothing can be wholly present at more than one place at once, nor wholly present at more than one time. With respect to the temporal case, he argues as follows:

> How does anything exist wholly at once (*totum simul*) at individual times, if these   1
> times do not exist at once? If it exists as a whole, separately and distinctly, at individ-
> ual times – just as a whole human being exists yesterday, today, and tomorrow – then   3
> it is properly said that it was and is and will be. Therefore its age, which is nothing
> other than its eternity, does not exist wholly at once, but is extended by parts in   5
> keeping with the parts of time. But its eternity is nothing other than itself. Therefore
> the supreme being will be divided into parts, according to the divisions of time. For   7
> if its age passes through periods of time, then with these times it has present, past,
> and future. (Ch. 21)   9

It follows from the nature of time, according to this argument, that what exists through time has distinct temporal parts: 'its age … is extended by parts in keeping with the parts of time' (lines 4–6). Hence temporal holochronicity is impossible: nothing can exist through time without acquiring temporal parts. An analogous argument for the spatial case leads Anselm to the general conclusion that God exists 'in no place or time, that is, nowhere and never' (Ch. 21).

Anselm thus faces paradox: he seems to have identified decisive arguments showing both that God is in time and space, and that God is outside time and space. His next chapter therefore attempts to resolve the apparent conflict, contending that since God is not contained by time and place, God is not bound by the nature of time and place. This means that, contrary to the argument we just saw him offer in Chapter 21, God can exist wholly at more than one place at the same time, and can exist wholly at more than one time. Anselm thus concludes:

> Since inevitable necessity requires that the supreme Being, as a whole, be lacking to no place or time, and no nature of place or time prevents it from being whole at once (*simul totam*) at every place or time, it is necessary for it to be present as a whole

at once in every individual place and time. For, because it is present at one place or time, it is not thereby prevented from being likewise and simultaneously present to this or that other place or time. Nor, because it was, or is, or will be, has any [part] of its eternity thereby vanished from the present time, along with the past that no longer exists; nor does it pass with the present that barely exists; nor will it come with the future that is not yet. (Ch. 22)

So Anselm in the end holds onto the initial arguments for God's being in every place and time, and rejects the arguments to the contrary. Holochronicity and holenmerism are possible for a being in space and time, and divine perfection in fact requires them.[14]

Modern theologians have spectacularly misunderstood medieval views in this domain. The mainstream of medieval Christian thought does not remove God from space and time, but rather invokes holochronic and holenmeric existence so that a simple, immutable being can nevertheless exist in all places and all times.[15] I do not,

---

[14]   The conclusions of the *Monologion* [1968] are reiterated in the *Proslogion* [1968], although so briefly that their significance might be (and generally has been) missed. *Proslogion* [1968], 13: 'Since, then, nothing is greater than you, no place or time contains you; but you are everywhere and always.' 'Uncircumscribed is that which exists all at once everywhere, which is understood of you alone.'   Readers have been thrown off by his remarks in *Proslogion* [1968], 19: 'You exist neither yesterday nor today nor tomorrow, but simply you exist, outside all time. For yesterday and today and tomorrow exist only in time; but although nothing exists without you, you nevertheless do not exist in place or time, but all things exist in you. For nothing contains you, but you contain all.' Out of context, this of course looks like atemporality. But read in the context of his other remarks, it becomes clear that Anselm is putting weight on the unsuitability of putting God *in* time, since 'in' implies containment. Thus, as *Monologion* [1968], 22, puts it, 'If the usage of language permitted, it would seem to be more fittingly said that [this Being] exists *with* place or time than that it exists *in* place or time. For a thing's being said to be *in* another signifies that it is *contained*, more than does its being said to exist *with* another.' Most modern readers of Anselm seem to have read him as committed to divine atemporality. Perhaps an exception is Rogers, but she adds the doubtful idea that Anselm ascribes to a tenseless (or B-series, or four-dimensional) conception of time (ROGERS, *Anselm on Eternity* [2006]). There is perhaps some evidence for this in the *De concordia* [1968], but it strikes me as thin – too thin for one to be confident about the matter, given how unprecedented it would be to defend a B-theory of time. For another paper associating a tenseless theory of time with Anselm, see LEWIS, *Eternity, Time and Tenselessness* [1988], although LEWIS thinks that Anselm (along with Boethius and Aquinas) were unwittingly committed to this consequence (p. 83). The only pre-modern author I have found expressly defending a tenseless conception of time, with all the attendant metaphysical consequences for the reality of past and future, is JOHN WYCLIF, *De ente praedicamentali* [1891], ch. 20 (see my *Metaphysical Themes* [2011], ch. 18).

[15]   In addition to being Anselm's view, I believe it is AQUINAS's: '[W]e ascribe to God words of all times, because he is absent (*deest*) from no time' (*In Sent.* I.8.2.3c); 'eternity is there as present (*praesentialiter adest*) to every time or instant of time' (*Summa contra gentiles* [1918], I.66.548); 'words of different times are attributed to God inasmuch as his eternity includes all times' (*Summa theologiae* [1888], I, q. 10, a. 2 ad 4). Admittedly, these passages

however, mean to brandish these historical remarks as an argument from authority. What Harold Bloom famously suggested about poetry in *The Anxiety of Influence*[16] is even more clearly the case in philosophy: what we call innovations are the result, very often, of our misinterpretations of the past. So it may be that entirely removing God from space and time is a step forward. Of course, I am doubtful whether this is so, in part because I think the general thrust of Anselm's remarks has a certain force. There is something quite unattractive about the picture according to which God created space and time and yet does not – perhaps even cannot – exist within it. Intuitively, one would expect God to exist at every place and every time, rather than at no place and no time. Still, there is nothing about Anselm's argument that *compels* assent. The two quick arguments for putting God in time and space, as quoted above, are the only ones that he gives, and they depend on two questionable assumptions: that what exists 'nowhere and never' is not real, or at least not fully real; and that for an agent to bring about some effect, it must exist at the time and place of that effect. These were standard assumptions during the Middle Ages, but they are ones that a proponent of divine atemporality will of course be ready to deny, and it is not clear how the issue might be adjudicated. Hence my earlier queries stand as open invitations to investigate the matter further.

---

are not decisive, because it is possible to suppose Aquinas has in mind some non-literal sense of 'presence'. See also SUÁREZ, who describes 'the whole eminent perfection by which eternity has the power (*vim*) of coexisting with every succession' (*Disputationes* [1866], 50.4.15).

LEIBNIZ takes it as a given, in his exchange with CLARKE, that 'God's immensity makes him actually present in all spaces. In like manner, God exists in all time' (*Leibniz-Clarke Correspondence* [1956], fifth paper, n. 45). The phrase 'in like manner' is significant because it is certain that Leibniz takes God to be literally present in space: that is just what the doctrine of divine immensity holds. So 'in like manner' suggests that 'in all time' should likewise be understood literally. Clarke, however, refuses to grant this: '[W]hen, according to the analogy of vulgar speech, we say that he exists in all space and in all time, the words mean only that he is omnipresent and eternal, that is, that boundless space and time are necessary consequences of his existence; and not that space and time are beings distinct from him, and *in* which he exists' (*Leibniz-Clarke Correspondence* [1956], fifth reply, n. 45). Of course, it is unclear whether Clarke's Newtonian view actually *removes* God from space and time.

Unsurprisingly (given his anti-realist views about space and time), Kant departs from this earlier tradition. He recognizes the position I am describing: 'Some have tried to prevent the difficulties which arise from representing God's existence as within time by insisting that all the consecutiveness of time be thought as simultaneous in God', but rejects it as incoherent: 'yet this is a pretension which requires us to think a contradiction: consecutive states of a thing, which are nevertheless *simultaneous*' (KANT, *Writings on Religion* [1996], p. 384). He reaches the analogous conclusion about spatial presence. Therefore, since Kant does insist on God's immutability, he concludes that God is wholly outside space and time.

[16] BLOOM, *The Anxiety of Influence* [1997].

1.3 What Exists All at Once?

Investigation by means of queries seems an appropriate way to proceed in a domain as obscure as this, where even the very existence of our subject matter – a perfect, necessarily existing being – is shrouded in doubt. Yet as obscure as these questions are, reflection on them helps to shed light on questions that are at least somewhat less obscure, regarding how ordinary material objects exist in and through time. As mentioned earlier, the notion of merechronicity is closely related to a thesis popular in modern metaphysics: that objects do not *endure* through time in such a way as to exist as a whole at each instant, but instead *perdure* through time, partly existing at one time and partly existing at another, and existing as a whole only when viewed as a four-dimensional object, extended through space and time.[17] This is an issue later medieval authors were also much concerned with, under the heading of the distinction between permanent and successive entities. Although medieval authors disagreed on how precisely to define the distinction between permanent and successive entities, they agreed that the central notion is of existing all at once (*tota simul*). Thus, according to Nicole Oresme's mid-fourteenth-century definition,

> ['Successive' is used] for that which at no time is such that what existed in its first part exists in its second part. Instead, for any time you take, some of that successive entity exists in one of its parts, and a totally different such exists in another part. 'Permanent' is used in the opposite way, when for some time, over some instants, the same thing exists all at once (*totum simul*), from one instant to another.[18]

The leading examples of successive entities were time and motion, which were judged to be successive on the grounds that neither could exist all at once, from instant to instant. The parts of motion and time do not endure, and moreover neither motion nor time even could exist at an instant. Motion-at-an-instant is not motion at all; time-at-an-instant is not time.

Not everyone was willing to postulate successive entities; Ockham, for instance, as one might expect from his generally parsimonious approach, thought there were no such things.[19] Most of the debate focused on motion, time, and other potential successive entities. But the debate is obviously relevant for the notion of eternality, given the unmissable affinities between the definition of a permanent thing and the definition of an eternal thing. Thomas Aquinas's discussion of eternity makes this connection explicit, defining the difference between eternity and time in these terms:

---

[17] One classic discussion is LEWIS's *Plurality of Worlds* [1986], pp. 202–5. For an accessible introduction, see LOUX, *Metaphysics* [2002], ch. 6.

[18] ORESME, *Questiones super physicam* [1994], III.6, dist. 1. A provisional edition of this section of the *Physics* commentary can be found in CAROTI, *La position de Nicole Oresme* [1994]. Caroti and others are preparing a critical edition of the whole of this recently identified and extremely important work.

[19] For a discussion of Ockham's view and other aspects of this debate, see my *Metaphysical Themes* [2011], ch. 18.

> Eternity is all at once (*tota simul*), which does not apply to time, because eternity is the measure of permanent being, whereas time is the measure of motion.[20]

Although Aquinas does not here use the term 'successive', readers would immediately have recognized motion as the paradigm of a successive entity. The passage might therefore seem to suggest that, for Aquinas, God is the only permanent entity, and that everything else is a successive entity, existing through time in virtue of having temporal parts, but never existing all at once. Indeed, the Boethian idea of eternality as holochronic, in contrast to the merechronic existence of temporal beings, might seem directly to entail this result. For if ordinary material objects count as permanent entities, then they must in some sense exist all at once, rather than being composed of temporal parts. But in that case it would seem that we have lost the distinction insisted on by both Augustine and Boethius, among others, between the part-by-part existence of creatures and the all-at-once existence of God. Divine eternality would turn out to be nothing special.

I have presented this puzzle in historical terms, but the issue is relevant to anyone concerned with eternality. If one wishes to characterize God's eternality in terms of holochronic existence, one must confront the question of how this differs from the existence of ordinary material objects. Do they not have all-at-once existence? Do I, for instance, not wholly exist right now? Is there really a part of me that existed yesterday, and that no longer exists? Insisting on the atemporal version of holochronic existence answers these questions only in part. To be sure, someone who goes down that road can draw a clear distinction between the existence of God and creatures, inasmuch as only God is atemporal. Divine eternality therefore *would* be something special. But the point of eternality, on the Boethian approach, was to avoid the successiveness of temporal existence, the inability of temporal creatures to 'encompass and embrace it [their life] all at once' (p. 13, line 10). It looks as if the only way to motivate eternality, when it is so conceived, is to insist that creatures have merechronic existence, which then allows God's mode of existence to distinguish itself as the only way of existing all at once. If creatures can themselves exist all at once, without temporal parts, then it becomes hard to see why God needs some special mode of existence. Our ordinary mode of existence might be perfect enough even for God.

A holochronically temporal account of eternality thus threatens to push us toward a merechronic account of how creatures exist – that is, in the usual modern parlance, toward perdurantist four-dimensionalism.[21] Even so, it seems to me that there is considerable room for defending holochronic eternality without treating

---

[20]   *Summa theologiae* [1888], I, q. 10, a. 4.

[21]   It should not be entirely surprising to find Boethian holochronic eternality pushing us toward perdurantism. For it is often held that divine eternality requires a tenseless, B-series conception of time (according to which the passage of time is an illusion) and there are strong affinities between that doctrine and perdurantism. Still, the two metaphysical doctrines – perdurantism and the tenseless conception of time – are logically independent, and I cannot see that anything in the present chapter depends on either a tensed or a tenseless theory of time. On the alleged link between eternality and a tenseless conception of time, see DELMAS

creaturely existence as merechronic. Indeed, medieval authors offer plenty of indications regarding how this might be done. Consider first Boethius's famous passage. Although it might seem at first glance as if he is committed to a merechronic conception of how creatures exist, in fact the passage is careful to say that it is the *life* of a creature – rather than the creature itself – that has temporal parts and cannot be 'embrace[d] all at once' (p. 13, line 10). Boethius does not say that 'you' fail to exist all at once. He does not say that temporal beings have temporal parts, but that their lives do; hence 'there is nothing located in time that can embrace the whole extent of its life equally' (p. 13, lines 3–4).

This is clearer still in Anselm. One might at first glance take him to be committed to the merechronicity of creatures, in view of his remarks regarding 'the nature of place and time'. But Anselm does not argue that the nature of time requires creatures to perdure part-wise through time. Rather, much as Boethius had done, Anselm distinguishes between a temporal entity and the ongoing event of its life. Thus Chapter 21's provisional argument against God's being in time runs by first establishing that being in time entails having an 'age' (*aetas*) that is extended part-wise. This would not ordinarily show that the temporal being itself does not wholly exist – indeed, Anselm is happy to say in this passage that 'a whole human being exists yesterday, today, and tomorrow' (p. 20, line 3) – but the inference holds in God's case, through the crucial middle premise of the argument: that God's age, his eternal life, is nothing other than God Himself (p. 20, line 6). Hence, if God's life has parts, then God must have parts. A creature, in contrast, can exist wholly at different times even if its life is an event that goes through time merechronically.

Both Boethius and Anselm are counting on a distinction between a thing and the events associated with that thing. When I first introduced the notion of merechronicity, I motivated it with the example of an event, kicking a football, and then suggested that this analysis in terms of temporal parts might be extended to a substance, like the boy kicking the football. But the only intuitively natural way to make that extension is to focus on the life of the boy, which seems to have parts just as much as does the act of kicking a football. This is a natural extension, because we are still talking about events, a life. To say that the boy himself has temporal parts – e. g., his six-year-old part and his seven-year-old part – strains our ordinary modes of expression. It is far more natural to say that the whole boy exists each and every day of his life. This is precisely how later medieval authors understood the distinction between permanent and successive entities. They were aware that, formulated incautiously, the distinction threatens to put all creatures on the successive side, and God alone on the permanent side. The result they wanted, however, was to put motion and other events on the successive side, and to put substances and properties on the permanent side. The way Nicole Oresme gets this result is to distinguish between two ways of being successive. A thing can be successive in some respect or another by being successive only in part, 'when

Lewis, *Eternity, Time and Tenselessness* [1988]; Padgett, *God, Eternity, and the Nature of Time* [1992]; and Craig, *God, Time, and Eternity* [2001].

a thing does not endure as a whole, but yet something of it always endures'. In contrast, something that is successive *simpliciter* is wholly successive – such a thing 'neither with respect to itself nor with respect to some of it endures through any time'.[22] Motion would therefore count as successive *simpliciter*, since there is no part of a motion that endures through time. Material substances, in contrast, will be successive in various respects, in virtue of constantly undergoing change. Still, even if some parts of a material substance do not endure, 'yet something of it always endures', as Oresme says. Elsewhere, he identifies this permanent core as the essence of a thing:

> Some things are so successive that they cannot endure in any way, like time and motion. Other things are permanent in such a way that although they have existence or endurance temporally, divisibly, and successively, nevertheless their essence remains the same for that whole time.[23]

On Oresme's account, then, material substances count as permanent because they possess a stable, enduring essence. This essence counts as existing *tota simul*, as wholly existing at every moment that it exists, and so as lacking temporal parts: the essences of material substances are, in this sense, holochronic. But the substance as a whole has parts that come and go with time: these parts might be changing properties (which themselves are permanent for as long as they exist), or they might be actions or events (which would be successive *simpliciter*).[24]

Oresme's approach offers a way of explaining what is special about God's holochronic existence without making all creaturely existence merechronic. On his account, material substances have a permanent core, but they are not permanent *simpliciter*, and so not holochronic *simpliciter*. This serves to distinguish them from God, who of course is entirely permanent and holochronic. Only something that is entirely unchanging could exist like that. Thus Oresme immediately continues the previous passage with the remark that 'God has neither a successive essence nor an existence or duration that is in any way successive. Instead, he indivisibly and infinitely endures through himself in his indivisible and illimitable eternity, which is the same as God himself'.[25]

To get these results, Oresme needs a distinction between a thing's essence and its changing attributes. Material substances can come out as permanent entities –

---

22 *Questiones super physicam* [1994], III.6.

23 *Nicole Oresme and the Medieval Geometry* [1968], II.13, p. 298.

24 Another, more extended treatment along these lines can be found in SUÁREZ's account of how the permanence associated with eternality is distinct from the permanence of creatures: 'Every created duration is such as to admit of succession either in itself or in the operations of its supposit. For although a substance can be created that is permanent and even immutable in its being (*esse*), no substance is or can be created that does not admit of some variation or succession at least in its accidents or internal motions' (*Disputationes* [1866], 50.3.7).

25 See also the similar discussion in Oresme's contemporary, ALBERT OF SAXONY, who remarks that 'we can imagine something being permanent *simpliciter* – namely, with respect to both its substance as a whole and also its states. In this way perhaps (*forte*) nothing is permanent except for the first cause' (*In Physicam* [1999], III.3, p. 483).

which is to say holochronic, which is to say enduring rather than perduring – only if they have some sort of unchanging core or essence. If one conceives of material substances as simply a bundle of ever-changing properties, then – at least by Oresme's lights – one would have to treat them as wholly successive entities, and therefore (in our modern parlance) embrace a four-dimensional perdurantist account. As Oresme conceives of the situation, this unchanging core must be distinguished not only from a thing's changing properties, but even from its 'existence or endurance'. This mirrors the way we saw Boethius and Anselm talking earlier. What makes created substances fundamentally successive and temporal is that their very existence – their 'life' or age – is an event that unfolds successively through time, no part of which endures through time. In this way, the famous but obscure medieval distinction between a thing's being and essence gets put to some extremely interesting work, inasmuch as it accounts for the intuition that in some sense (with respect to its essence) a material substance does wholly exist at each moment of time, whereas in another sense (with respect to its existence) it perdures through temporal segments.

To be wholly permanent, then, without any successive aspect, a thing's very life or existence must be possessed *tota simul*. There is perhaps room to wonder whether such a life could possibly be in time. This depends on an issue I have said almost nothing about: what does it mean to exist at a time, simultaneously with other things? I have been supposing that it is coherent for something – at least something divine – to be wholly holochronic, even with respect to its very life, and still be said to exist in and through time. One might instead think that this is incoherent, and that to exist in or through time just is to have a merechronic life. In that case, complete holochronicity would entail atemporality, and the conceptual space I have been attempting to carve out would disappear entirely. Yet I cannot see why this would be so. It seems to me that a thing might exist all at once, with respect both to itself and its life, while still the question would remain of whether that thing exists right now, at the same time that we exist. If this is an open possibility, then it seems to me there is a strong case to be made for thinking that a perfect being would have that kind of complete all-at-once existence, throughout all time.

1.4 Conclusion

When the notion of holochronic existence is distinguished from the notion of atemporal existence, it becomes important to reconsider the supposition that God exists outside of time. God's existing all at once, holochronically, is most naturally understood as a way of enduring through time, rather than being wholly outside of time. To be sure, such holochronically temporal existence is very different from the sort of temporal existence ascribed to God by some theologians today. To exist holochronically, a thing must be immutable, and so contemporaneous with creatures but still not responsive to creatures in the way proponents of a temporal conception of

God often seek.[26] Hence, a holochronically temporal account of eternality is not in any sense a compromise between atemporal and temporal approaches. Indeed, for all I have shown, the theory may bear some of the disadvantages of both approaches, without sufficient compensating advantages. Even so, the theory at least deserves serious consideration.

When eternality is understood as holochronically temporal, it satisfies the common view that eternity is a kind of duration. One might even say, as Eleonore Stump and Norman Kretzmann have urged, that eternity is the only 'genuine' and 'fully realized duration'.[27] This would follow if God alone endures through time, holochronically, whereas creatures exist merechronically. One need not, however, go so far. For it may be – as Oresme suggests – that even ordinary material substances have a genuinely enduring, permanent core, beneath their fluctuating, successive lives. This would not mean that the essences of material substances exist eternally. To count as eternal, a thing must have illimitable existence, holochronic in every respect. But it would mean that the mode of existence manifested by divine eternality is simply the perfect instantiation of a phenomenon displayed by ordinary substances all around us. What seems the very most mysterious of the divine attributes might therefore turn out to be very familiar.[28]

---

[26]   See, e. g., the classic discussions of PIKE, *God and Timelessness* [1970], and SWINBURNE, *Coherence of Theism* [1993].

[27]   STUMP AND KRETZMANN, *Eternity* [1981], p. 445.

[28]   I am grateful to Bradley Monton, Wes Morriston, Ryan Mullins, Allen Wood, and the Berlin conference participants for their helpful suggestions.

Chapter 2

Eternity, Simplicity, and Presence[1]

Eleonore Stump

2.1 Introduction

The doctrine of omnipresence implies that each point of space is equally *here* for God. On the doctrine, God is present to all places and to all persons. But what is it for God to be present? What is it for human persons to have God present to them? What does this presentness consist in?

Biblical stories portray God as personally present to human beings in the way in which one person is present to another, but in an especially powerful way. In Genesis, for example, Abraham hears God calling his name and responds with instant recognition of God. Abraham knows God when God calls, and God is present to Abraham then. When Rebecca is perplexed about what she feels happening in her womb, the text says that Rebecca went to inquire of God. She found God present to her when she turned to Him, and that is why she asked Him the question troubling her.[2] In these and many other biblical stories, there is a strong connection of some sort between God and a human person who finds God personally present to him. The ultimate expression in the Old Testament of a human being's experiencing God as present to him in this way is found in one of Job's last lines to God. Job says to God: 'I had heard of You by the hearing of the ear, but now my eye has seen You.'[3] Job not only experiences something he describes as seeing God, but he acknowledges that experience in terms of second person address to God. God's personal presence to Job is what Job is trying to express.

A similar point about God's presence to human beings can be found also in the New Testament in stories about Jesus. When Philip asks Jesus to show God the Father to the disciples, Jesus tells Philip that in seeing Jesus Philip is seeing God. The personal presence of Jesus to Philip is apparently somehow also the personal

---

[1]   This article was originally published in Doolan, *The Science of Being* [2011].

[2]   For the story of Abraham, see Gen 12–23. For this episode in Rebecca's life, see Gen 25:22.

[3]   Job 42:5.

presence of God to Philip. That is why Jesus maintains that, in knowing Jesus, his disciples are also knowing God.[4]

Biblical stories in both the Old and the New Testaments, then, portray God as able to be known directly and immediately by human beings and as able to be personally present to them.

This portrayal is in sharp contrast to the theological picture sometimes thought to be entailed by the doctrines of divine eternity and simplicity. In fact, some philosophers and theologians have rejected these doctrines, basic in the medieval Christian tradition, just because they suppose that these doctrines undermine or overturn the biblical portrayal of God's relations with human beings.[5] If God is eternal and so timeless, then in the view of the objectors to the doctrine of God's eternity God cannot be present to human beings, because human beings are in time. And if God is simple, then in the view of the objectors to the doctrine of God's simplicity God is unknowable by human beings; and because God is incomprehensible to human knowledge, God cannot be personally present to human beings either. One major reason for the rejection of the doctrines of eternity and simplicity on the part of some philosophers and theologians is therefore that they take these doctrines to imply a religiously pernicious disconnection between God and human beings.

In this paper, I will argue that these doctrines have no such implication. I will begin by looking more carefully at what it is for persons to be present to one another. Then I will consider and argue against an attempt to show that the doctrine of divine eternity rules out such personal presence between God and human beings. Next, I will consider the challenge posed by the doctrine of divine simplicity. I will give reasons for thinking that the doctrine of divine simplicity does not in fact entail the agnosticism frequently associated with it. I will also argue, however, that there is another kind of knowledge of God, which is compatible with the doctrine of simplicity even if, contrary to my arguments, that doctrine did imply a kind of agnosticism about God's nature. In my view, this alternative kind of knowledge of God is sufficient for God's being personally present to human beings in the way the biblical stories describe. Finally, I will show that Thomas Aquinas, one of the main medieval proponents of the doctrines of divine eternity and divine simplicity, recognizes this alternative kind of knowledge of God and supposes it is available to all Christians in this life.

For all these reasons, I will claim, neither the doctrine of eternity nor the doctrine of simplicity rules out God's being personally present to human beings.

---

[4]   John 14:8–9.

[5]   For one example of this sort of position, see WETTSTEIN, *Against Theology* [2008], pp. 219–45.

2.2 Personal Presence

What is it for one person to be present to another? In an earlier work, Norman Kretzmann and I tried to capture the relation of one person's being personally present to another in terms of one person's having direct and unmediated causal contact with and cognitive access to another.[6] I now think, however, that the attempt to capture personal presence in terms of direct and unmediated cognitive and causal contact misses something in the sense of personal presence even as between human beings. Consider, for example, one person, Paula, who is blind and falls over another person, Jerome, when he is unconscious in her path. Paula may cause Jerome to be moved by falling over him; and she may know by touch that it is a human person she has fallen over. Paula will thus have direct and unmediated causal and cognitive connection with Jerome; but she is not present to Jerome, in any normal sense of personal presence, in consequence of falling over him while he is unconscious.

What has to be added to the condition of direct and unmediated causal and cognitive contact for personal presence, I now think, is something psychologists call 'shared attention'. This is a cognitive state hard to define precisely but very familiar to us. Mutual gaze is one means for mediating a primary kind of shared attention; but there are many other kinds as well. Even newborn infants can exercise what seems to be an inborn capacity for shared attention. A newborn infant is capable of discriminating persons as persons, and the infant is also able to be aware of his mother's awareness of the infant. By two months of age, an infant can even exercise some control over shared attention. It can turn its face away, for example, and so avert mutual gaze with another person. The mutual awareness brought about by mutual gaze is a particularly powerful kind of shared attention. Psychologists call this 'dyadic shared attention'. But it is also possible for shared attention to be triadic. When a baby points out a dog to his mother, gazing alternately at the dog and at his mother, who is looking at the dog with him, then there is what psychologists call 'triadic shared attention' between them.

In each of the biblical stories I mentioned at the outset, shared attention between God and a human person is a notable feature of the story. God says to Abraham, 'Abraham, Abraham!', and Abraham replies, 'Here I am'. This conversation does not communicate information between God and Abraham so much as it establishes shared attention between them. When Rebecca turns to God in order to ask God a question, the point of the turning seems just to put her in a position to share attention with God before asking God her question. And when Job says to

---

[6] STUMP AND KRETZMANN, *Eternity, Awareness, and Action* [1992], pp. 463–82. By 'direct and unmediated' in this context, I mean only that the cognitive access or the causal connection does not have as an intermediate step the agency of another person; I do not mean that there is no intermediary of any sort. In this sense of 'direct and unmediated', if I am wearing my glasses when I see a person, I still have direct and unmediated cognitive access to him; and if I am on the phone with him when I cause him grief by telling him that his mother has died, I am still exercising direct and unmediated causality on him.

God, 'now my eye has seen You', he is using words to enhance what vision itself has somehow established for him: personal presence based on shared attention. This shared attention, mediated by hearing or even by some kind of seeing (as in Job's case), is a critical element in the personal presence of God to a human person in the biblical stories.

By contrast, consider, for example, Homer's depiction of Zeus. Wherever in physical reality he is, Homer's Zeus has direct and unmediated causal connection with the Trojans and also direct and unmediated cognitive access to them. That is, Zeus knows directly and immediately what is happening to the Trojans in the fighting with the Greeks, say, and he can affect the way the fighting goes just by willing it. But Zeus can continue to have such cognitive and causal contact with the Trojans even when he is (as Homer sometimes says) having dinner with the Ethiopians, for instance. While Zeus is among the Ethiopians, however, he is not present but absent from the scene of the Greek and Trojan war. So although Zeus has direct and unmediated causal and cognitive connection with the Trojans even while he is among the Ethiopians, he is not present to the Trojans then. Although he can affect and know the Trojans when he is in Ethiopia, Zeus cannot share attention with them when he is at that distance from them. While he is in Ethiopia, his power is present to the Trojans, we might say, but Zeus himself is not present to them. For this reason, Zeus is not omnipresent, even if he can know and control things at a distance from himself.

So for personal presence, not only does there have to be direct and unmediated causal and cognitive contact between persons, but there has to be the practical possibility of shared attention as well. *Mutatis mutandis*, the same point applies also to God. For real omnipresence, as distinct from mere power at a distance such as Homer's Zeus has, it needs to be the case that God is in a position to share attention with any human person able and willing to share attention with God.

In the example in which a blind Paula falls over unconscious Jerome in her path, Jerome is not present to Paula primarily because, in virtue of being unconscious, Jerome is not available to share attention with Paula. But shared attention can be ruled out for other reasons besides unconsciousness. As the example of Zeus among the Ethiopians makes clear, for knowers other than omnipresent God, physical distance can undermine shared attention.[7] There is also psychological distance, and it is at least as important an obstacle to personal presence as physical distance. If Jerome is in the same room as Paula but is totally absorbed in his work, for example, and never looks up at Paula or speaks to her, she will feel rightly that he is not present to her on that occasion. Or if Jerome is habitually secretive and self-absorbed, so that Paula is entirely shut out of his inner life, Jerome will not be present to Paula. The absence of psychological closeness undermines or obviates shared attention, and therefore vitiates or prevents personal presence, too.

---

[7]   On the other hand, perception is not necessary for shared attention. The internet, for example, can make shared attention even among people who are at some distance from each other. Two people engaged in animated discussion with each other by means of a computer are sharing attention as much as two people talking together on the telephone.

It is not possible to examine the notions of psychological distance or closeness in detail here;[8] but however exactly we understand these notions, it is clear that there will be psychological distance between persons if the mind of one of the persons in the relationship is hidden from the other. Distance of this sort can be a function of difference of abilities. If Jerome's chief work and chief joy is music, for example, but Paula is tone-deaf and musically illiterate, then Jerome will not be able to share attention with Paula in the part of his life that involves music. The distance resulting from this absence of shared attention between them will keep Jerome from being present to Paula, at least where the part of his life involving music is concerned. As an extreme of this sort of case, imagine that Jerome is incomprehensible to Paula, not just in his music-making and music-listening but in every way, entirely. In that case, the relationship between Paula and Jerome would be like the relationship between a dolphin and a human being who cross paths. A dolphin and a human being are each members of an intelligent species, but there will typically be little or no shared attention between them when they interact. Insofar as shared attention is necessary for personal presence, then to the extent to which Jerome is unknowable to Paula, to that extent he is not present to Paula either.

These conclusions obviously make a difference to the question of whether an eternal and simple deity can be personally present to human beings. And so, with this much reflection on the idea of personal presence, we can turn to the complaint that the doctrines of eternity and simplicity rule out personal presence between God and human beings.

2.3 The Doctrine of God's Eternity

It is easiest to begin with the doctrine of God's eternity. In *SCG* I.c.15, Aquinas describes God's eternity this way,

> God is entirely without motion ... Therefore, he is not measured by time ... nor can any succession be found in his being ... [Rather, he has] his being all at once (*totum simul*) – in which the formula of eternity consists.

In *STh* I, q. 10, a. 1, Aquinas cites the combination of illimitability and the lack of succession as the heart of the concept of eternity. As he explains there,[9]

> Two things make eternity known: first, the fact that what is in eternity is interminable, that is, lacking beginning and end (since 'term' refers to both); second, the fact that eternity lacks succession, since it exists all at once.

In *STh* I, q. 10, a. 2, Aquinas argues that God is His own duration; and in *STh* I, q. 10, a. 2 ad 2, he explains that God endures beyond all ages (*durat ultra quodcumque*

---

8   For detailed discussion of these notions, see my *Presence and Omnipresence* [2008].

9   For purposes of this paper, I have used the Marietti editions. Apart from the specific texts noted explicitly in the footnotes, the translations are my own. In the case of texts in *STh*, my translations are informed by the excellent translation of the Father of the English Dominican Province.

saeculum). These passages, combined with the preceding text, make it clear that
the interminability of God's existence is to be understood as the interminability
of unending duration of some sort, rather than as the interminability of a point
or instant.[10] It is evident from these texts and others as well that the concept of
eternity as Aquinas accepts it is the concept of a life without succession but with infinite atemporal persistence or atemporal duration, where 'duration' is understood
analogically with temporal duration.

There has been considerable debate in the secondary literature about the coherence of the doctrine of divine eternity. What is of interest to me here, however, is not
the objection that the doctrine is incoherent but rather only the complaint that the
doctrine is religiously pernicious because it rules out God's being present to human
beings, contrary to the portrayal of God in the biblical stories.

One person who has argued that, if God is not temporal but eternal, then God
cannot be present to human beings is William Hasker.[11] Hasker's argument for this
position depends on a claim which I will call 'Hasker's Principle':

(Hasker's Principle): To be present to temporal beings requires being temporal
    oneself.

Aquinas himself does not accept Hasker's Principle. On the contrary, Aquinas tends
to emphasize that the temporal things an eternal God knows are present to God in
His knowing of them. So, for example, Aquinas claims that God's eternal gaze views
future events 'presently' (*praesentialiter*).[12] On Aquinas's view, God knows future
contingent things in the same way He knows everything in time, namely, insofar as
future contingent things are present to God.[13]

In addition to the many passages in which Aquinas talks about God's knowledge
of temporal things as gaze or sight, or some other divine analogue of a kind of direct
awareness, there are also many passages in which Aquinas expresses forcefully his
sense that (eternal) God is personally present to (temporal) human beings. For
example, in his commentary on Galatians, in discussing the relation of eternal God
to human persons, Aquinas says,

> the ultimate perfection, by which a person is made perfect inwardly, is joy, which
> stems from the presence of what is loved. Whoever has the love of God, however,

---

[10] Cf. also *STh* I, q. 39, a. 8 obj. 1 and corpus; *STh* I, q. 46, a. 1 obj. 8 and ad 8. In *STh* I, q. 10,
a. 4, the first objection takes as a premise the claim that eternity, like time, is a measure of
duration; in the reply to the objection, AQUINAS disputes only the assumption that time and
eternity are the same kind of measure of duration, not that eternity is a measure of duration.
In *STh* I, q. 10, a. 4 ad 3, this point is developed. In that reply, Aquinas maintains that time as
a measure of duration is the measure of motion, whereas eternity as a measure of duration
is the measure of permanent being.

[11] HASKER, *God, Time, and Knowledge* [1989]; cf. especially p. 169. For more discussion of
Hasker's argument and others related to it, see the chapter on eternity in STUMP, *Aquinas*
[2003].

[12] *QDV* 12.6 corpus.

[13] *STh* I, q. 14, a. 13.

already has what he loves, as is said in 1 John 4:16: 'whoever abides in the love of God abides in God, and God abides in him'. And joy wells up from this.[14]

Aquinas develops the same idea in discussing the mission of an eternal divine person. In that context, Aquinas says,

> There is one general way by which God is in all things by essence, power, and presence, [namely,] as a cause in the effects participating in his goodness. But in addition to this way there is a special way [in which God is in a thing by essence, power, and presence] which is appropriate for a rational creature, in whom God is said to be as the thing known is in the knower and the beloved is in the lover … In this special way, God is not only said to be in a rational creature but even to dwell in that creature.[15]

So Aquinas does not suppose that being present to something temporal requires being temporal oneself. On the contrary, on Aquinas's understanding of the nature of divine eternity, an eternal God can be more present to a human person than any temporal being could be. The one, infinitely enduring present of eternity is simultaneous with each moment of time as that time is present. Since that is so, each moment of the life of a human person is always present at once to eternal God. By contrast, when Paula is present to Jerome in her middle age, her childhood is past and gone; and her old age is not yet here. What Jerome has present to him of Paula's life is only the temporally thinnest part, that part which is temporally present *now*; and he has this part available to him only instant by instant. By contrast, God has present to him, all at once, the whole of Paula's life.

Aquinas would therefore reject Hasker's Principle. And, in my view, he would be right to do so. Hasker's Principle can be generalized in this way:[16]

(General Principle): One person can be present to other things or persons only if he shares their mode of existence with them.

But this general principle is not true. If the general principle were true, it would follow from it that a non-spatial God could not be present to spatial beings. But virtually no serious theologian would accept such a claim; presumably Hasker himself would not be willing to accept it. If the general principle is unacceptable as applied to space, however, why should we suppose that it is acceptable as applied to time? If God can be present to His creatures without sharing their *spatial* mode of existence,[17] why should we not suppose that God can be present to His creatures without sharing their *temporal* mode of existence?

---

[14] *In Gal.* 5:6. There is an English translation of this work: AQUINAS, *Commentary on Saint Paul's Epistle* [1966]; for this passage, see pp. 179–80. I have used my own translation here.

[15] *STh* I, q. 43, a. 3.

[16] HASKER disputes the claim that this principle can be generalized in this way in *The Absence of a Timeless God* [2002]. But Hasker's argument is effectively refuted by SENOR, *The Real Presence* [2009]; and so I will not deal with it further here.

[17] Consider relationships of direct awareness in which the subject and object are of different orders of dimensionality. A three-dimensional observer can be and very frequently is effortlessly aware of a two-dimensional object as such; an imagined two-dimensional observer could not be aware of a three-dimensional object as three-dimensional.

2.4 The Doctrine of God's Simplicity

Even if the complaint as regards the doctrine of divine eternity could be dispatched in this way, however, there is a worse problem raised by the doctrine of divine simplicity. It seems that an eternal, *simple* God could not be personally present to human beings even if an eternal non-simple God could be.

The doctrine of divine simplicity is perhaps the most difficult and controversial piece of medieval philosophical theology but also one of the most important.[18] It derives from the conviction that God is a being whose existence is self-explanatory, an absolutely perfect being.[19] Aquinas was among the most influential expositors and defenders of this doctrine. But Aquinas is often enough interpreted as holding the view that, because of the doctrine of simplicity, it is not possible for human beings to have any positive knowledge of God. On this interpretation of Aquinas's views, Aquinas maintains that because God is simple, human beings can know what God is *not*, but they cannot know anything of what God is. This is sometimes thought to be the heart of the *via negativa* in theology.

Aquinas puts a discussion of God's simplicity near the beginning of his treatment of the nature of God in the *Summa theologiae*,[20] and he begins that discussion with a short prologue. In the prologue, he says,

> When we know with regard to something *that* it is, we still need to ask about its mode of being (*quomodo sit*), in order to know with regard to it what it is (*quid sit*). But because we are not able to know with regard to God what he is, but [rather] what he is not, we cannot consider with regard to God what the mode of being is but rather what the mode of being is not ... It can be shown with regard to God what the mode of being is not by removing from him those things not appropriate to him, such as composition and motion and other things of this sort.

This passage and others like it have sometimes been pressed into service as evidence for a thorough-going agnosticism on Aquinas's part with regard to knowledge of God. So, for example, Leo Elders says,

> The comprehension of God's essence is altogether excluded. This conclusion is presupposed in the Prologue to the Third Question ... Even if we say that God is perfect, good or eternal, we must realize that we do not know what these terms mean when predicated of God.[21]

---

[18]   This doctrine has also been the subject of a voluminous literature. The most sustained and sophisticated attack on Aquinas's position can be found in HUGHES, *Complex Theory* [1989]. Hughes's attack, however, seems to me based on misunderstandings of crucial elements of Aquinas's metaphysics, as reviewers have pointed out (see, for example, BURRELL, *Review of Hughes* [1992], pp. 120–21), and so I will not consider it here.

[19]   The derivation of divine simplicity from such considerations is apparent in AQUINAS's *QDP* 7.1, as JORDAN has recently pointed out in his article *Names of God* [1983] in FREDDOSO, *Existence and Nature of God* [1983], pp. 161–90; see esp. pp. 176–9.

[20]   *STh* I, q. 3.

[21]   ELDERS, *Philosophical Theology of Aquinas* [1990], p. 143.

But caution is warranted here. It is true that Aquinas explains divine simplicity only in terms of what God is not – not a body, not composed of matter and form, and so on. On the other hand, however, in the course of showing what God is not, Aquinas relies heavily on positive claims about God. So, for example, Aquinas argues that God is not a body on the basis of these claims among others: God is the first mover; God is pure actuality; God is the first being; God is the most noble of beings. In arguing that God is not composed of matter and form, Aquinas actually makes a huge substantial positive metaphysical claim about the nature of God. He says,

> a form which is not able to be received in matter but is subsistent by itself (*per se subsistens*) is individuated in virtue of the fact that it cannot be received in something else. And God is a form of this sort.[22]

In fact, in *STh* I, q. 13 Aquinas repudiates the sort of agnosticism some scholars in effect attribute to him. Aquinas himself associates such a position with Moses Maimonides and rejects it explicitly. Elsewhere, Aquinas bluntly denies the view that human beings can have no positive knowledge of God. In *QDP* q. 7, a. 5, for example, he says,

> the understanding of a negation is always based on some affirmation. And this is clear from the fact that every negation is proved by an affirmation. For this reason, unless the human intellect knew something affirmatively about God, it would be unable to deny anything of God.

These texts and others like them strongly suggest that it is a mistake to read the prologue to *STh* I, q. 3 as implying agnosticism with regard to the knowledge of God.

How, then, are we to understand that prologue? I am inclined to think that part of the problem in interpreting Aquinas's remarks in the prologue correctly has to do with the expression '*quid est*' in the text which claims that we do not know of God *quid est* (that is, *what he is*).[23]

The expression *quid est* is a technical term of medieval logic. Peter of Spain, for example, gives the standard medieval formula for a genus as that which is predicated of many things differing in species in respect of what they are (*in eo quod quid est*). In the terms of this technical understanding of *quid est* in medieval logic, it is certainly possible for someone who does not know the *quid est* of a thing nonetheless to know a great deal even about the essence of that thing. The *differentia* of a thing is also part of its essence, but the *differentia* is not predicated *in eo quod quid est*. So whatever exactly '*quid est*' means in Aquinas's thought, in the terms of medieval logic Aquinas's claim that we cannot know with regard to God *quid est* does not *by itself* imply that we can know nothing positive about God. On the contrary, the claim that we cannot know the *quid est* of God is apparently compatible in Aquinas's own mind with the many positive claims he makes about God. In examining Aquinas's understanding of the doctrine of divine simplicity, therefore, we should not simply assume on the basis of the prologue to the question

---

22   *STh* I, q. 3, a. 2 ad 3.
23   See, in this connection, particularly *SCG* I.14.

on simplicity in *STh* that Aquinas has adopted a thorough-going agnosticism as regards human knowledge of God's nature.

In addition, however, it is also important in this connection to note what a human knower *would* have, on Aquinas's views, if he did indeed grasp the *quid est* of a thing, any thing, including God. To see this, we need to remember something of Aquinas's philosophical psychology.

Aquinas thinks that the proper object of the intellect is the *quid est* or *quiddity* of a thing. Just as the external senses have their proper objects, such as colour, for example, so the intellect also has its proper object; the intellect apprehends quiddities as the eyes apprehend colours.[24] Aquinas calls the simple acts of cognition by which the intellect grasps the *quid est* of things 'the cognition of non-complexes'. This is what he thinks of as 'the first operation of the intellect', and it is the foundation for propositional knowledge.[25] The second operation of the intellect is what Aquinas calls 'compounding and dividing'. Composition or division occurs when the intellect combines its apprehension of quiddities or divides them to form affirmative or negative 'complexes' or propositional judgments.[26] These judgments are then available to the knower to use in discursive reasoning, which is the third operation of the intellect.

So when a person does have knowledge of the *quid est* of a thing, that knowledge is the first element in propositional knowledge and propositional reasoning.

2.5 The Knowledge of Persons

It is important to see, however, that propositional knowledge is not the only kind of knowledge possible for human beings. There is a different kind of knowledge available to human beings which is not reducible to knowledge *that* something or other is the case, and it does not depend on the grasp of the quiddity of a thing.

To get some intuitive feel for this non-propositional knowledge of persons, imagine a woman, Mary, who has been kept in an isolated imprisonment since birth by some mad scientist.   Imagine that Mary, in her imprisonment, has had access to any and all information about the world which can be transmitted in terms of propositions.[27] So, for example, Mary has available to her the best science texts for any of the sciences, from physics to sociology. She knows that there are other people in the world, and she knows all that science can teach her about them. But she has never had any personal interactions of a direct and unmediated sort with another person.   She has read descriptions of human faces, for example, but she

---

[24]   *STh* I, q. 85, a. 8.

[25]   For detailed discussion of this part of Aquinas's thought, see the section on the mechanisms of cognition in my *Aquinas* [2003].

[26]   See, for example, *In DA* lib. III, lect. XI, num. 746–60.

[27]   I am here adapting Frank Jackson's original thought experiment. For this thought experiment and the extensive discussion it has generated, see LUDLOW ET AL., *There's Something About Mary* [2004].

has never been face-to-face with another person.[28] And then suppose that Mary is finally rescued from her imprisonment and united for the first time with her mother, who loves her deeply.

When Mary is first united with her mother, it seems indisputable that Mary will know things she did not know before, even if she knew everything about her mother which could be made available to her in expository prose.[29] Although Mary knew that her mother loved her before she met her, when she is united with her mother, Mary will learn what it is like to be loved. And this will be new for her, even if in her isolated state she had as complete a scientific description as possible of what a human being feels like when she senses that she is loved by someone else. Furthermore, it is clear that this is only the beginning. Mary will also come to know what it is like to be touched by someone else, to be surprised by someone else, to ascertain someone else's mood, to detect affect in the melody of someone else's voice, to match thought for thought in conversation, and so on. These will be things she learns, even if before she had access to excellent books on human psychology and communication.

The way in which I have formulated what Mary learns – what it is like to be touched by someone else, and so on – may suggest to someone that Mary learns things just about herself, and that she learns them in virtue of having new first-person experiences. It seems, then, that whatever Mary learns can be explained adequately in terms of a first-person account.[30] But this is clearly wrong-headed. Even if Mary does learn new things about herself, what will come as the major revelation to Mary is her mother. Even this way of putting what Mary learns is misleading, because it suggests that Mary's new knowledge can be expressed in a third-person description of *her mother*. But neither first-person nor third-person accounts will be adequate for Mary to describe what is new for her. What is new for

---

[28] More than one person has suggested to me that if Mary had been kept from all second person experiences, she could not have learned a language, and she would be unable to read. But this objection seems to me insufficiently imaginative. We can suppose that Mary has been raised in a sophisticated environment in which carefully programmed computers taught her to speak and to read.

[29] Nicholas Wolterstorff has suggested to me in correspondence that if Mary had had the requisite sort of experience of personal interaction before her period of isolation, then it would have been possible to communicate to her in the expository prose of a third-person account what personal interaction with her mother would be like. On this view, the difficulty in communicating to Mary by a third-person account the nature of a second person experience with her mother is just a function of Mary's innocence of second person experiences. But I am inclined to think this diagnosis of Mary's difficulty is not correct. In ordinary circumstances involving persons socialized in the usual way, it remains true that when we meet a person for the first time, we learn something important which we did not know before we met that person, even if before the meeting we were given an excellent and detailed third-person account of that person.

[30] Although insofar as some of what is at issue for Mary in the relevant first-person experiences has to do with qualia, it may be that what she knows in that first-person experience is also not expressible in terms of knowing that.

her, what she learns, has to do with her personal interaction with another person. What is new for Mary is a second person experience.

This thought experiment thus shows that we can come to know a person and that this knowledge is difficult or impossible to formulate in terms of propositional knowledge.[31] The kind of knowledge at issue in the thought experiment about Mary is only the beginning of the examples of such non-propositional knowledge. To take one more example, consider this sentence:

(1)   Joseph saw his brothers in the crowd and knew them at once.

What is at issue in this sentence is Joseph's knowledge of the men before him, and so what is known in this case, we might suppose, is paradigmatically expressible in propositional form, in terms of knowledge *that*. This sentence is equivalent, we might think, to

(1')   Joseph knew *that* the men he saw in front of him in the crowd are his brothers.

It is true that in the recognition scene in Genesis Joseph does know *that* the men in front of him were his brothers, but this is not the same as seeing the men in front of him and knowing them as his brothers. Joseph might have known the identity of the men in front of him in any number of ways, but the sense of the first sentence is that Joseph knew their identity in virtue of knowing *them*, by face recognition, among other things.

It is clear that the brain of a normally functioning human being has the capacity to know a face, and it is equally clear that it is extremely difficult, if not impossible, to translate the knowledge conveyed by the sight of a particular face into a description of that face. As far as that goes, it is possible for one person, Paula, to see and describe appropriately the face of another person, Jerome, and yet *not* know Jerome in virtue of knowing his face, even though Jerome is a person otherwise familiar to Paula. In the neurological debility of prosopagnosia, a patient can see a face and describe it adequately, but on the basis of that perception alone the patient is unable to know the person whose face she is perceiving, however well acquainted she is with that person. By contrast, a normally functioning human being has the ability to identify a person on the basis of swift and reliable face recognition.

And so knowledge of a person on the basis of face recognition is another example of knowledge which is difficult or impossible to translate into propositional knowledge.

---

[31]   In correspondence, Al Plantinga has suggested to me that I am here in fact explaining in expository prose what it is that Mary learns, namely, what it is like to be loved by her mother, and so on. But that some sort of description of what Mary learns is possible does not mean that we can explain what Mary learns adequately with an expository account. Consider, for example, that while it is possible to describe the experience of seeing red to a person who has been blind from birth by saying that when a sighted person sees a red object, she knows what it is like to see red, this description is not an adequate explanation in expository prose of what the sighted person knows in knowing what it is like to see red.

The rapid, perplexing increase in the incidence of autism has led scientists and philosophers to a deeper understanding of the knowledge of persons and a new appreciation for its importance in normal human functioning. Various studies have demonstrated that the knowledge which is impaired for an autistic child cannot be taken as knowledge *that* something or other is the case. An autistic child can know *that* a particular macroscopic object is her mother or *that* the person who is her mother has a certain mental state. But the autistic child can know such things without the knowledge that a normally developing child would have. For example, an autistic child might know that his mother is sad, but in virtue of the impairment of autism he will not be able to know the sadness of his mother. And these are different items of knowledge. An autistic child might know that the person he is looking at is sad because, for example, someone who is a reliable authority for the child has told him so. But this is clearly not the same as the child's knowing the sadness in the face of the person he is looking at.[32]

In these cases, and in many other cases of perfectly ordinary human experience, it is arguable that it is not possible to express adequately what is known in terms of propositional knowing. Rather, it is a knowledge of persons.

Mutatis mutandis, the same distinction applies where God is concerned. Consider, for example, these two claims:

(2)   Thomas Aquinas knew that God is really present in the Eucharist.

and

(2')   Thomas Aquinas knew the real presence of God in the Eucharist.

These are clearly not equivalent claims, and the second cannot be reduced to the first. Obviously, the first could be true and the second could be false. Or consider this pair of claims:

(3)   Thomas Aquinas knew that God exists.

and

(3')   Thomas Aquinas knew God.

Here, too, the claims are not equivalent, and the second cannot be reduced to the first. In both these cases, what is at issue in the first sentence is propositional knowledge, and what is at issue in the second is the knowledge of persons with regard to God.

2.6 Knowledge and Presence

No doubt, propositional knowledge of another person can deepen and enrich the knowledge of persons, at least among adult human beings. Nothing in the claims I have made about the importance of the knowledge of persons should be taken to imply a discounting of propositional knowledge of persons. But for shared attention

---

[32]   See MOORE ET AL., *Components of Person Perception* [1997], pp. 401–23.

between two persons, and for the personal presence of one of them to the other that shared attention provides, the knowledge of persons is sufficient. That is why, no matter how much propositional knowledge of her mother the Mary of the thought experiment might have in her isolated condition, she cannot share attention with her mother or have her mother present to her without having the knowledge of persons of her mother.

What *undermines* personal presence, therefore, is not missing propositional knowledge. It is rather an absence of the knowledge of persons. As far as I can see, however, there is nothing about the doctrine of simplicity that rules out knowledge of persons with respect to God. Obviously, in the human case, it is possible for one person to have such knowledge of another even if he has little or no propositional knowledge with regard to that other person. Jerome can know Paula with the knowledge of persons without having much if any propositional knowledge about her. What the doctrine of simplicity rules out explicitly, however, is just propositional knowledge of the *quid est* of God.

So even if, contrary to what I have argued, the doctrine of simplicity gave us reason for accepting a general sort of agnosticism about God, that agnosticism would have to do only with propositional knowledge. The knowledge of persons with respect to God would still be available.

2.7 Aquinas's Position

Someone might suppose that whether or not this conclusion, informed by contemporary science and philosophical thought experiments, is right, it is nonetheless thoroughly anti-Thomistic. But this would be a mistaken supposition. In many places, Aquinas shows unequivocally that he recognizes and accepts knowledge of persons and thinks that it is available to human beings in this life as a mode of knowledge where God is concerned.

To begin with, in his commentaries on New Testament texts, Aquinas makes it clear that on his view human beings are in a position to know the incarnate Christ with the knowledge of persons. This is, of course, the case for the disciples living at the time of Christ; but it is also the case, on Aquinas's view, for people born after the earthly life of Christ. In the interest of brevity, I will illustrate these claims by considering just Aquinas's commentary on the Gospel of John.[33]

In that work, Aquinas clearly supposes that Christ can be known with the knowledge of persons even by people living after Christ's earthly ministry. Speaking to his own readers, Aquinas says,

> [i]f then, you ask which way to go, accept Christ, for he is the way … If you ask where to go, cling to Christ, for he is the truth, which we desire to reach …If you ask where to remain, remain in Christ because he is the life. (1870)

---

[33] For purposes of this paper, I found it convenient to use the translation of this text in AQUINAS, *Commentary on the Gospel of St. John* [1980].

That these descriptions of connection between human beings and Christ are not meant as metaphors for the acceptance of theological truths but are meant to be taken literally, as descriptions of personal relationship to Christ and personal knowledge of Christ, is attested by myriad texts in this same commentary. Consider, for example, this comment of Aquinas on Christ's claim that he is the true vine. Aquinas says,

> Christ is a true vine producing a wine which interiorly intoxicates us ... and which strengthens us. ... [T]hose united to Christ are the branches of this vine. (1979, 1983)

Without personal relationship to someone and personal knowledge of him, one could hardly be said to be *united* with that person.

Aquinas also clearly takes the knowledge of persons with respect to Christ to be the knowledge of persons with respect to God as well. For example, in commenting on Christ's rebuke to Philip that anyone who has seen Christ has seen the Father, Aquinas remarks,

> [Christ] shows that knowledge of the Son is also knowledge of the Father, [and] he ... [asserts] the disciples's knowledge of the Father. ... [T]here is no better way to know something than through its word or image, and the Son is the Word of the Father. ... Therefore, the Father is known in the Son as in his Word and proper image. (1876, 1878)

And Aquinas goes on to say,

> the Father was in the incarnate Word because they had one and the same nature, and the Father was seen in the incarnate Christ. (1881)

That is also, on Aquinas's view, the reason why Christ disapproved of Philip's request that Christ show them the Father. Aquinas says,

> [Christ] is displeased with ... [Philip's] request because the Father is seen in the Son. (1890)

In fact, not only is God the Father known in the Son, but, on Aquinas's views, part of the divine purpose in the incarnation is precisely to make the Father known. God wants human beings in this life to know Him, and that is why God provides an incarnation. Aquinas says,

> [n]o one can acquire a knowledge of the Father except by his Word, which is his Son ... [S]o God, wanting to be known by us, takes his Word, conceived from eternity, and clothes it with flesh in time. (1874)

As far as that goes, this knowledge of God is *necessary* for being in grace, in Aquinas's view. In commenting on the passage in which Christ says that those who persecute his followers will do so because they lack knowledge of God, Aquinas says of such persecutors that they will even kill Christians because, as he says, 'they have not known the Father ... or the Son.' (2076)

One should notice in this connection that Aquinas does not here ascribe a lack of propositional knowledge about God to these putative persecutors. What Aquinas says about them is that they lack personal knowledge of God: '[T]hey have not known the Father.'

Furthermore, on Aquinas's account, one of the great benefits of Christ's sending the Holy Spirit, which indwells in every one of those in grace, is that the Holy Spirit enables believers to know Christ – that is, to have the knowledge of persons as regards Christ. So, commenting on Christ's line that the Holy Spirit will glorify him, Aquinas says that for the Holy Spirit to glorify Christ is just for the Holy Spirit to give every believer knowledge of Christ (2106).[34] In fact, the wisdom which is one of the seven gifts of the Holy Spirit is the knowledge of God; that is why Aquinas allies it with *caritas*, the love of God (*STh* II-II, q. 45).

2.8 Conclusion

It is evident, then, that neither the doctrine of eternity nor the doctrine of simplicity gives a good reason for denying that God can be present to human beings, not only with direct and immediate causal and cognitive connection, but also with the shared attention which is the basis for personal presence. It is not necessary for God to share a temporal mode of existence in order to be present to a person in time, as long as God can be known by that temporal person. And the doctrine of simplicity gives us no reason for supposing that God cannot be known in the way necessary for personal presence.

As I explained in connection with the prologue to Aquinas's discussion of simplicity in *STh*, there are reasons for rejecting the view that, for Aquinas, human beings cannot have any positive propositional knowledge of God in this life even if they cannot apprehend the quiddity of God. But it is also true that human beings are ordinarily capable of a non-propositional knowledge of persons, which cannot be reduced to propositional knowledge and which does not depend on the apprehension of the quiddity of a thing. And this knowledge of persons is sufficient for personal presence. So, even if the doctrine of simplicity ruled out positive propositional knowledge of God, it would not rule out the knowledge of God necessary for personal presence.

That this is a view Aquinas shares is made clear from his commentary on the Gospel of John. In that commentary, Aquinas undoubtedly supposes that Christ's disciples had personal knowledge of this sort of the incarnate Christ, and he also clearly holds that in having this knowledge of Christ, they had personal knowledge of God the Father as well. As the passages cited above make clear, Aquinas also thinks that such personal knowledge of Christ, and through Christ of God the Father, is available to all Christians at any time through the operations of the Holy Spirit, without whose indwelling no human being can be saved.

---

[34] AQUINAS explains that claim in this way: '[T]he Son is the principle of the Holy Spirit. For everything which is from another manifests that from which it is. Thus the Son manifests the Father because he is from the Father. And so because the Holy Spirit is from the Son, it is appropriate that the Spirit glorify [i. e., make manifest] the Son' (2107).

For all these reasons, then, however we are to interpret Aquinas within the tradition of negative theology, it is not the case on his account that the doctrines of God's eternity and simplicity allow only negative knowledge of God or rule out the personal presence of God to human beings.

Chapter 3

Why We Need God's Eternity:
Some Remarks to Support a Classic Notion

Thomas Schärtl

Divine eternity is under fire and is subject to a lot of questions. Not only so-called Open Theists vote for some sort of divine temporalism. It has become almost a common opinion among contemporary Systematic Theologians that the classic idea of divine atemporality has to be replaced by some sort of temporalism. Contemporary philosophy shows, nevertheless, that the discussion is extremely overheated; the gaps between the different camps are deep. And the mutual accusations are harsh. Even the more or less "indecisive" thinkers reveal that it is not easy to give up the classic idea of eternity and that it is, on the other hand, equally problematic not to listen to some subtle arguments provided by so-called temporalists. So, why should one even try to argue in favour of classic eternalism? Before I develop some thoughts in order to introduce one (and, actually, it is just *one*) intuition that somehow forced me not to stay indecisive but to vote for divine eternity let me briefly define what I mean by divine eternity (but, as one can see, this definition is just a summary of what has been outlined by eternalists anyway):

1. An eternal being is not just an everlasting entity. It is, literally, not subject to the flow of time. Therefore:
2. An eternal being has no temporal parts. And:
3. An eternal being is 'simultaneous' to any points t_1 and t_2 in time even if t_1 and t_2 are not simultaneous.[1]
4. An eternal being is, based on this notion of simultaneity, fully present (omnipresent) to and at every point in time.

---

[1] Cf. STUMP AND KRETZMANN, *Eternity* [1987], pp. 219–52; cf. also STUMP, *Aquinas* [2003], pp. 131–58. It has been argued that Kretzmann and Stump's notion of 'ET-simultaneity' (which allows for God to be simultaneous to everything but does not allow temporal events to cross the line of eternity into total simultaneity) is not consistent. But there are many reasons to doubt such accusations since the concept of 'ET-simultaneity' works like the concept of 'relative identity'. However, this leaves a rather meta-philosophical question: What is the benefit of a logical and conceptual tool if its use is restricted to just one case of philosophical and theological reasoning?

Admittedly, these aspects are still pretty vague. They don't say much about 'eternity' and nothing about any reason why we should stick to the classic notion of divine eternity. As Brian Leftow has shown, much more conceptual work needed to be done in order to clarify if there is a connection between 1. and 2. or whether 1. and 2. already represent different notions of eternity (let us say an Augustinian versus an Anselmian concept of eternity).[2] Temporalists, on the other hand, point out that eternalists are in grave danger, since they cannot really show that the conjunction of 2. and 3. is consistent. Furthermore, 1. might threaten a Christian notion of God (or, to broaden the perspective, a concept of God which is typical for the monotheistic religions). The heart of any temporalist's counter-offer is tied to the idea that God needs to be able to act and react, to listen and to respond to temporal beings – actions which become pretty pointless, if not impossible, once we assume that God is in one way or the other "outside of time".

Before we turn to the nitty-gritty parts of my proposal, let me address a meta-theological and meta-philosophical problem: Who has to carry the *burden* of proof? Frankly, it is not so clear to me that the burden of proof lies with the eternalist, although Nicholas Wolterstorff is eager to point in another direction:

> We are obligated to understand as deeply and sympathetically as we can the considerations offered by our predecessors in favor of God's eternity. The burden of proof remains on them, however. They are claiming that we should not accept as literally true this aspect of the biblical representation of God [i. e., of God being temporal, T. S.]; for that we need cogent arguments. Otherwise what's left of the church's confession that Scripture, for it, is canonical?[3]

The problem consists, however, in Wolterstorff's hermeneutics. Since nobody can deny that the body of biblical scriptures is more like a choir of different voices, there is, after all, no such thing as a straightforward appeal to biblical testimony in order to support a temporalist's notion of God. As a matter of fact, for the most part of the Christian tradition the Bible has been read through the lenses of a certain tradition. And this tradition organically included a metaphysical concept of divine eternity. Apparently, at the level of theological interpretation nobody really perceived the slightest inconsistencies. Therefore, we cannot simply neglect the history of Christian hermeneutics which seemed to be able to reconcile the God of the Bible with the God of the philosophers – at least for the larger parts of this tradition. The situation would be different if we were forced to stick to a very rough idea of *sola scriptura*. But why should we do that theologically and, moreover, *philosophically*? What could be the role of the Bible in philosophical discourses concerning the concept of God and certain divine attributes? If we, instead, acknowledge the *interpretation* of the Bible in the light of theological and philosophical considerations as some sort of starting point – as a point of departure to get an idea of what Christian theism looks like – then the burden of proof clearly

---

[2]   Cf. LEFTOW, *Time and Eternity* [1991], pp. 73–111, 183–216.
[3]   WOLTERSTORFF, *Unqualified Divine Temporality* [2001], p. 189.

lies with those who want to *alter* the main course of tradition. In this case, the temporalist needs to do the homework and not the eternalist's camp.

Eternalists can claim to hold on to a position which is in accordance with larger parts of theological and philosophical traditions. Approached from the point of tradition, a temporalist would have to show that the traditional concepts are severely confused and inconsistent and that all the tools that are used to reconcile divine action with divine eternity (like the concept of providence) fall prey to further severe inconsistencies. But as the discussion has shown in the last two decades: God's eternity does not necessarily exclude divine action and, if we think of the foreknowledge problem, human freedom.[4]

But, and this is the oddness of doing philosophical theology, even if the eternalist might be able to show that there are no further inconsistencies (after purifying the concepts in question, for example) the result might not be enough to come up with a convincing argument to actually *support* eternalism. It is not enough to show that eternalism is not bad; actually, what we need to get out of the unfortunate tie-situation is to name some real benefits of eternalism – benefits that may, in the long run, outnumber or outweigh the benefits of temporalism. It has been argued that there are no benefits to eternalism apart from – let us say – a certain "coherence" with the so-called classic tradition. Is that true? And is there, on the other side, a price the temporalist would have to pay as well?

3.1 Systematic Theology's New Euphoria

It might be helpful, at least revealing, to turn to contemporary systematic theology in order to face some conceptual requirements for a Christian concept of God and to assess the destiny of a classic concept of eternity. Well, to put it mildly, the reputation of the classic notion of eternity in contemporary systematic theology is rather bad – if not disastrous. It seems that the theologian's conviction that the Christian God has to be an 'interactive' God excludes the heritage of classic metaphysics. Yes, systematic theology could be more than willing nowadays to lend a hand to the temporalist's endeavour.

It is helpful, even instructive, to look at a quote from Bob Russell – he is addressing certain needs and presuppositions of Christian eschatology and, therefore, tries to systematize different approaches as well as to work towards an 'integrative' understanding of 'eternity':

> A crucial argument shared widely among contemporary Trinitarian theologians is that eternity is a richer concept of temporality than timelessness or unending time. In essence, eternity is the source of time as we know it, and of time as we will know it in the new creation. Eternity is the fully temporal source and the goal of time. Barth calls it 'supratemporal'. Moltmann calls it the 'future of the future', and Peters refers to the future as coming to us (*adventus*) and not merely that which tomorrow brings (*futurum*). Pannenberg claims that God acts proleptically from eternity: God

---

[4] Cf. ZAGZEBSKI, *Freedom and Foreknowledge* [1991].

reaches back into time to redeem the world, particularly in the life, ministry, death and resurrection of Jesus. In this approach the relation between time and eternity is modeled on the relation of the finite to the infinite. Here the infinite is not the negation of the finite …; instead the infinite includes while ceaselessly transcending time.[5]

Let us be very fair and sober at this point: What Russell presents as an excellent overview of different concepts of eternity within contemporary systematic theology is, to put it mildly, somehow overstretching the rules of a literal understanding of the relationships between time and eternity. And the whole theological idea remains quite vague when it comes to the task of furnishing a "richer" concept of eternity. One might ask: 'Richer than what – richer than the above-mentioned notion of God's full presence at every moment in time or God's simultaneity?' And, is what Russell ascribes to Karl Barth as a 'super-temporal' aspect of eternity a vote for atemporalism or something "higher"? Completely stunning seems to be the idea that eternity is like a *source* of time. Just for the time being, try to imagine the model behind this very figurative expression. How could it be that time *flows* from eternity? Does this mean that eternity is some kind of past behind the past? Even more complicated is the notion of eternity being the future of our future. Would this insinuate that God, as an eternal being, is not yet present to us, that he still is in becoming and that he is, actually, somehow waiting for himself? And, the way in which Russell describes Pannenberg's idea of prolepsis looks a bit as if the famous German theologian would vote for some knot or tie in time which allows for a (please, forgive that expression) temporal overlap of present and future events. But, truth is, Pannenberg himself has, at least partially, a more classic concept of divine eternity than what Russell referred to.[6] And, one might add, a more classic notion of divine presence and simultaneity can be in a better position to account for the overlap between present and future Pannenberg is watching out for.

So, what happened to systematic theology? It is not the task of this paper to criticize the achievements of contemporary theology. But, and this is up for further debate, one could be inclined to think that systematic theology fell for the Heideggerian hex[7] (Heideggerians might hopefully excuse this phrase) and suffered from

---

[5]   RUSSELL, *Bodily Resurrection* [2002], pp. 26–7.

[6]   Cf. PANNENBERG, *Systematic Theology* [1991], vol. 1, p. 410: 'In distinction from creatures, who as finite beings are subject to the march of time, the eternal God does not have ahead of him any future that is different from his present. God is eternal because he has no future outside Himself. … Discussion of the eternity of God led to the thought that all things are present to Him. They are present to Him as what they are in their distinction from Him, whether they be past or future, actual or possible. The past remains present to the eternal God and the future is already present to Him. His eternity thus implies his omnipresence.'

[7]   Cf. HEIDEGGER, *Vom Ereignis* [1989], pp. 470–71: '*So reich gefügt und bildlos das Seyn west, es ruht doch in ihm selbst und seiner* Einfachheit. *Wohl möchte der Charakter des Zwischen (den Göttern und Menschen) dazu verleiten, das Seyn als bloßen Bezug zu nehmen und als Folge und Ergebnis der Beziehung der Bezogenen. Aber das Er-eignis ist ja doch, wenn schon die Kennzeichnung noch möglich ist, dieses Beziehen, das die Bezogenen erst zu*

some kind of eschatological overheating of the theological machinery. It seems that the Heideggerian notion of *being as event* became the *leitmotiv*, which was also applied as a leading concept to the theology of God. Furthermore, the promises seemed to be wilder than any other ontological dream. Is it not true that a God who is 'in becoming' can grow together with mankind and can respond seriously to human prayers and needs, at least better than an immovable and eternal God? However, there is no straightforward conclusion that might convince us to think that an eternal God cannot be a God of prayer and worship or a God of incarnation. Moreover, it might be argued that a temporal God's incarnation fosters the mythological conundrum that stems from a far too anthropomorphic idea of God's becoming and the relation of the two natures in Christ. If we follow Eleonore Stump's reading of Aquinas, we can say that for the Christian tradition it was possible to remain an eternalist *and* to stick to the God of the Bible, so to speak, i. e. to underline divine eternity while at the same time having a concept of divine action[8] and interaction (interpreted through the lenses of providence[9]).

But, let us take a closer look: Why exactly is it so problematic – within the genuine areas of systematic theology – to hold on to a notion of divine *eternity*?

---

ihnen selbst bringt, um in das Offene der Ent-gegnenden-Entschiedenen ihre Notschaft und Wächterschaft zu legen, die sie nicht als Eigenschaft erst annehmen, aus denen sie vielmehr ihr Wesen schöpfen. Das Seyn ist Not der Götter und als diese Nötigung des Da-seins abgründiger denn Jegliches, was seiend heißen darf und durch das Seyn sich nicht mehr benennen lässt. Das Seyn ist gebraucht, die Notschaft der Götter, und dennoch nicht aus ihnen abzuleiten, sondern gerade umgekehrt ihnen überlegen, in der Ab-gründigkeit seines Wesens als Grund.' In these dark remarks one notion is significant; Heidegger thinks that any true relation has to be realized as an event. When theologians start to adopt this view, the Trinitarian relations need to be spelled out as events – as a necessity that somehow dictates God's history with mankind. But this view is highly problematic; theologians need to be aware that *Seyn* has replaced the position held by God in a theistic worldview. What Heidegger says about the 'Gods' and the 'coming God' doesn't fit to classic theism or Trinitarian theology. The notion of being as event is over-stretching the requirements of timely existence and is, furthermore, blurring the lines between finite and infinite existence.

[8]   Cf. STUMP, *Aquinas* [2003], pp. 149–56, esp. p. 148: 'Since on Aquinas' views the life of God is all at once and so atemporal, that is God must be different in important ways from a temporal, human mind. Considered as an atemporal mind, God cannot deliberate, anticipate, remember, or plan ahead, for instance, since all these mental activities essentially involve time, either in taking time to be performed ... or in requiring a temporal viewpoint as a prerequisite to performance (like remembering). But it is clear that there are other mental activities that do not require a temporal interval or viewpoint. Knowing seems to be the paradigm case. ... Willing, for example, unlike wishing or desiring, seems to be another. Furthermore, nothing atemporal can be material, and so the mind of God cannot be material; perceiving is therefore impossible in any literal sense for the mind that God is. But nothing in the nature of incorporeality or atemporality seems to rule out the possibility of awareness.'

[9]   Cf. STUMP, *Aquinas* [2003], p. 151: 'If an eternal God is also omnipotent, he can do anything it is not logically impossible for him to do. Even though his actions cannot be located in time, he can bring about effects in time unless doing so is logically impossible for him.'

It is not the divine impassibility that bothers us (and, please note, there is no analytic truth that may derive impassibility from eternity; this follows only if one is conceptually "glued" to a very anthropomorphic idea of passion that is inspired by an idea of anxiety and affection that grow over time). It is – and here we might follow the Lutheran theologian Robert Jenson – the Trinitarian and Christological formula that forces us to think that Jesus Christ *is* the divine *Logos* in a very straightforward and unequivocal sense. The classic notion of eternity, so it seems, becomes an obstacle for the understanding of this unequivocal 'is'. According to Jenson, the metaphysical burden lies in the need to establish some kind of parted or doubled Christology which has to make a difference between an eternal and a (rather) temporal son while confirming the "identity" of the two. Jenson is offering a very different solution; in order to avoid the problems of traditional Christology (problems that have to do, in his opinion, with the classic concept of theistic metaphysics which was intoxicated, so to speak, by Greek philosophy) he proposes the provocative idea that the second person of the Trinity is precisely the "temporal" Jesus Christ. In order to say something like that he has to develop a somewhat different understanding of the relations between past, presence, and future and of the relations God has to past, presence, and future. His key to spell out the identity of the Trinitarian persons (without abandoning their difference) is the role of the Holy Spirit *as* the future:

> The future whose oncoming temporalizes us is an appropriation to each other of the specific event of Jesus and all created history. Therefore the very process of time is in fact a *reaching back* in *anticipation*, 'a process into the depths of our present lives.' Past and future do cohere for us despite everything. They do not cohere because some third fact (e. g., a timeless present) bridges the gap. They cohere because the future that is before us is the *interpreting* of all prior occurrence – of all that is then or at any penultimate time past – by a specific temporal occurrence. And the very specificity of this occurrence – love – is such that the interpreting is inexhaustible.[10]

It is quite interesting to see that Jenson is mixing a variety of entirely different notions. There is, on the one hand, this idea of temporal occurrences that are bound together by the future. On the other hand, the classic notion of eternity, which has brought God into the position of simultaneously accessing past and future, is straightforwardly replaced by a theological idea of the future. But how can the *distant* future ever guarantee the coherence of *past events*? How should it be possible that the future as the *future* creates a *whole*? The worldview Jenson describes does not have any characteristics of simultaneity at all. Why is that?

Admittedly, there are certain benefits to this worldview: the relations among the Trinitarian persons are spelled out in temporal terms. This can be a framework to understand Karl Rahner's famous "axiom" (i. e., 'the economic Trinity is the immanent Trinity and vice versa'[11]) better or to interpret the 'is' which is the crucial part of the formula in terms of identity: in a way Jenson would say that

---

[10]   JENSON, *Triune Identity* [1982], p. 177.
[11]   Cf. RAHNER, *Trinity* [1970], pp. 99–103.

the immanent Trinity is identical to the economic Trinity (because there is no such thing as a reality "beyond" the history of salvation). The fact that the future remains distant allows for the 'identity' of the 'non-identity' of the Trinitarian persons. Although Father and Son are part of the very same temporal move towards the future, the basic openness of the future keeps a distance between Father and Son. The Holy Spirit, as the basis of this openness, needs to be part of this grammar of 'identity' and 'non-identity'.

> Truly, the Trinity is simply the Father and the man Jesus and their Spirit as the Spirit of the believing community. This "economic" Trinity is eschatologically God "himself," an "immanent" Trinity. And that assertion is no problem, for God is himself only eschatologically, since he is Spirit.
> As for God's freedom, only this proposal fully asserts it. The immanent Trinity of previous Western interpretation had but the spurious freedom of unaffectedness. Genuine freedom is the reality of possibility, is openness to the future; genuine freedom is Spirit. And it is only if we interpret God's eternity as the certainty of his triumph that we are able without qualification to say that God is Spirit. If we so understand God's freedom, we are indeed unable to describe *how* God could have been the selfsame triune God other than as the "economic" Trinity now in fact given.[12]

In other words: the divine *Logos* is nobody else but Jesus Christ, Jesus of Nazareth. His divinity consists – according to Jenson – of his directedness towards an endlessly promising future (which is anticipated in his resurrection), a future which promises his arrival at the Father's realm. The difference between Father and Son is bridged by the Holy Spirit's gift of sheer endlessness. The second person of the Trinity is the temporal Son. But thanks to the Father's basic involvement in the future and his ongoing "becoming", the Father is always a father, i. e., he is standing in a defining relation to the Son. And since the Son's "essence" is the directedness towards the future, the Son is always and necessarily related to the Father as the ultimate goal and meaning of his very existence. But in Jenson's theology the Son we are talking about is always and primarily the God *incarnate*. If we cross out the classic concept of divine eternity, the question what the incarnation might add to the immanent Trinity simply disappears because the immanent Trinity *is* the economic Trinity, the economy of salvation (and therefore of history and time) is the only framework of the Trinity and of God's divinity. The embeddedness of the Trinity in the economy of salvation (and, therefore, in time) might look like this:

---

[12]   JENSON, *Triune Identity* [1982], p. 141.

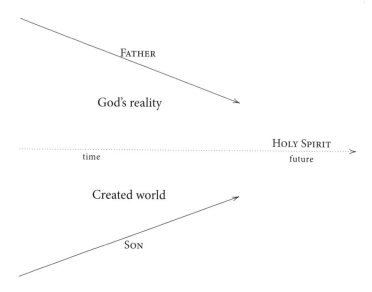

Jenson's approach is – just to use a cliché – a modification of a more Hegelian system of spelling out the relationship between God and the world.[13] The Son is entirely coming from the world; through the Easter event the Son is approaching the divine reality. Since the future makes 'eternity' in Jenson's view the concept of an eternal pre-existence of the Son seems to be entirely meaningless. Jenson does not deny such a concept; but he would underline its meaninglessness given that the coordinates in which this concept could make sense presuppose an old-fashioned contraposition of time and eternity – a contraposition which has to be overcome:

> If we ... ask who is the second identity of this eternal triune life, in which the created life of the son is decreed, we must answer that it is that same incarnate Son. This answer will seem circular only if we, perhaps subliminally, persist in plotting the triune life on a time line, or as a timeless point from which all points on the time line are equidistant. But the triune God's eternity can be plotted neither way. The triune God's eternity is precisely the infinity of the life that the Son, who is Jesus the Christ, lives with the Father in their Spirit. It is in that infinity that Christ precedes himself.[14]

3.2 The "Eternal" Son

Coming from a classic tradition one might wonder what Jenson's motives really are. As a matter of fact: one motive seems to be a very rigid reading of the 'is' in

---

[13] Cf. HEGEL, *Die vollendete Religion* [1995], p. 151: '*Dieser Sohn ist erhoben zur Rechten Gottes. In dieser Geschichte also ist für die Gemeinde die Natur Gottes, der Geist durchgeführt, ausgelegt, expliziert. Dies ist die Hauptsache, und die Bedeutung der Geschichte ist, daß es die Geschichte Gottes ist. Gott ist die absolute Bewegung in sich selbst, die der Geist ist, und diese Bewegung ist hier an dem Individuum vorgestellt.*'

[14] JENSON, *Triune Identity* [1982], pp. 140–1

the basic Christological formula ('Jesus Christ *is* the divine *Logos*') why Jenson is eager to abandon divine eternity or atemporality. The price he has to pay is a pretty overheated Trinitarian situation: the divine persons are pushed to the future, which is in principle out of reach. Does Jenson even provide a framework which allows us to speak of a co-presence of the Trinitarian persons? Is the price he pays to keep the non-identity of the Trinitarian persons their embedded-ness in the three "modes" of temporal existence? Furthermore, do expressions like 'Christ infinitely precedes himself' make sense at all once you cross out any notion or form of divine eternity?

But what happens if we turn our heads towards a classic notion of eternity and the resulting concept of incarnation? In her defence of Thomas Aquinas's classic concept of divine eternity Eleonore Stump writes:

> The divine nature of the second person of the Trinity, like the divine nature of either of the other persons of the Trinity, cannot become temporal; nor could the second person at some time acquire a human nature he does not eternally have. Instead, the second person eternally has two natures; and at some temporal instants, all of which are ET-simultaneous with the existence of each of these natures in their entirety, the human nature of the second person has been temporally actual. At those times and only in that nature, the second person directly participates in temporal events.[15]

Stump is not too clear at that point; however she admits that her concept of incarnation remains a brief sketch. But could it be the case that she falls prey to the problems she herself has pointed at in examining Nelson Pikes' problem and verdict, i. e., the difference between 'being eternally related to something' and 'being related to something eternal'? Her remarks sound like the second person of the Trinity needs to have a human nature eternally. And, at face value, this looks like the required human nature would be an eternal "attribute" of the second person of the Trinity. But clearly, the doctrine says something different. Although the divine *Logos* keeps the *natura assumpta* after resurrection forever, he never was eternally born out of the Father's "womb" having a human nature. Stump seems to be aware of the problems; so she introduces the notion of 'being temporally actual.' This notion – somewhat underdeveloped in these remarks – forces us to think that there are temporally actual and temporally non-actual natures, maybe in addition to "eternally" actual natures. How can we get a hold of these differences? Do they make sense? Or can they be reduced to actual and merely potential attributes of something? If the latter is true then what Eleonore Stump says is not an explanation of incarnation but a statement that holds that the eternal *Logos* had the potential to take on a human nature. A temporalist or a speculative theologian like Jenson might wonder how it works that a divine being can take on and does take on a human nature. But would it not be better – instead of using the expression 'the divine *Logos* had the human nature eternally' to cross out the 'have' and to talk about an eternal relation between the divine *Logos* and the human nature (a relation that could be spelled out in terms of ET-simultaneity) because doing so would not make the *relatum* an eternal being?

---

[15] STUMP, *Aquinas* [2003], p. 156.

There is, nevertheless, something worth keeping and underlining in Stump's pro-posal: the divine *Logos* is related to the human nature. And along the lines of the creed we might want to add: the *Logos* is *eternally* related to the human nature. But we have to be careful, too. This relation is not meant to make human nature by itself eternal. Eleonore Stump might have seen this very problem; and therefore she introduced the notion of 'being temporally actualized' which makes human nature look like some kind of abstract entity which can or cannot become actualized (but within Christology it is not the human nature as such which is the subject of actualization; it is the human nature of Jesus Christ – and one might ask if we should treat this ontological reality like an abstract entity or a universal). Again, it is the idea of 'having' that bothers us, because this notion somehow insinuates that there is a divine part within a human entity or the other way round. But the Christological doctrine does not really allow the use of any parthood-relation. The idea of *enhypostasis* forces us to look for another tool. But, it will be this tool that brings us back to the classic notion of eternity.

Indeed, there is an alternative tool that is able to keep a classic notion of eternity and that is capable of presenting an understanding of *incarnation* and *hypostatic union* along the lines of the doctrine while using sign-theoretical terms. In this framework the aspect of "becoming" (as an event in time) is left to the human being Jesus of Nazareth who – as the authentic sign – "is" (in a more subtle understanding of 'is') the divine *Logos*. Along these lines we can say: 'Jesus' life is and became an authentic sign for the essence of God and, moreover, it became, as a sign, an instance of God's eternal Word.'[16] The presence of unrestricted love as a principle of God's self-identification is the same as the role, the reality and the properties of the eternal Word. As a sign of God's unrestricted love to human beings Jesus signified the eternal Word. And in doing so he gave evidence of "being" the eternal Word – the one and only authentic sign of God's liberating self-identification in history. The full human nature (with a full human freedom and will) became the "material" to *signify* God's overflowing divine reality. To say this is to abandon every mythical understanding of a divine messenger hidden in the "clothes" of human nature and existence. A sign-theoretical grammar (focusing on the modes of exemplification and denoting) will help. Adopting this view we can hold[17]:

1.   Jesus *exemplifies* true humanity. He is truly human because he is familiar with all the constituents of human life: suffering and passion, desire and virtue, decision and choice.

2.   Jesus *denotes* the reality of God because he transcends the coordinates of the world in the ways in which he "defines" himself. His call and his authority points to the "otherness" – and in doing so, in pointing to this otherness, he is and he becomes the sign of the otherness to this world.

---

[16]   I have developed these ideas in a broader version in another article, cf. SCHÄRTL, *Zeichen der Freundschaft* [2007].

[17]   Cf. SCHÄRTL, *Zeichen der Freundschaft* [2007], pp. 98–9.

3.   Jesus *exemplifies* the reality of God any time when he expresses God's infinity in his life: the infinite divine goodness in his forgiveness, the infinite love of God as the healing love for a sinful and ill world, the infinite divine patience – revealed on the cross.

4.   The *Logos exemplifies* God's nature because he is the truth and wisdom in the godhead, the instance of God's self-knowledge and self-signification.

5.   The *Logos denotes* the reality of Jesus insofar as he is the instance of otherness in God and insofar as he correlates this otherness to God's identity and to God's self. The otherness of the world is foreshadowed in the otherness of the *Logos*.

6.   The *Logos exemplifies* the reality of Jesus insofar as he is the sign and the expression of self-giving love, which gives everything he receives back to its origin in a way that makes the immeasurably loving God visible and "touchable".

The idea of a hypostatic union is ensured in this grammar of *exemplifying* and *denoting*[18] because we can substitute the names 'Logos' and 'Jesus' for each other without changing the meaning and the validity of the sentences in question. While the act of denoting presupposes or, at least, enables a certain kind of "distance" and distinction, the act of exemplifying presupposes that the exemplifying entity belongs to the kind that is exemplified by it. Denoting and exemplifying are interconnected and belong to one act of signifying.

Signification, in this case, is a two-way street. The *Logos* signifies the human nature; he has an *eternal* relation (in the framework of ET-simultaneity) to the human nature. But this does not make human nature eternal. Jesus *signifies* the divine reality. This signification happens in time and is, therefore, temporal. The interconnection of significations, however, makes it possible to talk about the different ways of signification in terms of ET-simultaneity. Although for Abraham Jesus was a future entity and for a historian of the 21st century he is a person of the past, this is not the case for the divine *Logos*, since for the divine *Logos* the notions of 'past' and 'future' have no true bearing within the coordinates of ET-simultaneity. Within this framework we can say that for the divine *Logos* the human nature of Jesus Christ is *eternally* present – a presence which is the presupposition of eternal signification

---

[18]   Both concepts are mentioned along the lines of Nelson Goodman's understanding of *exemplifying* and *denoting*. Cf. GOODMAN, *Languages of Art* [1976]. Within this framework we can stipulate: whenever x exemplifies F, x is an instantiation of the kind F stands for whereas whenever x denotes G, x does not belong to the kind G stands for. The different aspects of kind-membership involved in the above mentioned propositions allow us to stick to the more or less paradoxical formulas of orthodox Christology. The idea of signification needs, of course, a more advanced ontology which permits us to use a stronger, even a basic notion of signification – saying, for example, that signification is a basic mode of being. The discussions (and especially the CDF-notification in 2004) concerning HAIGHT, *Jesus* [1999], document the need for an ontologically strong concept of symbol and symbolization. It was Karl Rahner who prepared such a deeper concept. Cf. RAHNER, *Zur Theologie des Symbols* [1967].

(by denoting and exemplifying). But at the same time we can avoid saying that the divine *Logos* eternally *had* a human nature. Within the mentioned framework and thanks to the relation of signification two "realities" are brought together without confusing their very different features.

3.3 Super-Presentism

Actually, it would be worthwhile to say more about Trinitarian conceptualizations and the new euphoria of systematic theology to think about divine existence in temporal terms. For the moment, it might be enough to have pointed out the most intricate problem which, in the end, leads to the intuition which serves as my basis to defend eternalism. Let me call this problem the 'Christological frame of reference'; it means that whenever we talk about the divine *Logos* we, instantaneously, refer to Jesus Christ, the 'word incarnate'. Jenson thinks that this frame of reference can be established by "temporalizing" the Trinitarian relations as such – saying that the immanent Trinity is the 'Trinity in time and history'. Even from God's perspective – given that God is seated in time – this frame of reference would be valid. And for the divine Father the Son would 'always' be the 'word incarnate'.

But, taking a closer look at Jenson's approach, we will detect two related problems: a modal problem and – one might be inclined to call it – a rather metaphysical problem. The modal problem lies at the very heart of the concept of the so-called hypostatic union in Christ. While the divine Father is necessarily a Father, we cannot simply and straightforwardly say that incarnation is necessary – there are no possible worlds in which the divine Father does not have a Son. But there might be possible worlds in which we find no word incarnate (because these worlds are, to allude to a Thomistic tradition, free from original sin). In theological terms, we would have to insist that incarnation is a gift of grace which is somehow related to the ways our actual world is. Thus, the distinction between the eternal *Logos* and the 'word incarnate' pays tribute to this problem; it is necessary and essential for God to be Trinitarian (in a Christian perspective, of course) but the incarnation isn't necessary since its modal status is tied to the modal status of the created world. Therefore, it is not a surprise that some theologians responded rather critically to Rahner's famous axiom and pointed out that the immanent Trinity is not in every respect the economic Trinity and vice versa.[19]

---

[19]   KASPER, *The God of Jesus Christ* [2005], p. 277: 'If, then, the axiom which states the identity of the immanent and the economic Trinities is not to lead to the dissolution of the immanent Trinity instead of to its substantiation, this identity must not be understood along the lines of the tautological formula $A = A$. The "is" in this axiom must be understood as meaning not an identification but rather a non-deducible, free, gracious, historical presence of the immanent Trinity in the economic Trinity. We may therefore rephrase Rahner's axiom as follows: in the economic self-communication the intra-trinitarian self-communication is present in the world in a new way, namely under the veil of historical words, signs and actions, and ultimately in the figure of the man Jesus of Nazareth.'

The metaphysical problem has precisely to do with the frame of reference Jenson is alluding to: how can we ever think that in addressing the divine *Logos* we are (somehow simultaneously) addressing Jesus Christ if even God is temporal and if we would have to say that (at a certain point) for a 'temporal' God Jesus of Nazareth once was a future entity? Jenson tries to avoid the rather complicated consequences of this problem by seating God in the future. But this is not a real solution; it just turns the whole framework of reference upside down and begs the question whether a 'futurized' God is still a temporal God (and, honestly, I have no idea of how one can distinguish a futurized God from a here and now absent God). So, if we want to keep the idea that in addressing the divine *Logos* we also refer to Jesus of Nazareth, and if we, furthermore, want to keep the above mentioned insight that the divine *Logos* himself refers to Jesus of Nazareth (whenever he refers to himself) we need a strong concept of *co-presence*, a co-presence which has to be understood in terms of *simultaneity*. Such a notion, as one can see, presupposes a classic notion of eternity which is the prerequisite for talking about ET-simultaneity. In other words: The Christological frame of reference is stable only if we can say that the divine *Logos* is simultaneous to every event that happens in time. Only if this is true the business of addressing Jesus of Nazareth in addressing the *Logos* will work accurately, and only if this is true the tools of denoting and exemplifying are useful.

The metaphysical problem that has been identified as the problem of co-presence leads to my basic intuition: if presentism is true, then we really need divine eternity (seen as the prerequisite of ET-simultaneity) to keep the above-mentioned frame of reference. Presentism holds that past events do not exist any longer, while future events do not exist yet.[20] Only present events deserve the notion of 'existing'. It might be worthwhile to discuss the notion of existence which is involved in these remarks. I'd like to call it the purely ontological side of the problem. There is, however, a more epistemological and semantic side to it – a side which may serve as a basis to trust presentism: how can we refer to past and future events? A clear examination of this question might show that such a reference is possible only through some detour-features. Thus, one can say, for example, that referring to past events is possible because there *are* mind-gifted persons who were co-present with these events and who mediate the previous presence through the means of memory etc. Comparable insights might hold for future events: referring to future events is possible only because there are mind-gifted persons who will be co-present with these events and who mediate the mode of not yet being present through the means of anticipation and imagination. It might be questionable to say that past events do not exist any more while future events do not yet exist, because a rather liberal understanding of 'existence' according to the semantics of possible-worlds talk might allow for a liberal usage of the phrase 'existence'. But maybe we can agree on the fact that only present events are 'immediately' *referable*, since immediate reference (like the notion of immediate awareness) is the standard and model of reference.

---

[20]   For a discussion of presentism, cf. MARKOSIAN, *A Defense of Presentism* [2004].

But, of course, the epistemological-semantic problem and the ontological problem are tied together since we can raise the question what might happen in a situation in which we do not have the guarantee that there were or will be any mind-gifted entities that might be co-present with certain past or future events? Would this not lead to the most unwelcome situation in which a stable framework of reference (for which immediate reference is the centre with mediated reference revolving around) must collapse at a certain point? The danger of collapsing, which threatens the whole business of reference at the very end, is one of many reasons for German philosopher Robert Spaemann to develop, using his very own words, the 'last proof of God's existence'.[21] Although I do not want to discuss the validity of his considerations under the category of 'proofs' let me draw attention to Robert Spaemann's insight which, in my opinion, clearly points towards a classic notion of divine *eternity*. Robert Spaemann writes:

> Das Futurum exactum, *das zweite Futur ist für uns denknotwendig mit dem Präsens verbunden. Von etwas zu sagen, es sei jetzt, ist gleichbedeutend damit, zu sagen, es sei in Zukunft gewesen. In diesem Sinne ist jede Wahrheit ewig. … Wenn wir heute hier sind, werden wir morgen hier gewesen sein. Das Gegenwärtige bleibt als Vergangenheit des zukünftig Gegenwärtigen immer wirklich. Aber von welcher Art ist diese Wirklichkeit? Man könnte sagen: in den Spuren, die sie durch ihre kausale Einwirkung hinterlässt. Aber diese Spuren werden schwächer und schwächer. Und Spuren sind sie nur, solange das, was sie hinterlassen hat, als es selbst erinnert wird.*
> *Solange Vergangenes erinnert wird, ist es nicht schwer, die Frage nach seiner Seinsart zu beantworten. Es hat seine Wirklichkeit eben im Erinnertwerden. Aber die Erinnerung hört irgendwann auf. Und irgendwann wird es keinen Menschen mehr auf Erden geben. Schließlich wird die Erde selbst verschwinden. Da zur Vergangenheit immer die Gegenwart gehört, deren Vergangenheit sie ist, müssten wir also sagen: Mit der bewussten Gegenwart … verschwindet auch die Vergangenheit, und das* Futurum exactum *verliert seinen Sinn. Aber genau dies können wir nicht denken. … Wenn gegenwärtige Wirklichkeit einmal nicht mehr gewesen sein wird, dann ist sie gar nicht wirklich. … Wir müssen ein Bewusstsein denken, in dem alles, was geschieht, aufgehoben ist, ein absolutes Bewusstsein.*[22]

Robert Spaemann's reflections on the correct understanding (and the ontological commitments) involved in the use of '*x will have been* such and such' allude to the problem of the frame of reference. Even if some less Platonist philosophers may try to get out of this problem using some advanced possible-worlds talk, the status of past and future beings and events as addressees of acts of denoting and referring to remains vague if we do not have an absolute frame of reference. If presentism is true, the ideas that only finite and temporarily seated beings are entrusted with the business of referring causes a riddle or a semantic atrocity. Only if there is a super-present mind-gifted being – a being which is co-present with every being or event in the past and in the future – the framework of reference we need remains entirely stable and the problems of mediated reference (which will occur for every

---

[21] Cf. SPAEMANN, *Der letzte Gottesbeweis* [2007].
[22] SPAEMANN, *Der letzte Gottesbeweis* [2007], pp. 31–2.

finite being at a certain point) are counter-balanced by a super-present instance of immediate reference.

Of course, there is a watershed: to be a super-present being is to be different from any finite being we can think of. For finite beings the "logic" of presentism is unavoidable: *past events disappear; and future events are not yet here.* But the situation is different for a super-present being since 'past' and 'future' do not apply to its mode of existence. To exist as a super-present being entails being co-present with every event and being. And for this being there is a stable framework of reference which – as a benefit – stabilizes the framework of reference used and required by human (i. e., finite and temporal) beings. It should be obvious at this point that the mode of existence applied to a super-present being is nothing less than the classic notion of divine eternity. Even if we might think that we can do without a stable framework of reference, it is, at least, the very heart of the Christian doctrine (coming from Christology) that requires nothing less but the stable framework of reference provided by super-presentism. Still, one can question the consistency of this answer: if presentism is true, how can there be super-presentism? But at that point we have to be aware of some traditional answers coming from the classic doctrine of God: if it is consistent to think that there are *two different modes of being,* (namely an infinite and a finite mode of being) then it is not logically impossible to assume that there are two different modes of presentism – super-presentism and "normal" presentism. Furthermore, if presentism is right and if a stable framework of reference is unavoidable, then to postulate the existence of a super-present being (as a guarantee of stabilized immediate reference) remains a requirement.

However, one could argue that the introduction of super-presentism (as an understanding of divine eternity) leads to a very unwelcome consequence. To illustrate this problem, let us listen to Paul Helm's interpretation of the outcomes of an eternal perspective:

> [A]ccording to the eternalist, there need to be no temporal first moment of creation, and so the universe need not have begun (temporally) to exist, for from the divine standpoint the universe is eternal, even though it exists contingently. And even if we suppose a first moment of creation it does not follow that God existed before the creation, before that first moment. For if there was a first moment of creation, then there was no time prior to the first moment during which God might exist.[23]

As you can see, Paul Helm falls prey to the age-old problem of slipping from 'God is eternally aware of *x*' to 'For God *x* is eternal'. The two propositions do not, as one can easily see, express the same state of affairs. And one cannot derive the second sentence from the first one since God's awareness (which is an outcome of his super-present mode of being) does not necessarily make anything he is aware of eternal. For to be eternally aware of something does not include being aware of something eternal. It just requires that the entity which is eternally aware of something (temporal) is eternal. And the same holds for the related acts of mind-gifted existence: like acts of referring to and, in general, acts of signification.

---

23 HELM, *Divine Timeless Eternity* [2001], p. 48.

So, to put my core argument in a nutshell: *If it is true that referring requires a stable framework of immediate reference and if it is true that, from the heart of Christian doctrine, we cannot do justice to Christology without a stable framework of reference* (which allows for the divine *Logos* to "signify" the human nature of Christ eternally), *then we cannot do away with divine eternity* – interpreted as the mode of super-present existence.

Part II

Divine Omniscience and Human Freedom

Chapter 4

Eternity and Fatalism

Linda Zagzebski

4.1 The Fatalist Argument

Fatalism is the thesis that we have no control over future events. Since the past used to be future, fatalism is actually the thesis that we do not have control over any events and never did. But the influential fatalist arguments conclude that we do not control *future* events. The futurity of the fated events is essential to the claim that they are fated. We allegedly have no control over the future because we have no control over the past and we do not control the connection between past and future identified by the fatalist. In the first part of this paper I want to investigate this link between fatalism and temporality, and I will then explore the issue of what happens to fatalist arguments when we move outside the temporal domain.

At the most general level, the three historically most important fatalist arguments all have the same form: We cannot control the past; the past entails the future; therefore, we cannot control the future. This is the basic form of standard arguments for logical fatalism, for theological fatalism, and for causal fatalism. In each case, the proponent of the argument is usually *not* a defender of the fatalist thesis. Rather, the proponent typically takes for granted that the fatalist conclusion is false and proposes the argument as a way to force us to reject one or more premises of the argument. Other philosophers reject the validity of the arguments. I am not going to focus on the specifics of either of these responses since I am interested in investigating the general form of the fatalist threat and its connection with time.

Although the standard fatalist arguments say, in effect, that we cannot control the future because we cannot control the past, none of the arguments says that we cannot control the future only because we cannot control the past. Each of the arguments identifies something else that we cannot control in addition to the past and the argument then has the form: (1) We cannot control the past, and we cannot control x. (2) The past + x entails the future. Therefore, (3) We cannot control the future. Let us look briefly at how each kind of fatalist argument has this structure.

(Logical Fatalism) The logical fatalist argues that we cannot control the past truth
    of propositions about the future, nor do we have any control over the fact that

the truth value of a proposition is immutable. Together these assumptions entail that the future will be what it will be. Therefore, we cannot control the future.[1]

(Theological Fatalism) The theological fatalist argues that we cannot control the fact that God had the beliefs He had in the past, nor can we control the fact that God is infallible. God's past beliefs together with His infallibility entail the future. Therefore, we cannot control the future.[2]

(Causal Fatalism) The causal fatalist argues that we cannot control the state of the world billions of years ago, nor can we control the laws of nature or the principle of determinism (which we presuppose for the purposes of the argument). The state of the world in the distant past plus the laws of nature entail the future, given determinism. Therefore, we cannot control the future.[3]

Since the proponent of the argument generally rejects the fatalist conclusion, a common strategy is to use the argument as a way to force the denial of one of the premises – e. g., the truth of future contingent propositions, divine foreknowledge, or the thesis of determinism. Each of these arguments has a large literature, particularly the second and third. Curiously, many philosophers take the first argument to be obviously fallacious, yet rarely does anybody make the same claim about the second or third argument.

I have presented the general structure of these arguments in order to highlight the fact that each argument crucially depends upon the assumption that we cannot control something in the past. Presumably we cannot control it *because* it is past. In addition, each argument depends upon the assumption that there is something else we cannot control – a principle about the fixity of the truth value of propositions, God's nature, or causal determinism and the laws of nature. In each case the argument gets its conclusion by using a transfer of necessity principle. This principle is modelled on axiom (K), an axiom of every system of modal logic:

(K)   If $\Box(p \rightarrow q)$, then $\Box p \rightarrow \Box q$.

It is tempting to accept principles of this form for types of necessity other than logical necessity, including principles that substitute the informal operator 'we cannot control the fact that p' for '$\Box$ p' in the consequent of axiom (K). If we make that substitution, the principle becomes the following Transfer of Lack of Control Principle (TLC):

---

[1]   The Master Argument of Diodorus Cronus was widely discussed by post-Aristotelian logicians and its general form has remained unchanged for millennia. The argument is roughly of the form given above.

[2]   The foreknowledge dilemma is mentioned by CICERO in *De Fato* and by AUGUSTINE in *On the Free Choice of the Will*. The contemporary version, of course, has an enormous literature.

[3]   A well-known variation of this argument is given by VAN INWAGEN, *Essay on Free Will* [1983]. It has been called the 'consequence argument' for the incompatibility of causal determinism and free will.

(TLC) If $\Box(p \to q)$, then if we cannot control the fact that p, we cannot control the fact that q.

Fatalist arguments use this principle or some variation of it. If something in the past along with something else entails the future, then if we cannot control the former, we cannot control the latter. There are objections to (TLC), but it has many variants,[4] and my focus in this paper is not a critique of (TLC).

Is there any way we could get a plausible and important argument for fatalism without the assumption that we cannot do anything about the past? I do not know of any historically important argument that does not include lack of control over the past as a premise, and lack of control over the future as a conclusion, but notice that there is nothing in (TLC) that refers to temporality. The past is allegedly one of the things we cannot do anything about, but there are others. I think we should keep in mind that the fatalist argument relies on (TLC) or a variation of it, since later we will discuss the possibility of an argument for fatalism that makes no reference to time.

I have drawn attention to the similarities among the arguments for logical, theological, and causal fatalism, but I do not want to exaggerate the similarities. It could turn out that one argument is invalid or has a false premise but another does not. Perhaps the argument for theological fatalism fails to show that infallible fore-knowledge leads to fatalism, but the causal fatalist argument succeeds in showing that causal determinism leads to fatalism. Or perhaps the logical fatalist argument fails to show that past truth about the future leads to fatalism, but infallible fore-knowledge does lead to fatalism. My point in calling attention to the similarities in the structure of the arguments and their assumptions about the past is not to claim that they stand or fall together, but to reveal the reference to past and future in fatalist arguments, and to raise the question whether reference to temporality is crucial in generating an argument for fatalism.

4.2 Escaping Fatalism by Escaping Time

The logical fatalist and theological fatalist arguments have something in common that distinguishes them from the causal fatalist argument. Both of the former arguments have a premise that we cannot control something in the past that arguably is not in the past because it is not in time. Propositions can be plausibly understood as non-temporal entities, if they are entities of any kind, and if so, they do not have properties in the past. If so, a proposition p was not true yesterday, nor is it true today, nor will it be true tomorrow. Similarly, according to an important tradition in Christian philosophy notably defended by Boethius and Aquinas, God is not in time and so He does not have beliefs in time. There is nothing God believed yesterday, nor does He believe anything today, nor will He believe anything tomorrow. So one

---

[4] Variations include the stipulation that p is true, or the stipulation that q is false. Another variation requires that q is about something later in time than p. For the latter proposal, see O'CONNOR, *Persons and Causes* [2002], ch. 1.

traditionally important way out of both logical and theological fatalism attempts to escape fatalism, not by denying (TLC), nor by denying the assumption that we cannot do anything about the past, but by denying the pastness of that which we allegedly do not control as presented in the first premise of the respective arguments.

Notice that the denial that God is in time need not involve any positive claim about the nature of divine eternity in order to avoid commitment to the fatalist conclusion in the argument for theological fatalism. For example, God need not be eternal in the full Boethian sense of having the complete, simultaneous, and perfect possession of illimitable life.[5] It is sufficient that God has no temporal properties and, in particular, God did not have beliefs in the past. Similarly, the denial that propositions have truth values in time need not involve any commitment about the nature of propositions beyond the claim that they have no properties in time.

There are some differences between the use of the timelessness move to avoid logical fatalism and the use of the move to avoid theological fatalism. Here is one difference. Even if propositions are outside time, they seem to have temporal correlates – sentence tokens or, perhaps more obviously, utterances. An utterance occurs at a particular moment of time and utterances seem to be the sorts of things that are true or false. You can speak truly or you can speak falsely, and if what you say is true, being true seems to be a property of the utterance at the time of the utterance, which may be in the past. So even if propositions are timeless entities, what you said yesterday was true yesterday. If so, the logical fatalist gets his argument. He only needs to formulate it in terms of utterances, or what people say, rather than propositions. In contrast, if God's beliefs are timeless, there is nothing that is a temporal correlate of God's timeless beliefs. That is to say, there is no x that occurs in time and is related to divine timeless beliefs as utterances are related to timeless propositions, and which permits a reformulation of the fatalist argument. In this respect the timelessness move looks better as a way out of theological fatalism than as a way out of logical fatalism.

But is there not something in the past correlated to God's timeless beliefs in the relevant way? Suppose I make the utterance, 'God timelessly believes p'. Is my not utterance true or false for the same reason that my utterance 'p' is true or false? If my utterance yesterday that God timelessly believes p was true, do we not have something in the past which we do not control due to its pastness, and which permits a reformulation of the fatalist argument? If so, the eternity move does not help.[6]

But that response is too fast. The theological fatalist argument is a different argument than the logical fatalist argument. The former begins with the pastness of God's past beliefs; the latter begins with the pastness of the past truth of propositions – or utterances, in the revised version. If God (with His beliefs) is outside of time, then there is a straightforward escape from the theological fatalist argument. The

---

[5]   BOETHIUS: *The Consolation of Philosophy* V. VI.

[6]   PLANTINGA gives a version of this objection to the timelessness move in *Ockham's Way Out* [1986], p. 240.

reply that it falls prey to an argument about the past truth of utterances about God's timeless beliefs is just the reply that this way of escaping theological fatalism is not also an escape from logical fatalism. But the defender of divine timelessness as a way out of theological fatalism can quite rightly point out that he was not offering a way out of logical fatalism. He was responding to a standard form of theological fatalism, and that is given by the doctrine of divine timelessness. What remains is not an argument about God or His infallible beliefs, but an argument about the past truth of utterances, and that is a different problem which has, presumably, a different solution. The problem with the past truth of the utterance, 'God timelessly believes p' is the same as the problem with the past truth of the utterance 'p'. It is the same problem and it has the same solution, if there is one. I think, then, that if God's beliefs are timeless we do not yet have a reason to think that they are tied to something in time in a way that permits a reformulation of the theological fatalist argument. Divine timelessness does not escape the argument for logical fatalism, but we knew that anyway.

There is, however, a way God's timeless beliefs could be tied to something in time in a problematic way. Assuming that God infallibly knows outside of time that an event occurs at time t, could He not reveal His knowledge to a temporal being prior to t? Suppose God infallibly and timelessly believes that the Treaty of Versailles is signed on June 28, 1919. Surely, God could reveal this knowledge to a human being a hundred years before the signing of the treaty. Or suppose, as Peter van Inwagen proposes, that God causes a monument to come into existence *ex nihilo* in 1900 on which are inscribed the following words: 'On 21 September, 1942, a human being named Peter van Inwagen will be born. On 23 December, 2006, at 11:46 a. m. Eastern time, he will have to choose between lying and telling the truth. He will choose to lie.'[7] Van Inwagen argues that this possibility poses a fatalist threat for a timeless being. He says, 'Is it true in any of the possible continuations of the then-present state of affairs that the words inscribed on the monument did not express a true proposition? No, for in that case God would either have been mistaken or have been a deceiver, and both are impossible. My act (my telling the lie), was therefore not a free act.' Van Inwagen goes on to say that 'a divinely inspired human prophet who has foretold certain actions of human beings would also be a Freedom-denying Prophetic Object' (ibid). He concludes that the foreknowledge problem can be reconstructed for a timeless deity and retains 'much of the force' of the original argument.

Let us look more closely at whether the possibility of a revelation of the future in the form of van Inwagen's monument permits a reconstruction of the theological fatalist problem. Since it is belief in what the monument says that leads to a foreknowledge dilemma, let us begin by considering the reason why fallible human knowledge of the future does not pose the same fatalist threat as infallible foreknowledge. Whether a fallible human belief about the future is one of knowledge depends upon how things turn out. For instance, suppose I believe in September

---

[7] VAN INWAGEN, *What Does an Omniscient* [2008], p. 219.

2008 that final exams in the fall semester at my university end on December 19, and suppose that the belief is true and that it is warranted or justified or has whatever other property knowledge requires in addition to truth. In that case I know that final exams end on December 19. But since I am fallible, no matter how justified I am in my belief in September, it is possible that final exams do not end on December 19. There might be a big ice storm that results in the cancellation of the last day of finals, or the university President might, on a whim, move the exams up a week. Of course, that probably will not happen, and so it will probably turn out that my state of belief in September is one of knowledge. But if finals do not end on December 19, it will turn out that I did not know in September that finals would end on that day even if I am as justified as I can be in such matters. Possessing the best of justification or whatever other property knowledge requires in addition to truth is compatible with having a false belief. Of course, since knowing entails truth, it is necessary that *if* I know, I have a true belief, but it is not necessary that the state I am in in September is one of knowing since I am not infallible.

This is the reason the problem of divine foreknowledge rests on the combination of the pastness of God's beliefs and their infallibility. Although we cannot do anything about the fact that somebody in the past believed what he believed, we sometimes *can* do something about the fact that the belief he had was true and was a case of knowing – if the belief is about something that has not yet happened. Somebody can, in principle, make a belief that finals end on December 19 false by cancelling the exams, in which case they also make it the case that anybody who believed that exams end on December 19 did not know that they do. But unfortunately, we do not have this power when the belief is infallible. There is nothing anybody can do to make an infallible belief false.

Now let us go back to van Inwagen's monument. Is there anything anybody can do to make a belief in what the monument says false? Given that the words on the monument are written by God in plain English, and assuming some human Sam is a normal English speaker and the monument is easy for him to read, and assuming also that Sam believes the inscription is veridical, then if Sam reads it and comes to believe what he thinks is written there, there is not much chance he will make a mistake in believing what God timelessly believes and which was divinely inscribed on the monument in 1900. But even though there is not much chance, there is nonetheless some chance. Given the fallibility of Sam's powers and the lack of a perfect match between him and his environment and his understanding of the intentions of the inscriber, it is still possible that what he comes to believe when he reads the monument is false. If so, the state he is in does not entail the truth of what he believes, and so his believing in 1900 that van Inwagen will tell a lie in 2006 does not entail that van Inwagen will tell the lie.

Van Inwagen asks, 'Is it true in any of the possible continuations of the then-present state of affairs that the words inscribed on the monument did not express a true proposition? No, for in that case God would either have been mistaken or have been a deceiver, and both are impossible.' But there is a confusion in this claim. There *is* a possible continuation of the then-present state of affairs in which the words Sam *believes* are inscribed on the monument do not express a true proposition. God cannot be mistaken, but Sam can. Since God is not a deceiver, we can assume that God makes sure that Sam believes the truth. Even so, God does not make Sam believe infallibly. As long as we interpret the monument example as one in which a timeless infallible God reveals the future to fallible temporal beings, there is no fatalist dilemma arising from believing the inscription on the monument. And the same point applies no matter how a fallible being obtains knowledge from God. As long as the recipient is fallible, we do not get a problem like the problem of theological fatalism.

But there is another interpretation of van Inwagen's claim that has nothing to do with God being a deceiver because it has nothing to do with the belief of a human knower. When van Inwagen says that there is no possible continuation of the then-present state of affairs in which the monument did not express a true proposition, he might think that the mere existence of the monument poses a fatalist problem even if nobody reads it and comes to believe the inscription. Perhaps he thinks of the monument as a piece of a vast History of the World, containing all true propositions about the past, present, and future, and no false ones. In that case, fatalism seems to be implied by the *truth* of the inscription which records a particular proposition God infallibly believes and which he inscribes with perfect accuracy. On this interpretation of the monument example, infallibility is not relevant since infallibility is not a property of inscriptions or of the propositions expressed on inscriptions. It is a property of a conscious believer. On this interpretation, if there is a fatalist problem, it arises from the fact that a truth about the future is "written" and cannot be unwritten or changed; truth necessarily stays the same forever. On this interpretation, the problem of the monument is the problem of logical fatalism, not theological fatalism, and as I have said, the two problems are distinct and should be treated separately. The problem of the monument is therefore either a version of logical fatalism, which has nothing to do with anybody receiving a revelation from God, or it is not a fatalist problem because the recipient is not infallible. Either way it is not the problem of infallible foreknowledge.

So far we have not found a reason to fear that if God is timeless, His timeless knowledge can have a temporal counterpart, thereby generating another version of theological fatalism. Surely, God can reveal His knowledge to a temporal creature, but as long as the creature is fallible, that creature's epistemic state will not entail the truth of what He believes. But this leads to a harder problem. Can we not imagine that God reveals His knowledge to an infallible temporal being? To make the strongest case for a temporal correlate of timeless knowledge, all we need to do is postulate the possibility that God Himself enters time with His infallible knowledge intact. And that is exactly what some versions of the doctrine of the incarnation maintain. If Jesus Christ had a divine mind in time that knew the future infallibly, there is a threat of theological fatalism even if we accept the doctrine of divine timelessness.[8] Of course, there might be reasons why this version of the doctrine does not make sense, but the worry is that if it does make sense, it would mean that the doctrine of divine timelessness loses any advantage it would otherwise have in solving the problem of theological fatalism.

Furthermore, I suspect that the problem exists as long as it is even *possible* that God enters time with infallible foreknowledge, and this point can be generalized. Van Inwagen makes it clear that he is not worried that God's inscription on the monument would prevent human freedom only if God actually created such a monument. Presumably, he thinks there is no such monument, but he thinks the mere possibility of the monument threatens fatalism. And this is the usual position of incompatibilists about infallible foreknowledge and free will. If I am right about that, we cannot save the timelessness solution as a way out of fatalism unless it turns out that it is not even possible that a timeless God enters time with infallible foreknowledge, nor can He reveal His foreknowledge to an infallible temporal being.

In this section I have argued that the timelessness solution to the foreknowledge dilemma succeeds in evading the theological fatalist argument only if there is no temporal counterpart of divine timeless knowledge, and I think that the defender of the Boethian way out can succeed in avoiding such a temporal counterpart under the assumption that the incarnate Son of God does not have infallible knowledge at moments of time, and could not have such knowledge, nor can any other temporal being have infallible foreknowledge. But in the next section we will look at a different reason for thinking that escaping time does not escape fatalism.

4.3 Fatalism and a Timeless Knower

If fatalism is a problem about the relation between past and future, escaping time ought to escape the fatalist threat. But we do not yet have a secure solution to theological fatalism unless the timeless realm does not also have a problematic relationship with human contingent acts. In past work I have argued that the Boethian moves avoids one fatalist argument only to fall prey to another.[9] To identify the problem, let us go back to the essential idea of fatalist arguments in (TLC): If p entails q, then if we cannot control p, we cannot control q. Standard fatalist arguments begin with the fact that we cannot control the past and we cannot control something else, and argue from there to the conclusion that we cannot control the future. But (TLC) does not include any reference to time, and I think the lack of reference to time in (TLC) is important. There are many things we cannot control in addition to the past. The fatalist arguments themselves rely upon premises referring to our lack of control over things other than the past – the laws of nature and the

---

8   I am thinking of a position like the two minds view of MORRIS in *Logic of God Incarnate* [1986], pp. 102–7, or the divided mind view of SWINBURNE in *Christian God* [1994], pp. 194–209.

9   ZAGZEBSKI, *Freedom and Foreknowledge* [1991], pp. 60–63.

logical principles used in the arguments. Presumably, there are many other things we do not control as well. One would think that a paradigm case of something we cannot control is anything in the timeless realm. How could finite temporal beings hope to have power over a transcendent domain, a domain wholly outside of time (and, presumably, also outside of space)? The prime candidates for timeless objects – properties, propositions, numbers, possible worlds – are as necessary as anything can be. I am not suggesting that God's timeless beliefs are abstract objects. Nonetheless, there is a prima facie connection between the timeless realm and the realm of what we cannot do anything about, a connection that requires a closer look.

One way to examine our intuitions about what we can and cannot control is to think about why we believe we cannot control the past and why we think that it is at least arguable that we can control the future. We can then apply these intuitions to the timeless realm.

I think there are two different reasons why we believe we cannot do anything about the past. The first is the metaphysical principle that there cannot be backwards causation. This principle is often thought to be intuitively obvious, but there are at least two distinct ways the principle can be understood:

(i)   A cause cannot be later in time than its effect.
(ii)   A cause must be prior in time to its effect.

Most philosophers who discuss causation distinguish (i) and (ii) only because they notice that (ii) rules out the possibility that a cause is simultaneous with its effect, whereas (i) does not. I doubt that in the context of most discussions another difference is noticed: (ii) rules out a causal relation between a temporal event and something outside of time, whereas (i) does not. The principle that there cannot be backwards causation rules out a temporal cause and a timeless effect only if the principle is interpreted as (ii). Furthermore, it is not clear that either version of the principle is relevant to the issue of whether we can have some control over the timeless realm since 'doing something about' x or 'having some control over' x is broader than 'causing' x. Causing x is one way to have some control over x, but it is not the only way. Even if we do not and cannot cause God's timeless beliefs, it might still be the case that God believes what he believes *because of* something we do; perhaps he believes timelessly *in virtue of* something we do in time. I am not able to offer an account of the because-of relation, but I think that it is worth noticing that whatever the relation is, it is very doubtful that it reduces to the causal relation. So if the principle ruling out backwards causation is interpreted as (i), it does not rule out causing something in a timeless domain, and even if the principle is interpreted in the strong sense of (ii), that does not rule out the possibility that something in the timeless domain occurs because of something in the temporal domain, assuming that the because-of relation is not causal.

I conclude that if our lack of power over the past is due to the principle that there cannot be backwards causation, there is no reason to think that we lack power over the timeless realm. At least, it would take quite a bit of work to demonstrate the application to the timeless realm. However, I do not insist upon this point because there is a second reason why we believe we cannot do anything about the past that comes much closer to applying to the timeless realm. Writers on time and fatalism sometimes refer to the idea that the past is ontologically determinate, fixed, complete, whereas the future is ontologically indeterminate, unfixed, in need of completion by an injection of free choice (and maybe also pure chance) into the ontological mix.[10] This point is often associated with the claim that the past is more real than the future. These claims are obviously vague, but they are probably clear enough to permit the following conjecture. The reason why we cannot do anything about the past is that there is nothing left to be done; the past is complete. We can in principle do something about the future because the future is in process of construction. It is in need of something to complete it.

This reason for thinking we cannot do anything about the past certainly appears to apply to the timeless realm. The timeless domain is at least as real as the past. In fact, the origin of the idea of the timeless realm in Parmenides and Plato suggests that it is more real than anything temporal. Furthermore, the timeless domain is determinate, fixed; it has no need for something outside of it to make it complete. It surely does not need the temporal domain. It would exist just as it is even if no temporal domain existed at all. At least, it is tempting to think that. And that suggests that on grounds of ontological reality and fixedness, the timeless realm is like the past and unlike the future. In fact, it is more of what makes the past beyond our power than the past is. So if we think we cannot control the past, we have at least as much reason for thinking that we cannot control the timeless domain. Therefore, if God's beliefs are outside of time, it appears that we would have no more control over them than we would if God's beliefs were in the past. Both are in the category of what we cannot do anything about.

I think this means that we have reason to adopt a principle of the Necessity of Eternity that is parallel to the reason for adopting a principle of the Necessity of the Past. Admittedly, the two principles differ in their hold on our intuitions. The latter is enshrined in such common sense aphorisms as 'There is no use crying over spilled milk', whereas there is no parallel aphorism that says there is no use crying over something timeless. But that should not make us feel any more secure about our ability to influence the timeless realm. People do not have sayings about our relation to the timeless realm only because most of us have very few ideas at all about the timeless realm. Philosophers do not have much to say about it either, but I have suggested that what philosophers say pushes us in the direction of thinking that we have no control over it. I am not arguing that the principle of the Necessity of Eternity is true. In fact, I hope that it is false. My point is that it is supported by some of the same intuitions that support the Necessity of the Past and for that reason should be taken seriously.

---

[10]   The traditional contrast between past and future given here does not mention the present. Recently, presentism, the view that only the present is real, has gained popularity. I will not discuss presentism in this paper.

The principle of the Necessity of Eternity permits the formulation of a fatalist argument for timeless knowledge parallel to the argument from infallible foreknowledge. To formulate the argument, we need three principles:

(1)   Either the necessity of the past or the necessity of eternity
(2)   (TLC)
(3)   A principle Quine called 'semantic shift'.[11]

By 'semantic shift', I mean a principle permitting semantic ascent or semantic descent. An illustration of semantic ascent is standardly given by the following:

> If snow is white, the sentence 'Snow is white' is true,

or alternatively,

> If snow is white, the proposition that snow is white is true.

Semantic descent is the converse:

> If 'Snow is white is true', then snow is white,

or alternatively,

> If the proposition that snow is white is true, then snow is white.

We can now formulate two fatalist arguments, one for a temporal deity and one for a timeless deity. Take an example of a future human act that is intuitively freely chosen, if anything is. Suppose it is my act of flying to Los Angeles on December 23, and let F be the proposition I express by the sentence, 'I will fly to L. A. on December 23'.[12]

The argument in which God has beliefs in time runs as follows:

Theological fatalist argument for temporal deity

(1)   God infallibly believed F in the past.   (Assumption)
(2)   I cannot do anything about the fact that God infallibly believed F in the past.   (Necessity of the Past and lack of power over God's infallible nature)
(3)   Necessarily, if God infallibly believed F in the past, then F is true.   (Definition of 'infallibility')
(4)   If (2) and (3), then I cannot do anything about the fact that F is true.   (TLC)
(5)   Therefore, I cannot do anything about the fact that F is true.   (Modus ponens)
(6)   Therefore, I cannot do anything about the fact that I fly to Los Angeles on December 23.   (Semantic shift)

An exactly parallel argument with the assumption that God is timeless runs as follows:

---

[11]   QUINE, *Philosophy of Logic* [1970], p. 12.
[12]   If my use of the indexical 'I' leads to questions about whether my words express the same proposition as that expressed by somebody else who says 'Linda Zagzebski will fly to Los Angeles on December 23', then replace the former by the latter in the arguments above. For the purpose of this paper, we can leave issues about the first person pronoun aside.

Theological fatalist argument for timeless deity

(1') God infallibly believes *F* timelessly. (Assumption)

(2') I cannot do anything about the fact that God infallibly believes *F* timelessly.
(Necessity of Eternity and lack of power over God's infallible nature)

(3') Necessarily, if God infallibly believes *F* timelessly, then *F* is true.
(Definition of 'infallibility')

(4') If (2') and (3'), then I cannot do anything about the fact that *F* is true. (TLC)

(5') Therefore, I cannot do anything about the fact that *F* is true. (Modus ponens)

(6') Therefore, I cannot do anything about the fact that I fly to Los Angeles on December 23. (Semantic shift)

In offering these arguments, I am not proposing that there are no ways to escape their conclusion. My view is that there are ways out of the temporal version of theological fatalism, and I also think there are ways out of the timeless version. My point here is that timelessness itself does not solve the dilemma and it may not even have any advantage in escaping theological fatalism. Possibly a stronger case can be made for the rejection of (2') than for the rejection of (2), given the fact that the Necessity of Eternity has a weaker hold on our intuitions than the Necessity of the Past. Even so, the intuitions supporting (2') are strong enough that it cannot be rejected out of hand. The Boethian solution to the problem of infallible foreknowledge cannot be declared victorious without further argument.

4.4 Logical Fatalism and Timelessness

Does the timelessness move do any better as a solution to logical fatalism? I argued in section 4.2 that even if propositions are timeless, there are temporal counterparts to propositions that permit a reconstruction of the argument for logical fatalism, so we already have one reason to think that timelessness is not useful in avoiding the problem. The argument of section 4.3 gives us another reason to think that timelessness does not escape logical fatalism. If the timeless realm is as fixed as the past, the timeless truth of propositions about the future are as fixed as the past truth of propositions. So if the timelessness move generates a parallel dilemma of theological fatalism, it would also permit a parallel dilemma of logical fatalism. As we will see, however, there is an interesting difference in the timeless truth dilemma. The fatalist argument it generates is much shorter than the other arguments.

Let *F* be my utterance, 'I will fly to Los Angeles on December 23, 2008', or alternatively, the proposition I express by that utterance.

Logical fatalist argument for temporal propositions (or utterances)

(1_L)   *F* was true in the past (e. g., the time of utterance).   (Assumption)

(2_L)   I cannot do anything about the fact that *F* was true in the past.
                                                                (Necessity of the Past)

(3_L)   Necessarily, if *F* was true in the past, *F* is true forever.
                                                         (Immutability of truth value[13])

(4_L)   If (2_L) and (3_L), then I cannot do anything about the fact that *F* is true forever.
                                                                                      (TLC)

(5_L)   Therefore, I cannot do anything about the fact that *F* is true forever.
                                                                         (Modus ponens)

(6_L)   Therefore, I cannot do anything about the fact that I fly to Los Angeles on December 23.   (Semantic shift).

The principle of the Necessity of Eternity permits an even shorter fatalist argument for timeless propositions, without requiring the Transfer of Lack of Control Principle (TLC):

Logical fatalist argument for timeless propositions

($1_{L'}$)   *F* is timelessly true.   (Assumption)

($2_{L'}$)   I cannot do anything about the fact that *F* is timelessly true.
                                                                  (Necessity of Eternity)

($3_{L'}$)   I cannot do anything about the fact that I fly to Los Angeles on December 23.
                                                                          (Semantic shift)

If propositions are timeless, and assuming that the semantic shift at line ($3_{L'}$) is innocuous, it follows that premise ($2_{L'}$) had better be false. We can see, then, that the move from (1_L) to ($1_{L'}$) is hardly an advantage! The timelessness move either has no advantage in escaping either kind of fatalism, or only a weak advantage due to the somewhat weaker intuitive support for the Necessity of Eternity over the Necessity of the Past.

4.5 The Urgency to Find a Compatibilist Solution to the Timeless Knowledge Dilemma

Let us return to theological fatalism. So far we have seen that the doctrine of divine timelessness escapes theological fatalism only if it can overcome two hurdles. The first is that there must be no temporal counterpart to timeless knowing which permits a reconstruction of the temporal fatalist argument. I have argued that it can overcome this hurdle. The second is that there must be no apparent fatalist

---

[13]   A variation on the view that propositions are immutably true is that there are truth value links between tensed versions of the same proposition that hold necessarily. Dummett argues for these links in *Truth and the Past* [2006].

consequence of timeless knowing. In the previous section I argued that the doctrine does not overcome this hurdle since there is a timeless knowing dilemma parallel to the foreknowledge dilemma. This does not mean that timeless knowing leads to fatalism, but it does mean that there is a fatalist argument for a timeless deity that requires a response, just as there is a fatalist argument for a temporal deity that requires a response. Perhaps it is easier to get out of the timeless knowledge dilemma than the temporal knowledge dilemma. Nonetheless, a way out is required, and timelessness does not escape fatalism in one move. If the doctrine of divine timelessness comes out ahead of the doctrine of divine temporality with respect to fatalism, it is only by the degree to which the Necessity of the Past is more compelling than the Necessity of Eternity. I will leave it to my readers to decide how much that is, but in this section I want to argue that there is one respect in which the timelessness doctrine has a disadvantage when compared with the doctrine of a temporal deity.

The problem is this: there is no incompatibilist fall-back position if God is timeless. Christian philosophers who believe that infallible foreknowledge is incompatible with human free will typically conclude that free will exists, but there is no divine foreknowledge. That is, the incompatibility they perceive between foreknowledge and free will is resolved in favour of free will. The denial of divine foreknowledge, then, is a backup position for those philosophers who want to retain as much of the traditional conception of God as they think they can, while retaining the belief in human freedom. This is the position taken by Peter van Inwagen in the paper mentioned above, and it has been defended by philosophers such as Hasker who advocate what has been called 'Open Theism'.[14] Hasker's idea is that an omniscient deity foregoes possessing infallible foreknowledge of human choices in order to save human freedom. God has complete, detailed, and infallible knowledge of the past and present and the tendencies of each creature, which allows him to know the objective probability of each possible future event and the gradually changing likelihood of each possibility's being realized. But God does not know the contingent future infallibly. Christian philosophers who take this position typically also say that nothing of religious importance is lost by this qualification of God's omniscience. God's ultimate control over the world does not require meticulous knowledge and control over every detail of the creation. We can still trust in God and rely upon his providential care even without infallible foreknowledge.[15]

Now notice that there is no analogous incompatibilist position on timeless knowledge that preserves free will. If a timeless knower "gave up" timelessly knowing the contingent future, he would have to give up all infallible knowledge of human contingent affairs. For a timeless God, there is no possibility of temporarily foregoing an infallible grasp of the future. Either a timeless God infallibly knows that I fly to Los Angeles on December 23 or he does not. Either he infallibly knows

---

[14]   See HASKER, *God, Time, and Knowledge* [1989] and PINNOCK ET AL., *The Openness of God* [1994].

[15]   See HASKER, *God, Time, and Knowledge* [1989], ch. 10.

van Inwagen tells a lie on a certain date in 2006 or he does not. And the same point applies to every other act in human history. On the view of incompatibilists like the Open God theists, God eventually finds out what happens in the world when it occurs, and ever afterwards He knows it infallibly. But if God is timeless and does not know human free acts infallibly, He never knows infallibly. The unavoidable conclusion is that human free will had better be compatible with infallible timeless knowing because if it is not, there is no incompatibilist qualification of omniscience that will save anything close to the traditional conception of a God for the adherent of divine timelessness.

I have presented this feature of the timeless knowledge dilemma as a disadvantage of the doctrine of timelessness, but that judgment may not be fair. If you are confident that there is a good compatibilist solution to the problem, you will not be dismayed by the fact that there is no appealing fall-back position. Or maybe you think the fall-back position is not very appealing anyway, so the foreknowledge dilemma is no less threatening than the timeless version. But for people who find the view that God lacks infallible foreknowledge a viable option, the loss of that option makes the need to resolve the timeless knowledge dilemma urgent.

How urgent is the need to solve the dilemma of logical fatalism? It seems to me that the fall-back position that propositions or assertions about the contingent future have no truth value is not very appealing. There are good logical reasons for accepting that propositions are either omnitemporally or timelessly true, so there is a pressing need to solve the logical fatalist problem. Given a choice between the position that propositions are timeless and the position that they are temporal, I have argued that there is no reason to prefer the view that propositions are timeless because of its alleged advantages in escaping logical fatalism. We should acknowledge that if any human being can do anything about anything, there is a proposition the truth of which somebody has some control over. If propositions are temporal entities with truth values that remain fixed throughout time, then somebody can do something about something in the past. Alternatively, if propositions are timeless entities with timeless truth values, then somebody can do something about something in the timeless realm. Is the latter implication any easier to accept than the former? Or to pose the question the other way around, is the former implication any harder to accept than the latter? I think not, and I think the situation is much the same with the problem of divine foreknowledge. How much harder is it to say that God knew p in the past because of something that happens in the future than to say that God knows p timelessly because of something that happens in time?

4.6 Conclusion

Every historically important argument for fatalism argues that we have no control over the future because we have no control over the past. In this paper I have concentrated on the arguments for logical and theological fatalism. The past truth of propositions about the future and God's past infallible knowledge of the future both seem to lead to fatalism, and in both cases, it is tempting to think that fatalism can be escaped by escaping time. If propositions are timelessly true rather than true in the past, the logical fatalist argument collapses. If God's knowledge of our future is timeless rather than in the past, the theological fatalist argument collapses. But I have argued that escaping fatalism by escaping time solves the fatalist problem only if the timelessness move can overcome two hurdles: (1) There must be no temporal counterpart that permits a reformulation of the fatalist argument. I argued that the timeless knowledge of God can overcome this hurdle, but the timeless truth of propositions cannot. (2) There must not be a reason to think that the timeless realm shares with the past the feature of being outside our control. I argued that the timelessness move does not overcome this hurdle for either argument. There is a principle of the Necessity of Eternity that permits the formulation of a parallel timeless truth dilemma and a parallel timeless knowledge dilemma. The necessity of eternity may have a weaker hold on our intuitions than the necessity of the past, and to that extent the timeless knowledge argument for fatalism may be easier to escape than the temporal version, but the timeless knowledge problem is worse in one respect: there is no fall-back position that saves human free will by qualifying divine omniscience. If God is timeless, there had better be a mistake in the timeless knowledge argument.

I conclude that the escape from fatalism does not turn on the issue of temporality vs timelessness. There are many reasons why a Christian philosopher should be attracted to the traditional conception of divine timelessness, but I do not think the need to escape fatalism is one of them.

Chapter 5

Molina on Foreknowledge and Transfer of Necessities

Christoph Jäger

5.1 Introduction

In disputation 52 of part IV of his *Concordia*,[1] Luis de Molina reconstructs, and rejects, seven arguments against the compatibility of divine omniscience with human freedom. Let us call the position of Molina's opponent 'theological incompatibilism' and its negation 'theological compatibilism'. The second argument Molina considers is widely regarded as one of the most powerful objections to theological compatibilism. Molina closely follows Aquinas's exposition of the problem (*STh* I, q. 14, a. 8) but offers his own, original solution. This solution, I believe, contains one of the most insightful and systematically promising ideas developed in the *Concordia*. In fact, it anticipates an argument about causal determination and moral responsibility that has recently reentered the philosophical stage and is hotly debated in the contemporary free will literature. Molina's reconstruction of his opponent's reasoning is couched in terms of 'absolute necessity':

> Quote A:
> If a conditional is true and its antecedent is absolutely necessary, then its consequent is likewise absolutely necessary; otherwise, in a valid consequence, the antecedent could be true and the consequent false, which is in no way to be admitted. But the conditional 'If God knew that this was going to be, then it will so happen' is true, or else God's knowledge would be false; and the antecedent is absolutely necessary, both because it is eternal and because it is past-tense and there is no power over the past. Therefore, the consequent will be absolutely necessary as well, and hence no future thing foreknown by God will be contingent.[2]

---

[1]   MOLINA, *Concordia* [1953]. The first edition appeared in 1588 in Lisbon, the second in 1595 in Antwerp. The full title is *Liberi Arbitrii cum Gratiae Donis, Divina Praescientia, Providentia, Praedestinatione et Reprobatione Concordia* (*The Compatibility of Free Choice with the Gifts of Grace, Divine Foreknowledge, Providence, Predestination and Reprobation*).
[2]   Disp. 52, 3, pp. 337–8/pp. 164–5. '*Si conditionalis aliqua est vera et eius antecedens est absolute necessarium, consequens est etiam absolute necessarium; alioquin in bona consequentia esse posset antecedens verum et consequens falsum, quod nulla ratione est admittendum. Sed haec condicionalis est vera: si Deus scivit hoc esse futurum, id ita eveniet, alioquin*

Since all human actions and decisions are among the "future things" in question, this argument would demonstrate that unrestricted divine omniscience entails that no human action (or decision) is contingent. From this the critic concludes that no human action (or decision) is *free*.

This argument has a certain surface clarity. However, on closer inspection, some perplexing questions arise, both with respect to what exactly it states and to what Molina responds. A key question is whether the argument should be understood as maintaining that for every human action and decision God knew at any given prior point *in time* that it was going to occur; or that He enjoys eternal knowledge about all human actions and decisions, where 'eternal' is construed in an extratemporal sense. As we shall see, whether Molina offers a viable solution to the problem depends essentially on whether we opt for an intratemporal or an extratemporal reading. According to what I shall call the 'standard interpretation', Molina adopts a temporal reading and rejects his opponent's argument because he rejects a modal closure principle about some temporal kind of necessity. Thus, Alfred Freddoso,[3] and following him Linda Zagzebski,[4] John Martin Fischer,[5] and others, suggest that Molina rejects the above argument because he dismisses the view that so-called 'accidental necessity' is closed under entailment.[6] Roughly, accidental necessity is a time-relative kind of necessity that pertains to states of affairs that are already past and thus "over and done with". If a state of affairs is accidentally necessary, no one can affect it anymore. However, under that interpretation, I shall argue, Molina's attempt to refute the argument presented in quote A fails. Moreover, Molina shares the Thomistic view that God's mode of existence is timeless eternity. In this respect, he is strongly committed to the Augustine-Boethius-Aquinas tradition.[7] Strictly speaking, Molina's official position thus does not allow God to be described as having knowledge at certain times. Instead, the sentence 'God

---

scientia Deo esset falsa; et antecedens est absolute necessarium, tum quia aeternum, tum etiam quia praeteritum et ad praeteritum non est potentia. Ergo consequens erit etiam absolute necessarium ac proinde nullum futurum praescitum a Deo erit contingens.' Here and in what follows the English translation follows Freddoso's (in FREDDOSO, *Molina: On Divine Foreknowledge* [1988]), with page references, in this order, to Rabeneck's Latin edition and Freddoso's translation.

[3]   FREDDOSO, *Molina: On Divine Foreknowledge* [1988], pp. 56–8.

[4]   ZAGZEBSKI, *Divine Foreknowledge and Free Will* [2002], ZAGZEBSKI, *Freedom and Foreknowledge* [1991], pp. 131–3.

[5]   FISCHER, *Molinism* [2008].

[6]   Though FISCHER, *Molinism* [2008] does not seem to question Freddoso's *interpretation* of Molina on this topic, he presents an extensive critique of Freddoso's Molinism, the core of which is that the account does not provide a solution to the foreknowledge dilemma, but presupposes that divine omniscience is compatible with human freedom. I think that Fischer is right here. After all, the very notion of divine middle knowledge, as Molina construes it, comprises God's *knowledge* as to what every possible human creature would *freely* do in any possible situation. In what follows, I argue that Molina successfully defends the *coherence* of that notion by rejecting a certain modal closure principle.

[7]   Cf. for example disp. 48: 2, pp. 10–11.

knew that this was going to be' should be taken as saying that, as Molina often puts it, only 'in our way of understanding' (*nostro intelligendi modo*) God may be said to have known things as coming to be. Talk about divine 'foreknowledge' or about the fact that God's knowledge of certain events is now past should in the *Concordia* be understood as referring to the fact that God has extratemporal knowledge of matters that only from an intratemporal point of view can be described as past, present, or still coming to be. However, in that case the 'absolute necessity' Molina talks about in quote A is not some kind of temporal necessity. Instead, I suggest, what is at issue is a kind of necessity constituted by lack of power on the part of human subjects to exert any causal impact on the states of affairs in question. Interpreted in this way, the closure principle Molina discusses is indeed false and the argument he reconstructs on behalf of the critic, and dismisses, collapses.

5.2 The argument from absolute necessity

Let us begin with some of the more obvious features of the argument presented in quote A. (i) Molina invokes the familiar distinction between absolute and hypothetical necessity. The consequent of a conditional is 'hypothetically necessary' iff, assuming the antecedent holds, it is impossible for the consequent not to obtain; the consequent is necessary only on the hypothesis that the antecedent is true. A proposition or state of affairs is 'absolutely necessary', by contrast, if the necessity operator operates unconditionally on the proposition or state of affairs in question. For example, although it is not absolutely necessary that Adam existed (for he might not have existed), it is necessary in the hypothetical sense that, if someone knew at a given time before Adam existed that Adam would exist, Adam existed. Sometimes Molina makes a related point by employing the distinction between *necessitas in sensu diviso* and *necessitas in sensu composito*, or the distinction between *necessitas consequentiae* and *necessitas consequentis*. The statement 'Whatever God knows must (necessarily) obtain' is ambiguous. It is true if the whole conditional falls within the scope of the necessity operator. Otherwise, Molina argues, i. e., if the necessity in question is taken *in sensu diviso*, or as a *necessitas consequentis*, the statement is false. (Not every proposition God knows is a necessary proposition.)[8]

(ii) At first blush, one may nevertheless be tempted to reject the argument Molina reproduces in quote A as *obviously* misguided – and hence wonder why he takes it seriously at all. Thus, if we interpret the necessity operator as referring to metaphysical necessity[9] and the phrases 'if a conditional is true' and 'valid consequence' as referring to material implication, the argument would employ the (false) modal principle: 'If necessarily p, and p (materially) implies q, then necessarily q.' However, Molina does not construe his opponent's reasoning in this way. He is thinking of an argument that is much harder to refute (if it can be refuted at all). This emerges

---

8   Cf., for example, *Concordia*, disp. 52, sect. 32, 35, 36.
9   A state of affairs is metaphysically necessary iff it obtains in every possible world.

from his response, as he presents it in sections 32–34 of disp. 52. There Molina explicitly says, first, that the conditional under consideration 'is *necessary* (because in the composed sense these two things cannot both obtain, namely that God foreknows something to be future and that the thing does not turn out that way)'.[10] Molina construes the argument as assuming – correctly – that it is a conceptual truth that, if God knows that *p*, then *p*; he reads his opponent as maintaining that the conditional 'If God knows that *p*, then *p*' is *necessarily* true.

Second, as regards the 'absolute necessity' that allegedly transfers from the antecedent and to the consequent of the conditional in question, it seems clear that what is under consideration is *not* metaphysical necessity. The fact that God "foresaw" a given state of affairs (Adam's existing, Judas' betrayal of Christ, etc.) is metaphysically contingent. Had He chosen to actualize a different world, things would have gone differently, and consequently God would not have known what in fact He did know about what would happen. Molina, it seems, does not want to portray his opponent as (falsely) maintaining the contrary. Given these observations, the principle referred to in the first sentence of quote A appears to be of the following general form:

(P)   If (i) it is necessary in some sense (which is not that of metaphysical necessity) that *p*, and (ii) *p* entails *q*, then (iii) it is necessary in some sense (which is not that of metaphysical necessity) that *q*; in short: $Np, \Box(p \supset q) \vdash Nq$

According to this view, what, if not metaphysical necessity, is at issue?

5.3 The standard interpretation

The distinction between 'absolute' and 'hypothetical' necessity is a purely syntactical distinction that does not tell us anything about the metaphysical nature of the modality thus characterized. However, Molina says that the antecedent of the critic's argument is absolutely necessary because, among other things, it is 'past-tense and there is no power over the past' (see quote A). This invites an interpretation in terms of the temporal necessity that Ockham and before him William of Sherwood dub 'accidental necessity' (henceforth for short: A-necessity). William of Sherwood writes:

> That is accidentally necessary which neither now nor in the future can be false, but once might have been false. (*Necessarium autem per accidens est, quod non potest nec poterit esse falsum, potuit tamen.*)[11]

The core idea here may be captured by saying that a true proposition (or state of affairs) *p* that is metaphysically contingent is A-necessary at *t* if it is beyond anyone's power at and after *t* so to act that *p* would not have been true. For example, that Caesar crossed the Rubicon on January 10, 49 B.C., is now A-necessary. The event

---

[10]   '*In sensu composito cohaerere non possunt ista duo, quod Deus aliquid praesciat futurum et illud non eo modo eveniat*' (disp. sect. 34, p. 353/p. 189, my emphasis).
[11]   WILLIAM OF SHERWOOD, *Introductiones in logicam* [1995], 11, p. 34.

in question is already past and hence no one can prevent it any more from having occurred. As Freddoso remarks in his helpful introduction to his translation of part IV of the *Concordia*,[12] a distinctive feature of this time-relative kind of modality is that a metaphysically contingent state of affairs which is still A-*contingent* at a given time T_0 may yet be wholly determined by causes that operate at or after T_0. Molina himself does not employ the term 'accidental necessity'. However, Freddoso and other interpreters have suggested that Molina's reasoning can best be captured in terms of this notion.[13] Reconstructed in terms of accidental necessity, the argument Molina discusses would run as follows.[14] Suppose that, due to His omniscience, God knows at T_1 that S will do X at a given later time T_3. (To borrow one of Molina's favorite illustrations: Suppose that God foreknows that Peter will deny Christ three times on the night before Christ is crucified.) Consider the state of the world at some time T_2 between T_1 and T_3. The theological incompatibilist may reason as follows:

Argument I: the accidental-necessity argument

(1) It is (absolutely) A-necessary at T_2 that God foreknew at T_1 that S would do X at T_3.

(2) The fact that God foreknew at T_1 that S would do X at T_3 entails that S does X at T_3.

(3) Hence it is (absolutely) A-necessary at T_2 that S does X at T_3.

(4) If it is (absolutely) A-necessary at T_2 that S does X at T_3, then S does not do X freely at T_3.

(5) So, S does not do X freely at T_3.

Note that T_2 could be any time before, and however close to, T_3. In general, the reasoning of Argument I can be applied to any times, (human) subjects, or their actions or decisions. The upshot is that this argument, if sound, would show that, if there is unrestricted divine foreknowledge, then no human action or decision is free.

(5) obviously follows (via *modus ponens*) from (3) and (4). Premise (2) is also beyond dispute. However, are (1) and (4) acceptable, and does the intermediate conclusion (3) really follow from (1) and (2)? First, a comment on (4). Why would the fact that an action is necessary *per accidens* rule out that the agent performs

---

[12] Cf. FREDDOSO, *Introduction* [1988], p. 14.

[13] Cf. FREDDOSO, *Introduction* [1988], pp. 56–8.

[14] The following presentation is inspired by, but deviates somewhat from, Freddoso's. It is also inspired by Zagzebski's formulation of the foreknowledge dilemma (cf. ZAGZEBSKI, *Freedom and Foreknowledge* [1991], ch. 1). One difference between the following argument and Zagzebski's reconstruction is that she works with the notion of God's believing what his creatures will do, while my presentation talks, with Molina, about divine knowledge of human actions.

it freely? The answer requires a somewhat more precise characterization of A-necessity. Let us say, again following Freddoso,[15] that

(A-Necessity) A proposition p is accidentally necessary at t iff p is (i) metaphysically contingent and (ii) true at t and every moment after t in every possible world that has the same history as our world at t.

Thus understood, A-necessity entails that if p is A-necessary at t then no one has the power at or after t to contribute causally to anything that would render p false. Consider an instantiation of p that describes some human action. If that proposition is A-necessary at t then no one has the power at or after t so to act that p would have been false, i. e., no one – including the agent – has the power to see to it that the action in question is, or was, not performed. Premise (4) maintains that, if this is the case, the action is not performed freely. Hence (4) subscribes to the principle of alternate possibilities (PAP). PAP maintains, in its most prominent version, that an agent performs an action freely only if she could have done otherwise. A-necessity, however, rules out 'alternative possibilities control'.[16] However, PAP is controversial. It may be questioned on the grounds of Harry-Frankfurt-style reasoning according to which acting freely does *not* require the agent to be able to do otherwise, but only that she sufficiently identify with the relevant desires.[17] This is an initial potential weakness of Argument I. Those who like Frankfurt, John Martin Fischer and others reject PAP can immediately reject the above argument because it implicitly relies on PAP.

Molina, however, accepts that freedom requires alternative possibilities, and here I shall not pursue the question whether he is right on *that* issue. I will shortly discuss premise (1), but let us first consider the deduction of (3) from (1) and (2). What general rule, or principle, does that deduction rely upon? Deducing (3) from (1) and (2) would be licensed by an instantiation of (P), complemented by a time index, in which the necessity in question is construed as *accidental necessity*. That is, (3) would follow from (1) and (2) if the following principle were true:

(P*) If it is A-necessary at t that p, and p entails q, then it is A-necessary at t that q.

According to Freddoso,[18] Zagzebski,[19] Fischer,[20] and other commentators who follow Freddoso in this respect, Molina is discussing something like Argument I in the relevant passages of disp. 52 and rejects this argument because he rejects (P*). In support of this interpretation, these authors point to Molina's official response

---

[15]   *Introduction* [1988], p. 55.

[16]   This label is due to John Martin Fischer, cf., for example, FISCHER, *Metaphysics of Free Will* [1994], pp. 160–184.

[17]   For a more detailed discussion of this point, see ZAGZEBSKI, *Freedom and Foreknowledge* [1991], pp. 154–162.

[18]   *Introduction* [1988], p. 58.

[19]   *Divine Foreknowledge and Free Will* [2002], *Freedom and Foreknowledge* [1991], pp. 131–2.

[20]   *Molinism* [2008].

to the argument. Here is the relevant passage, from which we have already quoted, *in toto*:

> Quote B:
> In such a case, even if (i) the conditional is necessary (because in the composed sense these two things cannot both obtain, namely, that God foreknows something to be future and that the thing does not turn out that way), and even if (ii) the antecedent is necessary in the sense in question (because it is past tense and because no shadow of alteration can befall God), nonetheless the consequent can be purely contingent.[21]

At first sight, the wording of this passage does seem to support a reading of the argument Molina wishes to refute in terms of A-necessity, plus the idea that he attempts to do so by rejecting (P*). On closer inspection, however, a number of worries arise. (i) First, a notorious question is *on what grounds* Molina might dismiss the closure principle he regards as central to his opponent's argument. Perhaps the hardest problem for the above proposal is that there would not seem to be any good reason for rejecting (P*). If a proposition is now accidentally necessary since it is can no longer be false, then any proposition it entails is accidentally necessary as well and can no longer be false either. If it is now accidentally necessary that Caesar crossed the Rubicon in 49 B.C., how could it now fail to be accidentally necessary that Caesar crossed a river in 49 B.C., or that he *existed* at that time? Given Molina's generally great logical competence, it is hard to believe that he should – mistakenly – reject the view that accidental necessity is closed under entailment. Freddoso notes this difficulty and argues that Molina must thus reject the above understanding of *accidental necessity*.[22] However, perhaps Molina does not in fact deny that A-necessity is closed under entailment, because he does not construe the argument he wishes to refute in terms of A-necessary. This is the view that I shall argue for.

(ii) Another problem with the accidental-necessity interpretation is, as Zagzebski notes[23], that A-necessity is distinctive of the temporal asymmetry between past and future. Necessity *per accidens* pertains to past states of affairs. But then nothing is necessary *per accidens* at all moments of time. This should, Zagzebski warns us – correctly, I believe – immediately alert us to a problem with any argument for theological determinism that employs *this* notion of necessity. If the distinguishing feature of A-necessity is pastness, how could any future event be A-necessary?

(iii) Third, remember that one of the reasons Molina cites for the absolute necessity of the antecedent is that it is 'eternal' (see quote A). To be sure, in the *Concordia*, Molina frequently oscillates between portraying God and His cognitive and voluntary states as eternal, and using temporal language for describing these states. Moreover, Molina often does explicitly ascribe 'foreknowledge' (*praescientia*,

---

[21] *'Tunc enim, esto conditionalis sit necessaria, quia in sensu composito cohaerere non possunt ista duo, quod Deus aliquid praesciat futurum et illud non eo modo eveniat, et esto antecedens illo modo sit necessarium, quia praeteritum et quia in Deum nulla possit cadere vicissitudinis obumbratio, nihilominus consequens potest esse mere contingens.'* (disp. 52, sect. 34, p. 353/p. 189)

[22] Cf. *Introduction* [1988], p. 58.

[23] Cf. *Freedom and Foreknowledge* [1991], p. 15.

praecognitio) to God. However, as we have already seen, Molina's official position is the Thomistic view that God's mode of existence is extratemporal eternity. From the standpoint of extratemporalism, however, it is incorrect to maintain that He holds knowledge *at certain points in time*. Hence, when Molina slips into temporal lingo, he may best be interpreted as trying to say that God enjoys extratemporal knowledge of matters that only from an intratemporal point of view – only *nostro intelligendi modo* – can be described as past, present, or still coming to be. If this is true, then Molina could, and should, immediately reject premise (2) of Argument I. Molina should reject this premise since, according to his timeless view, God has no foreknowledge of *anything*, and none of His knowledge of metaphysically contingent states of affairs is necessary (in whatever sense) at any time. This observation, too, suggests that the accidental necessity interpretation of the argument Molina reproduces in quote A is not on target. Even though it may at first appear as if he is concerned with some kind of temporal necessity, on closer inspection this interpretation runs into trouble.[24] What kind of modality then, if not accidental necessity, is at issue?

5.4 The 'causal-impact argument'

The relevant kind of necessity that human agents may confront, I claim, is lack of power on their part to exert any causal influence on the necessary states of affairs in question. Call this kind of necessity 'causal impact necessity'; for short: CI-necessity. Somewhat more precisely:

(CI-Necessity) A metaphysically contingent proposition or state of affairs p is CI-necessary for a given agent at t iff it is not within the agent's power at t to contribute causally to something that constitutes, or grounds, a necessary or sufficient condition for p.

---

[24] FALES, *Is Middle Knowledge Possible?* [forthcoming] argues that Molina's general conception of freedom makes middle knowledge impossible. According to this conception, Fales thinks, two doppelgangers who have exactly the same prior character, desires, beliefs, etc., and who face exactly same choice under the same circumstances are such that one could freely choose to do X and the other not. But if *that* is so, Fales maintains, there are no truth-makers for counterfactuals of freedom. However, he then argues that both foreknowledge and middle knowledge, though at first sight problematic, turn out to be possible after all because they do have truth-makers. Both kinds of knowledge, Fales argues, are possible because rational human actions are determined by agents' practical deliberations. Since such deliberations do not *causally* determine the agent, both futurefactuals and counterfactuals of freedom have truth-makers that do not prevent the action from being performed freely. I shall not go into the so-called grounding objection here, but would like to note that, if what I argue is on target, strictly speaking for the Molinist there is no divine foreknowledge. This might not cause too much trouble for Fales' with respect to middle knowledge, for he could restrict his practical-deliberation argument to this kind of knowledge.

Every proposition that is A-necessary at t is also CI-necessary at t (for any subject); A-necessity entails CI-necessity. The converse however does not hold. That Caesar crossed the Rubicon in 49 B.C. is both A- and CI-necessary for us now. However, while, for example, the laws of nature are, for every human being at every time, CI-necessary, they are not, at any time, neccessary *per accidens*. The reason why natural laws defy our causal influence is not that they are past, and it is logically possible that they will change in the future.

Deploying the notion of CI-necessity puts us in a position to state what seems to be an undeniable requirement for an action to be free:

(RF) An agent performs an action freely at t only if it is not CI-necessary for him at t.

This is a moderate and very plausible condition. If an event is such that the agent has no causal influence whatever upon it, how should it qualify as a freely performed action? (Indeed, many would say that in such a case it does not qualify as an action at all.) Moreover, Molinists accept (RF). It is part of their doctrine, which was widely endorsed by medieval Aristotelians, that human agents must be 'secondary causes' of their freely performed actions. According to this view, the 'primary cause' of everything is God. Yet a human action is free only if the creaturely agent gives God's 'general concurrence' that makes that action possible a particular direction by causally contributing to it as well. It follows that if it is CI-necessary for S that S do X, S does not do X freely.[25] We can now formulate the critic's reasoning against the compatibility of divine omniscience with human freedom in a way which, unlike Argument I, conforms to Molina's theological extratemporalism and thus meets him on his own ground. Two versions of such an argument must however be distinguished. The first considers God's knowledge about what actually happens in the actual world. Molina calls this kind of knowledge 'free knowledge' (*scientia libera*), because it depends on God's free decision as to which world shall be actual. This knowledge occurs 'postvolitionally' in God, for even He can avail Himself of it only (logically) after the creative act of His will by which He has actualized the actual world. The second version of the critic's argument concerns God's comprehensive eternal knowledge about what *would* happen were He to actualize a certain world. This kind of knowledge, which Molina famously dubbed 'middle knowledge' (*scientia media*), occurs 'prevolitionally' in God, i. e., it occurs (logically) before He actualizes a certain world. In particular, in the Molinist model God's middle knowledge comprises His knowledge what every possible free creature would *freely* do in every possible situation. I turn first to the anti-Molinist argument concerning God's postvolitional free knowledge about actual human actions.

Suppose again that some agent S does X at T (for example, that Judas betrays Christ when Christ and the disciples are gathering in the Garden of Gethsemane). According to Molina's official position God postvolitionally, but timelessly, knows that S does X at T. However, in Molina's view God's absolute sovereignty also entails that humans cannot exert any causal influence upon anything He knows. In section

---

[25] For more on this topic, see for example FREDDOSO, *Introduction* [1988], pp. 16–8.

21 of disp. 52, for example, Molina discusses the views of the 'holy Fathers' on the topic. Consider divine foreknowledge, as it occurs in Christ, of Judas's betrayal. Molina reports that Justin Martyr, for example, does say that 'Christ is not a cause of the betrayal, but rather [that] the betrayal is a cause of the Lord's foreknowledge'. However, Molina explains, Justin does not use the term 'cause' here 'to stand for a real cause; for the things are not a cause of Christ's foreknowledge'. Instead, what Justin really means, Molina argues, is the *reason* or *explanation* of why this foreknowledge exists.[26] If God is a timelessly eternal being, there is in any case a good reason for denying that human beings can ever have any causal influence upon Him and His knowledge. How could anything that happens in the temporal world act as a *cause*, even a partial one, of something that happens outside time? These observations yield the first premise of our second argument:

Argument II: the causal-impact argument regarding God's extratemporal postvolitional knowledge about actual human actions

> (1) At any time in S's life, it is CI-necessary for S that God know (postvolitionally, but from extratemporal eternity) that S does X at T.

However:

> (2) The fact that God knows (postvolitionally, but from extratemporal eternity) that S does X at T entails that S does X at T.

From (1) and (2) the theological incompatibilist infers that:

> (3) At any time in S's life, it is CI-necessary for S that she do X at T.

But from (3) it follows with our condition

> (RF) An agent performs an action freely at t only if that action is *not* CI-necessary for her at t.

that:

> (4) S does not do X freely at T.

Like Argument I, Argument II can obviously be applied to any action performed by any human being we may consider. The key difference between the two arguments is that Argument II, unlike Argument I, does not ascribe to God knowledge at times, and that it does not rely on the notion of divine *fore*knowledge. Still, Argument II only concerns God's postvolitional knowledge of actual human actions. How does human freedom fare under God's prevolitional middle knowledge?

---

[26] 'Non Christus proditionis causa sit, sed proditio causa est Domini praenotionis. ... Non sumit tamen causam pro vera causa, – res namque non sunt causa praescientiae Christi ... –, sed loquitur de ratione, quare illa sit' (disp. 52, sect. 21, p. 348/p. 181).

Here the critic can by analogous reasoning argue that, given (RF), the very notion of middle knowledge is not even coherent. Suppose once more that S, when placed in circumstance C at T, does X. For the reasons laid out above Molinists hold that:

Argument III: the causal-impact argument regarding God's extratemporal prevolitional middle knowledge

---

(1) At any time in S's life it is CI-necessary for S that God know (prevolitionally, and from extratemporal eternity) via middle knowledge that S, when placed in circumstance C at T, would freely do X.

(2) God's knowing (prevolitionally, and from extratemporal eternity) via middle knowledge that S, when placed in circumstance C at T, would freely do X, entails that S, if placed in C at T, freely does X.

(3) Hence, it is CI-necessary for S that, when S is placed in C at T, S freely does X.

Given (RF), however, this conclusion contains a self-contradiction. (3) says that S, when put in C, freely does X yet has no causal influence whatever upon doing so. Yet (RF) rules out that an action on which the agent has no causal influence is free. Hence, with (RF) we can deduce the self-contradictory statement from (3) that:

---

(4) S is not free in doing X freely when placed in C at T.

---

(4) is necessarily false. But (RF) is true (and part of the Molinist doctrine). (2) is true, and (3), Molina's opponent argues, follows from (1) and (2). If that is correct, then premise (1) is the culprit and Molina must give up the view that yields (1). That is, if Molina's opponent is correct, Molina must either give up the idea that divine knowledge is CI-necessary or abandon the claim that God enjoys middle knowledge. However, commitment to the view that everything concerning God is CI-necessary for every human being at any point in his life is one of the most funda-mental doctrines of Molinist theology. Hence, the critic concludes, the Molinist should abandon the notion of middle knowledge.

What can Molina respond to this argument? And how could he counter Argument II? Although Argument II and Argument III differ in certain important respects, Molina can take them in one package. In neither version is (1) a candidate for rejection. Molina is deeply committed to the doctrine that God's mode of existence is extratemporal eternity and that He enjoys middle knowledge. He also emphasizes frequently that because of God's absolute sovereignty no creature can have any causal impact on what He knows. Premise (2), again in both arguments, cannot reasonably be rejected either and (4) does follow, again in Argument II and III, from the respective (3) and (RF). But what shall we say about the deduction, in both arguments, of the intermediate conclusion (3) from (1) and (2)? As in Argument I, in versions II and III the deduction of (3) relies on a certain closure or transfer principle. It is a structural cousin of (P*), the difference however being that it deals, not with A-, but with CI-necessity. The principle in question maintains that:

(P**) If it is CI-necessary for a given subject at t that p, and p entails q, then it is CI-necessary for that subject at t that q.

The Molinist can reject both Argument II and III, I claim, because he can – rightly – dismiss (P**). This thesis fits well with what Molina says in the relevant passages, and it has some important advantages over Freddoso's reconstruction. It fits with what Molina says in quote B, namely that the antecedent of his opponent's argument (concerning divine knowledge of human actions) is necessary because it refers to the past (*quia praeteritum*), and because 'no shadow of alteration can befall God'. Clearly, this argument works not only for A-necessity but equally well for CI-necessity. Whatever is already past at T is necessary at T in the sense that it is impossible for anyone still to exert any causal impact on it at or after T. Granted, Molina does use the term 'foreknowledge' in this context and writes that God's foreknowledge is already past. As already noted, however, this should be read with a *nostro-intelligendi-modo* proviso. Speaking from an intratemporal perspective, we may say that at times which *for us* are already past God had knowledge about what *for us* was still coming to be. In the same vein we should also interpret the argument in quote A as claiming that the antecedent of the critic's argument is necessary because it is both 'past' and 'eternal'. God's knowledge of human actions is extratemporally eternal since it does not occur at any time. Yet for us that knowledge can also be described as necessary because there were past times in our lives, now causally inaccessible, when it was already present.[27]

There are at least three advantages of this account over the accidental-necessity interpretation of Molina's views on the transfer of necessities. First, unlike Freddoso's reading, the present reconstruction fits Molina's theological extratemporalism. Second, as laid out in this section, the CI-account is applicable both to an argument concerning God's postvolitional free knowledge and to an argument concerning His prevolitional middle knowledge about (possible) human actions. Third, and perhaps most importantly, unlike the analogous closure principle regarding A-necessity, (P**) is indeed false. In the following, penultimate section I shall corroborate this claim by presenting two counterexamples against (P**).

5.5 Is causal-impact necessity closed under entailment?

Consider cases of causal overdetermination in which an event to which an agent causally contributes would – due to other causes on which the agent has no causal

---

[27] This view implicitly invokes a concept that Eleonore Stump and Norman Kretzmann have dubbed 'ET-simultaneity' (*Eternity* [1981]). ET-simultaneity is a relation between timelessly eternal and temporal entities. Contrary to intratemporal simultaneity, ET-simultaneity is symmetrical, but neither reflexive nor transitive. Otherwise it would not be guaranteed that the *relata* are constituted by an extratemporal and a temporal entity. For a helpful critical discussion of the notion of ET-simultaneity that contains important objections against theological extratemporalism, see for example SWINBURNE, *God and Time* [1993] and FALES, *Divine Intervention* [2009], ch. 5.

influence – have ensued anyway. For example, remember Agatha Christie's *Murder on the Orient Express*. Hercule Poirot, the ingenious detective, eventually finds out that Mr. Ratchet has been stabbed by twelve different people (by Princess Natalia Dragomiroff, Hector Willard McQueen, Colonel Arbuthnot, Hildegard Schmidt, etc.). Each of them had their own go at the victim. We can easily construe such cases in such a way that each act of stabbing was causally sufficient for Ratchet's death, and that each stabbing caused his death via deterministic causal chains. Suppose that in addition none of the protagonists could have had any causal influence on any of his fellow conspirator's lethal actions. Then (i) for each conspirator the stabbing performed by any of his or her fellow murderers is CI-necessary. (ii) Second, it holds by assumption that, necessarily: If one of the relevant actions is performed, the victim will die; there is no possible world with the same laws of nature in which the victim is stabbed by one of the conspirators but survives. Yet (iii) Ratchet's death is not CI-necessary for any of the murderers, since each of them had some causal impact on that event. *Ex hypothesi* each individual act of stabbing was causally sufficient for the victim's death. This is a counterexample to (P**). We have instantiations of the fact that it is CI-necessary for some subject S that p; p entails q; but it is not CI-necessary for S that q.

Similar examples can also be found in contemporary philosophical debates about free will and moral responsibility. Some 400 years after the second edition of the *Concordia* appeared in print (in 1595), a fellow Jesuit of Molina's, Mark Ravizza, constructed a counterexample against Peter van Inwagen's famous closure principle for moral responsibility, known as (the responsibility version of) 'rule Beta'.[28] This rule says: (i) If p, and no one is, or ever has been, morally responsible for p; and (ii) p (materially) implies q, and no one is, or ever has been, morally responsible for the fact that this implication holds; then (iii) q, and no one is, or ever has been, morally responsible for q. When a growing number of counterexamples against this principle began to surface in the literature, Ted Warfield suggested a necessity version of rule Beta (call Warfield's rule 'Beta□Responsibility') which, he argued, was immune to the objections that had been launched against van Inwagen's original Beta.[29] In particular, Warfield argued that Ravizza's counterexamples against van Inwagen's Beta fail against Beta□Responsibility. The battle went on, and in a next movement Eleonore Stump and John Martin Fischer reformulated Ravizza-type counterexamples against Beta□Responsibility.[30] These counterexamples can be accommodated to fit our (P**) as well. One of the Ravizza-Stump-Fischer stories is *Avalanche* and goes as follows:

---

[28]   van Inwagen, *Essay on Free Will* [1983], pp. 183–189; Ravizza, *Semi-Compatibilism* [1994]; Fischer and Ravizza, *Responsibility and Control* [1998], pp. 154–162.

[29]   Cf. Warfield, *Determinism and Moral Responsibility* [1996]. Warfield's rule about responsibility is structurally equivalent to a principle David Widerker had suggested in an early criticism of van Inwagen's original rule Beta, as applied to the notion of having no choice about a state of affairs. See Widerker, *Argument for Incompatibilism* [1987].

[30]   Cf. Stump and Fischer, *Transfer Principles* [2000].

> Let it be the case that, necessarily, if the actual laws of nature obtain and the con
> ditions of the world at T_2 (some time just before T_3) are C, then there will be an
> avalanche that destroys [an] enemy camp at T_3. Let it also be the case that at T_1
> Betty *freely* starts an avalanche that is sufficient to destroy the camp at T_3 and which
> contributes to its destruction at T_3. Finally, let it be the case that Betty's freely starting
> an avalanche is the result of some suitable indeterministic process.[31]

In this example, it holds that (i), necessarily, if the laws of nature (L) obtain and the
condition of the world at T_2 is C, there will be an avalanche that destroys the camp
at T_3. Moreover, Stump and Fischer argue, we may assume that (ii) no one is even
in part morally responsible for L or the fact that the conditions of the world at T_2
are C. Though (i) and (ii) are true, however, (iii) it is not true that no one is, even
in part, morally responsible for the fact that there is an avalanche that destroys the
camp at T_3. After all, Betty freely and intentionally does something that is sufficient
for, and causally contributes to, there being an avalanche that destroys the camp at
T_3.

A critic may raise the following query with respect to this example. First, can
it reasonably be stipulated that no one is even in part morally responsible for C if
C stands for 'the conditions of the world', i. e., for the state of the world *in toto* at
T_2? This is a fair question, but I do not think it causes much trouble for Stump and
Fischer. Simply restrict C to those conditions of the world at T_2 that are causally
relevant to the avalanche (the one that has not been caused by Betty) and stipulate
that no one is morally responsible for this *partial* condition C of the world. Such
a scenario is certainly possible, but raises no worries as to whether people may at
least be partially responsible for the relevant state of the world.

Another worry may be that Betty's action is supposed to be the outcome of an
indeterministic process. This is required for the example in order to avoid begging
the question against incompatibilist views of the relation between causal determinism and moral responsibility. In the example, Betty's action must be free, and
she must be morally responsible for it. Yet if the story assumed that a free and
responsible action was the result of some *deterministic* process it would assume that
determinism and moral responsibility are compatible. Since this is precisely what is
at issue in the debate, such an assumption would beg the question against incompatibilism. On the other hand, L and C are supposed to necessitate the avalanche at T_2.
L and C are supposed to initiate some *deterministic* causal chain that leads to the
camp's destruction. (Otherwise the story would not constitute a counterexample
against Warfield's necessity version of Beta$_{\text{RESPONSIBILITY}}$.) Stump and Fischer's
example thus invokes a universe in which both deterministic and indeterministic
processes occur. However, while this may merit notice, I do not think the point can
be massaged into a problem for the story. Universes with both deterministic and
indeterministic features are clearly possible and, as many argue, even empirically
plausible.

---

[31]   STUMP AND FISCHER, *Transfer Principles* [2000], p. 49.

The debate between van Inwagen, Ravizza, Warfield, and Stump and Fischer concerns the notion of moral responsibility. However, the above example can easily be adapted to a corresponding argument regarding our notion of CI-necessity. After all, moral responsibility would seem to entail CI-contingency. (Arguably, if an agent is morally responsible for an event, he/she must have had some kind of causal impact upon it.) Suppose, then, that both the conditions C of the world, which together with L cause the avalanche at T_2, and the natural laws L themselves are CI-necessary for Betty. We then have: (i) It is CI-necessary for Betty that C and L obtain. Second, by hypothesis (ii) C and L entail that an avalanche destroys the camp at T_3. (iii) It is not the case, however, that the camp's destruction by avalanche is CI-necessary for Betty. For she performs an action (detonating the explosives) which is causally sufficient for the camp's being destroyed by an avalanche and which in fact contributes to the destruction. This is another counterexample against (P**). (P**), it emerges, is indeed false.

5.6 An objection

I have argued that while A-necessity is closed under entailment CI-necessity is not. However, I also said that A-necessity entails CI-necessity. Are these two claims consistent? Is it possible both that a certain kind of necessity N entails another kind of necessity N^* and that N is closed under entailment, but N^* is not? Compare the case to relations, not between alethic, but between epistemic modalities. A famous, though controversial, epistemic principle is that knowledge is closed, not just under entailment *simpliciter*, but under known entailment. Regarding that principle, Anthony Brueckner,[32] for instance, once argued that, 'if knowledge is closed under known entailment, then it seems quite plausible that each necessary condition for knowledge must also be so closed'. In another paper,[33] he even states without any moderation: 'Knowledge is closed under known implication only if each necessary condition for knowing is so closed.' (Brueckner here uses 'implication' in the sense of strict implication or entailment.) He then argues that certain necessary conditions for knowledge – such as believing, and having justification for the belief in question – are not closed under known entailment and that therefore knowledge is not so closed either. A critic of the argument laid out in the present paper may object in analogous fashion that, since accidental necessity entails CI-necessity and the latter kind of necessity is a necessary condition of the former, it is impossible that accidental necessity is closed under entailment but CI-necessity is not.

But such an objection would rest on a confusion. If A-necessity entails CI-necessity, but not *vice versa*, the set of things that are A-necessary is a proper subset of those that are CI-necessary. Hence items that are CI-necessary need not share all the logical properties of those that are A-necessary. What turns CI-necessity into A-necessity may remove precisely those items from the set that are not closed under

---

[32] BRUECKNER, *Structure of the Skeptical Argument* [1994], p. 831.
[33] BRUECKNER, *Skepticism and Epistemic Closure* [1985], p. 91.

entailment. For an analogous reason, Brueckner's argument against the closure of knowledge under known entailment is flawed.[34] It is not true that if some (alethic or epistemic) modality M entails another modality M^*, then if M is closed under (known) entailment, M^* must be closed under (known) entailment. So, just as it is coherent to maintain that knowledge entails, for example, belief and is closed under (known) entailment but belief is not, it is also coherent to maintain that while necessity *per accidens* is closed under entailment, causal-impact-necessity is not, even though the former entails the latter.

5.7 Conclusion

I have reconstructed and discussed a central step in Molina's treatment of the so-called foreknowledge dilemma, as he presents it in disputation 52 of his *Concordia*. I have argued that there are several reasons for which the standard interpretation, according to which Molina rejects a closure principle concerning accidental necessity, is problematic. The chief worry is that Molina officially commits himself to an extratemporalist account of divine eternity. This does not blend well with a construal of his response in terms of accidental necessity. However, Molinists can also, and more coherently, reject an argument for theological incompatibilism which is cast in terms of an extratemporal kind of postvolitional divine knowledge and which relies, not on a closure principle for accidental necessity, but on a structurally similar principle concerning the lack of power to exert causal impact on a given state of affairs. A related argument, which relies on the same closure principle, concerns God's prevolitional middle knowledge. I have argued that when Molinists reject these causal-impact arguments against the compatibility of divine omniscience with human freedom by dismissing the view that CI-necessity is closed under entailment, the palm goes to them.[35]

---

[34] For an illuminating discussion of this point, see HALES, *Epistemic Closure Principles* [1995].

[35] For helpful discussions of an earlier draft of this paper I am indebted to Evan Fales, Otto Muck, Katherine Munn, and Christian Tapp.

Part III

In Favour of a "Third Way"

Chapter 6

Eternity and Infinity

Christian Tapp

6.1 Introduction

When I tell people about an ongoing research project on the infinity of God, many of them will respond: 'Ah, yes, that is about eternity, right?' Then I will usually answer: 'Yes ... maybe'.

There seems to be an intuitive grasping of a relation between eternity and infinity. But can it be made explicit? How to conceive of this conceptual relation? That is the question this chapter is devoted to. There is, however, one problem I face right from the outset: 'infinity' and 'eternity' are both used in several different senses. According to some of them, infinity is related to eternity, according to others not, or not in the same way. So my goal can only be a modest one: collecting some kinds of conceptual connections rather than offering a comprehensive view.

6.2 Three Senses of Infinity

In the theological and philosophical tradition, the word 'infinity' is used in different ways. For example, in the sentence 'God may have created infinitely many beings' it denotes a quantity. It is an answer to the question: 'how many?' Call this the quantitative sense of infinity. In the sentence 'God is infinitely good' the word 'infinite' is used in a comparative way following Pseudo-Dionysius' method of *via eminentiae*. God is not called 'good' in the limited or restricted way we human beings could ever be good. When He is called good, He is meant to be good in a very special, a perfect way, exceeding the usual spectrum of meanings of this word. In a sense, He can be said to be not only good, but to be goodness itself.

Besides the quantitative and the comparative sense, there is another meaning of 'infinite' as it is used in the following sentence: 'The infinite God has created the whole universe of finite things'. One may call this the "metaphysical" sense of infinity – although I do not want to deny the metaphysical relevance of the other senses of infinity. I will call it the 'precategorical' sense for the following reason. Used in this way, 'infinity' is to draw a very basic distinction in the realm of what there is, namely, between finite and infinite things or – speaking theistically – created things and the one uncreated "thing", God. The Aristotelian categories of usual predication apply (in their standard sense) only in the realm of the finite while their use in the context of God, the infinite being, is not intended and may be misleading. So, in his treatise on divine Trinity, Boethius tries to show how the application of the Aristotelian categories has to be modified if they are used in the case of God.[1] As the finite/infinite distinction precedes the usual application of the categories, one might call this use 'precategorical'.

So, there are at least three senses of 'infinity', presented above in the order of decreasing vicinity to quantity or increasing metaphysical content (whatever exactly that is): 'infinite' in the sense of infinitely many, 'infinite' in the sense of unrestricted perfection, and 'infinite' in the precategorical sense. For infinity in the first, the quantitative sense, there are well-established mathematical theories that provide us with a precise way of defining this term. I will return to this later. As to what concerns the second sense, infinite goodness etc., some people tend to reconstruct this sense in terms of the quantitative sense. This can be done in an intensional way, as in the case when 'infinite goodness' is understood as goodness of an infinite degree, or in an extensional way, as in the case when 'infinite knowledge' is taken to be knowledge of an actually infinite set of states of affairs. I am not sure whether reconstructing the second sense of infinity in terms of the quantitative sense is a good thing to do, for what is actually needed here is not so much an infinite quantity of something, but rather some sort of maximality, totality or unsurpassability. (God is the *best* thing; he knows *everything* knowable, etc.) What I am most interested in is the third sense of 'infinity', infinity as a precategorical predicate which is used to draw the most basic metaphysical distinction, even before any category or categorical predicate can be applied. But this is also the sense which is the hardest to get a clear understanding of.

Having discerned these three basic senses of infinity, we may now proceed with examining some connections between infinity and eternity. To this end, it seems most promising to start with the clearest concept, the concept of quantitative infinity, for which there is something like a straightforward connection to (one kind of) eternity.

6.3 Quantitative Infinity and Sempiternality

There is quite a straightforward way in which one may think eternity and infinity are connected: if eternity is conceived of as an infinite amount of time. There is a precise sense in which a time interval can be called 'infinite', namely if it has no upper or lower bound (there is no number such that all numbers of the interval are above or below that number, respectively). Eternity, then, may be conceived of as such an infinite time interval.

---

[1]   See Boethius, *Quomodo trinitas* [1988].

6.3.1 Sempiternalism

This sense of eternity has played an important role in history. Philosophers since the ancient Greeks, up to the time of Kant and Hegel, and especially in the Middle Ages discussed the question whether the world was eternal and whether one could know if it were otherwise.[2] So, for example, Thomas Aquinas wrote a treatise *De aeternitate mundi*, on the eternity of the world. In this book, Aquinas came to the conclusion that an infinite extension of the world backwards in time is not logically or metaphysically impossible, so that the Christian belief in its opposite is proper faith, not knowledge by reason.[3] What was meant by 'eternity' in these contexts was that the time interval that had passed since the beginning of the world was infinite.

This meaning of 'eternity' is also relevant in the discussions about eternity as a divine attribute.[4] A minimal meaning of 'God's eternity' is frequently expressed by the following thesis

(BE)   God exists without beginning or end.[5]

In (BE), 'without beginning or end' indicates the relation to infinity. It may be doubted however whether (BE) really provides a *minimal* meaning of 'eternity'. Let us stipulate for a moment that it does. Then there can be different reasons for having no beginning or end: It can be for the reason that God is not in time, does not endure or has no location in time – this account is usually termed 'eternalism' – or it can be for the reason that God is in time, but he exists at each and every time instant, always, everlastingly, etc. – this is usually called 'the everlastingness account' or 'sempiternalism'.

So, sempiternalists understand God's eternity as everlastingness. Their main thesis is thus:

(Semp)   God exists at every point of time.[6]

---

[2]   See, for example, Schönberger's introduction to SCHÖNBERGER AND NICKL, *Bonaventura, Thomas von Aquin, Boethius von Dacien* [2000], pp. VII–XXXII.

[3]   See AQUINAS, THOMAS: *De aeternitate mundi / Die Ewigkeit der Welt*, in: SCHÖNBERGER AND NICKL, *Bonaventura, Thomas von Aquin, Boethius von Dacien* [2000], pp. 82–103. BOETHIUS, who has provided the generations after him with the most famous definition of eternity, spoke occasionally about 'going through the infinite spaces of eternity' (*Consolatio Philosophiae II*), but this passage remains unclear as it may be read as refering to spatial spaces. Later, to be sure, Boethius made clear that infinite duration is not really a kind of eternity, for it does not comprise the whole life at once, but is subdued to the 'no more' and the 'not yet'.

[4]   For the sake of simplicity, I simply speak of divine attributes, ignoring that one may discern between predicates proper, modifiers of predicates, etc. For the everlastingness account of divine eternity see, for instance, WOLTERSTORFF, *God is 'everlasting'* [2000].

[5]   See, for the formulation, *Eternity* [2003], p. 73, for its characterization as a minimal meaning of eternity, *Divine Eternity* [2009], p. 145.

[6]   I do not want to enter the discussion about whether there really are *points* of time. Suffice it to say that at least according to our best available scientific theories, time has the structure of the real numbers.

If sempiternalists want to provide an explication of God's eternity as it is determined by (BE), as we have stipulated for a moment, they face a certain tension between (BE) and (Semp), noticed for example by Brian Leftow.[7] In case there is only a finite time interval, the sempiternalist seems to claim that God's existence in time would have a beginning and an end, just for the reason that the interval is finite. But that would contradict the minimal understanding of eternity according to (BE). Leftow's conclusion is that the sempiternalist is committed to the thesis that there is an infinite amount of time and that God exists at all times of this infinite amount. So, according to Leftow, the sempiternalist is committed to a thesis much stronger than just that God exists always. I think, however, that this is not the only solution available to the sempiternalist, and, therefore, a charitable interpreter should not impute such a strong thesis to the sempiternalist, in particular if he sets out to criticize him as Leftow does.

Let us suppose there is only a finite interval of time. Then, there are at least two ways of defining what it means to have a beginning in time (or an end, *mutatis mutandis*):

(Beginning$_1$) s has a beginning$_1$ in time iff there is a point of time "before s", i. e., there is a point t_0 at which s exists and there is a point $t < t_0$ at which s does not exist.

(Beginning$_2$) s has a beginning$_2$ in time iff there is a first point of s's existence in time, i. e., there is a point t_0 at which s does exist and for all points $t < t_0$ s does not exist.

The first definition does not lead to any problems for the sempiternalist. Since there are no points at which God does not exist, there are *a fortiori* no points to the left of an arbitrary t_0 at which God does not exist. So, with respect to beginning$_1$, the sempiternalist's thesis (Semp) secures (BE).

This is not the case if one holds on to the second definition of 'beginning' as having a first point of existence in time. In this case it depends on whether the finite interval of time is open or closed. To be closed means that the interval comprises its end points, while to be open means that it does not. If the time interval is open, then (Semp) likewise secures (BE), for in this case there is for every point of time an earlier point of time and since God exists at all points of time (Semp), for every possible t_0 there is an earlier point t at which God does exist. Hence, in case time is an open interval, a sempiternal God cannot have a beginning$_2$ in time. The situation is different however if the time interval is closed. For then, there is a first point in time (the left border of the interval), and this first point is also the first point of God's existence: At all earlier points it is true that God does not exist, simply because there are no earlier points. Hence, in case time is a closed interval, a sempiternal God has a beginning$_2$ in time.

The preceding analysis has shown that there is one case in which the sempiternalist's thesis (Semp) does not imply the minimal understanding of eternity (BE), namely when the second definition of beginning/end is applied and (created) time

---

[7]   See *Eternity and Immutability* [2005], pp. 49–52.

is taken to form a closed finite interval. So, under certain circumstances, Leftow's view that the sempiternalist may be committed to more than (Semp) hints in the right direction. But the sempiternalist has more resorts than Leftow suggests: with respect to the interval formed by all points of time, he may argue that the interval is infinite in both directions, that it is finite but open, that the second definition of beginning/end has to be replaced by the first or a third one, or that (BE) does not provide a minimal meaning of eternity.

6.3.2 Finiteness and Embeddings

If one is interested in the infinity assumptions of a particular philosophical position with respect to time, one has not only to deal with the macrostructure of time – the question whether time extends over a finite or an infinite interval – but also with its microstructure. This can be seen by the following consideration.

One can smoothly transform finite open intervals into infinite ones and *vice versa*. Consider the following example: if x is in the open time interval (t_1, t_2), one may, in a first step, transform this into the interval $(0, 1)$ by mapping x onto $x' = \frac{x - t_1}{t_2 - t_1}$. In a second step, one may further transform the interval $(0, 1)$ into the interval $\left(-\frac{\pi}{2}, +\frac{\pi}{2}\right)$ by mapping x' onto $x'' = \pi \cdot x' - \frac{\pi}{2}$. And in a last step one can transform the interval $\left(-\frac{\pi}{2}, +\frac{\pi}{2}\right)$ into the whole range of real numbers by using the tangent function mapping x'' onto $x''' = tan(x'')$. Putting all three steps together leads to the function $f : x \mapsto x''' = tan\left(\pi \cdot \frac{x - t_1}{t_2 - t_1} - \frac{\pi}{2}\right)$, which maps the arbitrary finite open interval (t_1, t_2) one–one onto the whole range of real numbers.

Therefore, in a certain sense, it is mathematically equivalent to speak about an infinite interval or an open finite interval. If we consider only the interval of time as such, the tangent transformation shows that there is no relevant difference between the infinitely extended and the finitely extended case if the metric of the finite interval is suitably adjusted.[8]

Things change, however, if one takes the embedding in the full line of real numbers into consideration. (And this embedding is presupposed in the above definition of 'finite intervals' as having no bounds.) Then it makes a difference whether the interval is finite or not. Firstly, one then has the metric on the finite interval induced by the embedding into the real numbers, and this metric is not equivalent to the one induced by the inverse of the tangent function above. Secondly, then there are real numbers farther left than the first point of God's existence in time. But these points are by definition not points of time. This may also explain why many people think that the question of what God did 'before time' makes sense. And it may explain the fact that most people do not see that in case of a finite open interval, something existing at every point in that interval does not have a beginning or end according to the second definition.

---

[8]   Therefore, it is not true that an allpowerful God can shrink space to a finite volume only if space is not infinitely extended (LOWE, *Metaphysics* [2009], p. 255).

Note, that all these considerations depend on two important assumptions that one may discuss: that it is open intervals that matters and that time has the micro-structure of real numbers. It may be interesting to note also that the transformability depends of course on infinity assumptions lying at the foundations of the real numbers. That the line of real numbers is in a sense 'continuous' means that there is, so to speak, enough room for smoothly squeezing the whole number line into a finitely extended interval. Temporal infinity in the sense of interval extension is intimately connected with the microstructure of time.[9] This fact will play an important role in the following considerations.

6.4 Infinity *via eminentiae*

From a Christian point of view, the sempiternalist account seems to have some advantages over the eternalist account. The temporal conception of God[10] seems to fit better to what the Bible and the other traditions of the Church tell us about God: that He created the world, led the people of Israel through the desert, spoke, revealed Himself, saved, was incarnated in Jesus Christ, resurrected him, sent the Holy Spirit, etc. In a word: Christian faith believes in a God who is acting in history. Conceptually, it is much harder to see how a completely timeless God could act in history than in case of a temporal God (albeit, it is nevertheless quite hard to understand how God as a non-spatial being can act in spacetime in any usual sense of 'acting' as derived from the context of human actors). Many philosophers even think that personhood in general is tied to time. Maybe, a temporal God is also more appropriate to our religious experience, our feelings, our prayers, and our lives. So from these points of view, the conception of a temporal God seems more appropriate to Christian faith.

But being close to the biblical scriptures and being close to our religious experience comes at a certain price: how to secure the divinity of God? The temporalist faces the danger of putting Him on the level of worldly entities. He, therefore, sometimes tries a certain move in order to keep up the difference between creator and creatures. Paul Helm reports it as the conception that God's 'powers of thought and action are infinitely more powerful than any human being's.'[11]

Such descriptions have a long history in the philosophico-theological tradition. They make use of infinity in order to heighten or increase the usual, mundane

---

[9]   The argument mentioned before is only an approximation. In reality, things are much more complex. So, intuitively one would suppose that if the world has a beginning, then it must have been the starting point of the time interval of our universe's history. But then the interval would probably be closed (not open) on, at least, one side. Then, the argument I presented must be modified, perhaps by compactifying the real number line by an infinitely distant point, etc.

[10]   I understand 'the temporal conception' always in the sense of the possibility of divine properties changing through time. That does not, of course, mean that *all* properties of God are variable. For this clarification, see KREINER, *Das wahre Antlitz Gottes* [2006], p. 413.

[11]   HELM, *Eternality* [1998], p. 78.

positive properties. Those properties are to be freed from all earthly limitations (especially from anthropological connotations) by saying that God possesses them in an infinite degree/intensity or that the degree in which God possesses them exceeds all creaturely degrees infinitely. So God is called 'infinitely more powerful' than we are, or His goodness is called 'infinite goodness', etc. In traditional theology, this method is known as '*via eminentiae*'. It is firmly grounded in the tradition. But it makes some assumptions that are by far not unproblematic, and it is disputable whether it really makes infinity assumptions.

One problem is the presupposition that all these properties come in objective degrees, that these degrees are objectively comparable, that there exists not only a maximum degree, but also an infinite one, etc. This seems to commit Christian faith to a certain extent to platonic-neoplatonic metaphysics. Furthermore, one sometimes finds problematic attempts to explain the eminency of predicates: to be infinitely good is explained as just the non-creaturely mode of being good, the mode in which God is said to be good. But that explanation is either circular, making use of what it was intended to explain, or it presupposes another, probably pre-categorical, concept of infinity that I will deal with in the next section. But it should be noted right here that in this case, the problem of the inscrutable mechanism becomes even more pressing. Generally, the suspicion may rise that the initial plausibility of the conception *via eminentiae* is due to its unclear status between the quantitative and the precategorical use. The concept of an unrestricted expansion lives on quantitative infinity while the idea of keeping the difference between creator and creation seems to require the precatgorical concept. Another problem is that it is not entirely clear what the meaning of infinity is in this context and how the mechanism is to work which is first of all merely *intended* as surpassing mundane properties '*via eminentiae*'.

But is it really infinity that is needed here? The concept in need must secure that God's perfections can never be reached by a creature. But creatures like us can increase their skills more and more. So, in order to secure the creator/creature difference, infinity seems to be necessary, for all finite degrees would stand in danger of being approached or even reached by creatures.

I do not want to assume that perfections and other properties come in quantifiable degrees, but let us pretend that they would do for the sake of the following argument. One may think that one could also do without infinity in this case, namely by using the inverse of the tangent function discussed above. The whole range of finite degrees would be mapped to a finite (half-) open interval, say, the interval $[0, 1)$. Creatures could be said to be capable of increasing their skills from 0.9 to 0.99, from 0.99 to 0.999, etc. without end, but without ever reaching the skills of God at level 1. Would this not show that infinite degrees are not necessary in order to secure the creator/creation difference? I think that one cannot get rid of infinity in this context so easily. For this argument veils the fact that even in this situation we have infinity assumptions in the play. They are hidden in what was called 'microstructure' of the real numbers before: the possibility of infinitely ascending $(0.9, 0.99, 0.999, \ldots)$ while staying finite in terms of absolute values (below 1).

6.5 The Metaphysical Sense of Infinity and Its Connection to Eternity According to Thomas Aquinas

Let me now turn to the precategorical or metaphysical sense of 'infinity'. In order to grasp this sense, I want to search a little deeper into the systematic thought of Thomas Aquinas who is not only one of the greatest philosopher-theologians, but also a "friend of infinity". He decisively makes use of this concept in the framework of a systematically structured thinking which is oriented towards arguments and clear concepts. These points suggest his suitability for an investigation of the third sense of infinity.

6.5.1 God's Infinity

According to Thomas Aquinas, God is to be considered as *actus purus*, as pure actuality. On this basis, Aquinas develops the complicated doctrine of the identity of *esse et essentia*, of essence and being in God. Being pure actuality, His essence consists in nothing but His existence, so He is the *ipsum esse subsistens*, the subsistent being-self. In God, one cannot find the divide between the principles of *materia* and *forma*, for He has no material side in the sense of no (unactualized) potentiality. He is pure form. And as pure form, He is infinite in that he is not limited in the way that matter usually limits a form in making it the form of this and that *concretum*. In contrast, creatures are always "composed" from *materia* and *forma*, where 'to be composed' must not be understood in the sense of putting two material things together. It is to be taken in the way that in each and every concrete being one can find two principles in action by virtue of which the concrete thing is: the principle by which it is what it is (form) and the principle by which it is this one, and not another individual of that species (matter, *materia signata*, as *principium individuationis*). To discern these two principles is not to discern two things that could exist separated from each other.[12]

In short, Aquinas' way is: God is *ipsum esse*, pure actuality, therefore the *maximum formale*, the entity (if 'entity' is to be used here) with the least material part possible, so to speak, namely, without any materiality. Therefore, God does not suffer from the limitations matter brings with it in the hylomorphism. That is what Aquinas means when he calls God 'infinite': As pure actuality, He does not suffer the limitations imposed by matter in composed beings.

Now, creatures may, according to the Thomist standpoint, have a qualified infinity, an *infinitas secundum quid*, infinity in a certain respect. This infinity may be privative as in the case of matter – matter is indeterminate with respect to forms so that matter *lacks* the determinateness or finiteness of a concrete thing – or it may be positive, like the form of angels which is unrestricted and therefore unlimited, and that is infinite. But creatures 'cannot be infinite in their *esse*'.[13] So, God is the only thing that is essentially infinite. Why?

---

[12] So, Aquinas is not a universal realist like a Platonist.

[13] SHANLEY, *The Thomist Tradition* [2002], p. 190.

Aquinas provides us with an interesting argument here (*STh* p. 1 q. 7 a. 2). He subscribes to a principle from Aristotle's natural philosophy, namely, that there cannot be essentially infinite effects in nature.[14] Hence, if something besides God were infinite, it could not have been created by God for then it would be an infinite effect of God as its (primary) cause.

Contrary to what some people hold, this argument does not show that, except in God's case, actual infinity is *per se* impossible. For the argument is completely dependent on Aristotle's principle of no infinite effects – a principle that can be made plausible, if at all, only as a principle in the domain of natural things, not as a general metaphysical principle. And even in the realm of natural things, the argument can be disputed, for it departs from assumptions that have been challenged by the development of modern mathematics.[15] At any rate, the argument shows that Aquinas holds a very broad conception of creation according to which God created everything, He created the world '*ex nihilo*'.

6.5.2 God's Eternity

As to what concerns the conceptual relation between infinity and eternity, Aquinas gives some hints in his commentary on the Sentences. There he explains the famous definition of Boethius' that eternity is '*interminabilis vitae tota simul et perfecta possessio*', the complete and perfect possession of illimitable life at once. And this explanation is interesting for, albeit it does not mention infinity explicitly, it explains eternity in quite a similar way: '*aeternitas dicitur quasi ens extra terminos*'. So, eternity is something like being 'outside the limits'. Aquinas distinguishes three senses in which 'outside the limits' can be meant:

- concerning the complete duration (of an event),
- concerning the succession of parts,
- concerning the limitation of received being.

---

[14] ARISTOTLE's argument is: everything is either an *arche* or it is from an *arche* (*ex arches*). But the infinite cannot have an *arche*, for such an *arche* of the infinite would be a limit to the unlimited. Therefore, the infinite must be an *arche*, i. e., it cannot be an effect of something else (*Physics* l. 3 c. 4, 203b). It seems, however, that there is a systematic ambiguity in this *arche*-talk. If *arche* means something like cause, then the *tertium non datur*-like premise in Aristotle's argument is plausible but I cannot see that being caused directly (i. e., without recourse to perfection, simplicity or the like) imposes a limitation. If, on the other hand, *arche* means something like a beginning or a principle, then it seems comprehensible that having an *arche* means a limitation, but then the *tertium non datur*-like premise becomes doubtful. It may be interesting to note that THOMAS AQUINAS was well aware of a similar ambiguity, saying that Aristotle uses *arche/principium* equivocally, for being from a *principium* means a principle of origin (*principium originis*) while the contradiction to infinity comes only from the infinity of quantities or sizes (*quantitatis vel magnitudinis*; *In Physicorum* [1954], L. III, l. vi, p. 166).

[15] For instance, the impossibility of actually infinite numbers or the necessary finitude of everything countable. See, for example, CANTOR, *Gesammelte Abhandlungen* [1932], pp. 370–439; see also my *Georg Cantor's Theory of Sets* [2005], pp. 161–2, and *Kardinalität und Kardinäle* [2005], pp. 90–99.

By bringing the elements of Boethius' definition in a one-one correspondence with these three senses of being 'outside the limits', Aquinas shows that there is no redundancy in Boethius' definition. '*Interminabilis vita*', 'illimitable life', excludes that the life of God – which, for Aquinas, is identical to His being – has ever had a beginning or an end (cf. the thesis (BE) above). '*Tota simul*', being completely at once, excludes the second sense, the succession of temporal parts. '*Perfecta*', being 'perfect', excludes the limitations of being that is received in something else and is thereby limited.

The first two aspects that are ruled out by the Boethian definition are well known in the contemporary discussion in the philosophy of religion. Brian Leftow, for instance, discerns inner and outer limits of life.[16] Outer limits are beginning and end of a life, inner limits the boundaries between different sections of a life, like between one's first and one's second year, or between what is past and what is future for a certain being at a certain time. Leftow points out that the inner limits are as real as the outer ones. Now, if God is conceived of as a perfect being, lacking the typical creaturely constraints we experience every day (for example, when rising in the morning makes manifest all the heavy burdens of life), then He must not suffer from these two limitations. That He has no *outer* limits is what (BE) says: His life has neither beginning nor end. But having no *inner* limits precludes God from being in time like we are: He cannot have past and future for that would mean that He would suffer inner limits that become manifest in losing parts of His life to the deep oceans of the past. To this end, by the way, Leftow adds a speculative argument according to which the worth balance of God's life in total must be positive every day, so losing a day would mean losing something positive, decreasing perfection – which is impossible for a perfect being.

In Aquinas' view, being thus without inner and outer limits stands in connection to the concept of '*aevum*': Being in the sense of *aevum* or, say, sempiternality is distinct from God's eternity for it is a creaturely mode of being. Sempiternal entities like angels or heaven are creatures. They participate in the being of God and do not have their act of being in themselves. Hence, their being is limited by their essence. As Leftow puts it: 'The writers of Scripture see God as unlimited, free from creaturely constraints.'[17] This being free from constraints is what is usually termed 'infinite'.

6.5.3 Eternity and Infinity

For Aquinas this basic metaphysical sense of infinity is closely linked to eternity. Although this link is hardly ever made explicit, one can read it off from many passages in which infinity and eternity are treated separately but strikingly parallel. So, for example, in the *Summa theologiae*, Aquinas describes an infinite being as a being having '*esse non receptum*', something that has its act of being not received

---

[16]   See LEFTOW, *Eternity* [2003], p. 74.
[17]   See LEFTOW, *Eternity* [2003], p. 74.

from something else. In the commentary to the Sentences, in turn, it is eternity that is described this way. As was the third point in the explanation of Boethius' definition, eternity precludes the inner and the outer limits of life and the limits imposed by the creaturely mode of received being.

It is interesting to take a closer look at how Aquinas deals with the question whether one could not define eternity in a different way. For questions like that usually show something about the systematic links in a thinker's 'web of concepts'. Aquinas deals with an objection to Boethius' definition. The objection is: '*interminabilis*' is a negative expression, it involves a negation. Therefore it should be avoided in definitions of concepts which are intimately related to the nature of God, the most perfect being.[18]

This argument makes use of a basic distinction between positive and negative properties I find hard to understand, especially in a logical perspective. To start with a predicate P and form a negated atomic sentence like $\neg Px$, or to start with the dual predicate P' and form an unnegated atomic sentence like $P'x$ seems not to make any significant difference from a logical point of view. But maybe there is a meaningful ontological distinction between positive and negative properties which is simply not reflected in the logical behaviour of the respective predicates.[19] Aquinas himself takes this distinction for granted, as he answers to this objection in a different way. First he refers to his general method of negative theology he has inherited from Pseudo-Dionysius. Our intellect cannot perfectly understand divine being, so it has to feel its way forward by the *via negativa*. That being pointed out, Aquinas also gives a systematic reason why one cannot get rid of the negation: Eternity, he says, is intimately tied to unity. And unity means undividedness, so it necessarily includes a negation.[20]

I have already pointed out that there are only very few passages in Thomas Aquinas' works in which eternity and infinity are explicitly linked. One of them is *Summa contra Gentiles* lib. 2, ch. 80, no. 4. By discussing it, I come back to the first connection of eternity and infinity: the eternity of the world.[21] Aquinas considers (and wants to disprove) arguments against the possibility of the existence of human souls, independent of the decaying corpse. For philosophers holding to the eternity of the world, he says, it seems completely impossible that souls can survive bodily death, for then, generation has started infinitely long ago, so that infinitely many human beings have died before us. But then an infinite number of souls must be actual right now, and that is – according to Aristotle's natural

---

[18]   See *In Sent.*, lib. 1 d. 8 q. 2 a. 1.

[19]   See, for example, PLANTINGA, *Warranted Christian Belief* [2000], pp. 52–5.

[20]   A similar point is touched by Eleonore Stump in her chapter on *Eternity, Simplicity, and Presence*, p. 29ff.

[21]   Another one is *In Sent.*, lib. 2 d. 1 q. 1 a. 5. There, Aquinas discusses the eternity of the world (*utrum mundus sit aeternus*) and presents an argument of 'the commentator', i. e., Averroes. In that article, there are many arguments dealing with infinity. For lack of space, they cannot be discussed here.

philosophy – impossible. Therefore it seems that souls without bodies cannot exist, at least not in the same number as before death, when the world is eternal.

I find it interesting to note that Aquinas completely subscribes to Aristotle's proof of the impossibility of an actually infinite number in nature.[22] But, he says, from all that stuff no difficulties follow for the catholic believers, for they do not hold the thesis of the eternity of the world. – An easy way out.

Why, then, mention this argument? One can see here, that Aquinas uses 'eternity' not only in the sense that one usually ascribes to him (the Boethian sense), but also in the sense of actually infinite amounts of time, for only if the 'eternal world' means that the world exists for an actually infinite number of days or years or whatever, eternity may be thought to imply the existence of an actually infinite number of souls.

6.6 An Analogy: Quantitative Infinity and God

As to what concerns the quantitative notion of infinity, I do not see how it can be used in connection with God in a literal or direct way – except for a sempiternalist's conception of eternity as discussed above. In my eyes, it is hardly convincing to use the quantitative concept of infinity in the case of other divine predicates, so, for example, if one conceives of 'omnipotence' as infinite power in the sense of having the power to bring about an infinite number of states of affairs, or 'omniscience' as infinite knowledge, i. e., that the number of propositions God knows is infinite. It appears doubtful to me whether those infinitarian concepts do really capture what traditional doctrine wanted to express by 'infinite power' or 'infinite knowledge' or, say, 'infinite goodness'. As I said before, in those cases a conception of maximality or unsurpassability is needed, not so much a conception of a certain infinite quantity.[23]

But maybe one can make use of it in an analogy or a mathematical metaphor for talking about God. In the mathematical definition, a set is called 'infinite' if it has proper subsets being equinumerous or, say, equivalent to the whole set. If one tries to connect this to the metaphysical way of talking about God, one may think of God's intrinsic properties as proper parts of God's nature. According to the classical doctrine, every essential property of God already coincides with his essence – a coincidence which is traditionally conceived of as part of the doctrine of divine simplicity. In a strong reading, God is simple not only in that He has no spatio-temporal parts, but also in that He has no *materia* and *forma* parts and no essence as distinct from His existence. This is one way in which Aquinas conceives of God's infinity (being pure form without matter). Hence, one might say that

---

[22]   Cf. Aquinas' response to the argument in no. 10 of *SCG* II, 80.

[23]   Another point is that one may also say that human beings know infinitely many propositions; for example, for every known proposition p we also know $p \wedge p$, $p \wedge p \wedge p$ etc., and for every natural number n we know, in a sense, the sentence 'n is a natural number'. A theory of knowledge from which it does not follow that we know $p \wedge p$ if we know p would have to use a theory of the individuation of properties I would be keen to learn more about.

this kind of theological infinity consists in that a proper part of God's nature (one of his essential properties) is, in a sense, equivalent to his nature. In conclusion, equivalence of a whole and some of its proper parts seems to be a very abstract feature that mathematical and theological senses of infinity have in common.

I do not want to elaborate on this analogy here, but present some considerations about the alleged impossibility of a third way. What follows is, admittedly, a little experimental in character.

6.7 The Alleged Impossibility of a Third Way

A timeless God seems quite remote from the believer and hard to be reconciled with Scripture's image of a God who acts in history. A temporal God, by contrast, seems hard to be conceived of as the creator of all, including time. Therefore, one may want to look for a third way combining the advantages of both, the sempiternalist and the eternalist account. Why not conceive of God as becoming temporal with creation, having been atemporal "before"?

6.7.1 Time and Ordering Relations

When Brian Leftow analyzed such a conception he came to a negative result: he has found 'that there is no coherent thought here to express'.[24] In my eyes, this conclusion goes beyond what is supported by his analysis. His analysis starts by saying that 'God becomes temporal' means that God's life has first a timeless and then a temporal part. But, Leftow says,

> God cannot first be timeless, then later be temporal. For then God's timeless phase is earlier than His temporal phase, and whatever is earlier than something else is in time.[25]

I do not find this argument fully convincing because of a systematic ambiguity concerning the use of 'phase' in it. If a phase is by definition something temporal, then the inference from the premise that one phase is earlier than another phase to the conclusion that both phases are in time seems perfectly valid. But then the premise is non-charitably formulated as it imputes the contradictory concept of a timeless *phase* to the criticized opponent. If, to the contrary, a phase is not necessarily something temporal, then the use of 'phase' is unproblematic here, while I have some doubts concerning the other premise that 'earlier than' can be used sensibly only as a relation between points or intervals of time. In my eyes, there are only two possible positions concerning talking of 'before' with respect to the beginning of time and world: either such talk of 'before' is completely senseless or it must be understood in a way different from, but not opposed to our usual understanding of 'before' as a relation between points of time. To be sure, usually with 'before', 'after', and 'earlier' we refer to relations in time. But when we talk

---

[24] LEFTOW, *Eternity* [2003], p. 75.
[25] LEFTOW, *Eternity* [2010], p. 280.

about creation and the beginning of time or about eschatology and the "time after death", we can of course not mean exactly the same as in our everyday usage of these words.[26] With these terms, we might refer to an ordering relation that extends the usual ordering of points of time to the topological environment into which the interval of time is embedded (see also section 6.3.2 above). Just as an example, one might think of time as the open interval $(0,1)$, and conceive of its natural embedding into the full real number line (such that there were infinitely many points "before" time) or into the closed interval $[0,1]$ (such that there were only one point "before" time, and one "after").

One might complain that this is not the literal meaning of 'before' and 'after', so that we use these words only figuratively or metaphorically. Well, probably this is true. But this is also true in many other cases, for example in a hard-core eternalist position which aims at being in line with the biblical tradition of a God who remembers, forgets, regrets, waits, foreknows, creates and sustains, incarnates and redeems, saves and salvages, listens and hears, understands and reacts, promises and fulfills, etc. All such predicates are temporal predicates not only because they are applied to temporal beings but also because they include a temporal component in their meanings. If we use these predicates in the case of an eternal, unchangeable God, something severe must happen to their meanings, for what is said in temporal terms is then said about something entirely atemporal. So, one frequently argues, sentences in which these predicates are used to talk about God are literally false, and can be found true only by means of taking them as metaphorical or symbolic language. Others, especially in the medieval tradition of Christian philosophy, tried to save as much of their meaning as possible within an eternalist framework, for example by developing theories that say that causes of temporal events do not have to be in time. It be necessary only to believe that the effects of God's action are in time, whereas He as their agent cause does not need to be in time. In my opinion, this interpretation does not help us with our problem, for it simply moves the problems from the realm of God's acting in time to the realm of a causal agent outside of time. So, even in the eternalist framework, there are lots of non-literal or metaphorical use of language in play.[27]

And the same holds also in natural sciences. In astronomy, for example, we call certain clouds of gas 'hot', although one may never experience them as hot. And this is not for the mere reason that one may not reach them. The thing is that the density of those clouds is so low that they consist only of some few atoms per cubic meter, these atoms having a very high average speed. So, according to the physical definition of heat (the average kinetic energy of atoms), the cloud is hot, but if one

---

[26]   Eschatological considerations are an important motivation for me in trying to keep the possibility of a coherent talk about 'before' and 'after' open with respect to an extension of our earthly time to point(s) 'before' creation and 'after'/'on' the Last Day. See my *Joseph Ratzinger on Resurrection Identity* [2010].

[27]   Something similar holds also with respect to Kant's *Dinge an sich* which are non-temporal (for time is an *Anschauungsform*), but which are said to affect us (*affizieren*). I am indebted to Christian Weidemann for pointing this parallel out to me.

would ever touch it, it would probably feel very, very cold – if there were anything to be "felt" in a near vacuum situation at all. So even in science we use our usual words for some phenomena in a non-literal way, redefining them appropriately for needs of fruitful and uniform theories. Why not do the same when talking about cosmogony and the limits of time? Why not say that in these circumstances we use a different order relation, or better: an extension of the usual order relation time induces, extending the relation 'before' to a realm of eternal life of God "before" creation?

If all of that is true, i. e., if there is no necessity to restrict the talk of 'before', 'after', or 'earlier than' to time, then 'God becomes temporal' need not be an empty self-contradiction. It might point to a third way somehow between eternalism and sempiternalism. I am not sure whether there is such a way that is viable, but I do not see that it were necessarily not.

6.7.2 God and Change

There is another argument against a third way I want to discuss. It goes approximately like this: if God is timeless, he cannot change. Therefore it is impossible that "before creation" God had no relation to temporal events and that after the world has been created God has a relation to temporal events. For first lacking a relation one later has would mean a change a timeless God cannot undergo.

A partial response to that problem, frequently given in tradition, was that it is not God who changes but only His relation to us. While these relations change, they leave Him completely untouched. In more recent terms, only God's extrinsic properties change while his intrinsic properties are changeless. This answer is only a partial answer, for it stays behind what religious language intends to express when talking about divine love and compassion, for example.[28] Is it true love and compassion if it leaves the loving one more or less untouched, unchanged?

What I want to call into question instead is the intimate relation between timelessness and impossibility of change. This relation is usually considered a conceptual relation, i. e., allegedly one cannot even think about change without thinking time. This goes back at least to Aristotle's influential natural philosophy with its famous description of time as the measure of change. But is it necessary to tie change to time? In Aristotelian terms: Is it necessary that time is the only measure of change, or may one think about other measures?

In our natural world, all changes need time. Think about one of the easiest digital systems we have, the light switch. If light is on and we switch it off, this action takes a little while, maybe half a second or so. Then, leave everything out of account that has to do with the lameness of my finger touching the switch, just take the time the switch needs from 'on' to 'off'. This is not something instantaneous, but it takes a very short amount of time, say 1/10 of a second. This seems always to be the case.

---

[28] See, among others, GEACH, *God and the Soul* [1969]; LEWIS, *Extrinsic Properties* [1986]; WEATHERSON, *Intrinsic vs. Extrinsic Properties* [2006].

Things do not happen instantaneously, but they need an, if short, amount of time. But is this necessarily so? In more abstract a perspective, what we have is a system with two possible states, and change taking place means that the one state is left and the other is taken. So, there must be two situations, one called 'before', and one 'after', and there is some quite simple predicate, namely 'on' or 'off', the truth value of which with respect to the light switch changes between 'before' and 'after'. Do I necessarily rely on time when talking about the two situations by using the words 'before' and 'after'?

In a similar fashion as above one may argue that I do not. What I am committed to is an ordering relation that allows distinguishing the two situations. This ordering relation usually is time or derived from time, but can we not conceive of others?

To be more precise, my point is that change does not conceptually presuppose duration, although processes of change in our natural world always do. Just consider two different (temporal) slices in spacetime, both point-thin but in finite (temporal) distance. Could change happen between the two? When, for example, one slice is this morning at 9 a.m., the other one is yesterday morning at 9 a.m., in the first I wear a grey t-shirt and in the second a blue t-shirt; is that not change? If it is, then one can conceive of change without duration. But maybe there is an ambiguity in talking about 'change' here, for it can mean both: a *result of comparing* two situations and the *process between* the two situations. I would agree that there are no processes without duration/time, but 'change' in the first sense could also be applied in cases where there is no duration between two situations. Change as a result of comparison presupposes an ordering relation according to which we can at least distinguish two states in at least two situations. In nature, to be sure, this ordering relation is time (or somehow derived from time).

Turning back to the eternity of God, that means it is not necessary that change in God is precluded by taking His eternity to mean timelessness. Maybe God's timelessness can be conceived of exactly in the way Leftow makes use of in his speculative argument mentioned above: that God is not into the 'before' and 'after' in the sense we are, in the sense in which we can be said to lose the past. Maybe this sort of timelessness is a viable way to understand the '*totum simul*' of Boethius. Maybe it does not exclude change and '*interminabilis vita*', illimitable life, from Him. And maybe it would make it possible to understand some quite intransparent formulations from theological tradition, as when Boethius says it is fundamental for Christian belief that the Trinitarian God with His interpersonal relations existed even 'before' creation, 'from eternity, that is, *before* time and world were constituted' ('*ex aeterno, id est* ante *mundi constitutionem*').

6.8 Summary

The aim of this chapter was to seek some traces of conceptual relations between infinity and eternity. A first relation was found in the debate about the eternity of the world in which 'infinity' is used in a quantitative sense. In the same sense, temporalists are sometimes said to make infinity assumptions about the time during which God exists. I argued (1) that it is unfair to presume that temporalists make such strong an assumption, and (2) that the issue of the infinite macrostructure of time is mathematically intertwined with the issue of the microstructure of time – a problem that is not specific to the temporalist. Then I switched to Thomas Aquinas as a famous exponent of an eternalist standpoint. In his explanation of Boethius' definition a threefold sense of eternity showed up: no outer limits, no inner limits, and no limits of received act of being – the last point corresponding to his precategorical usage of 'infinity'. Eternity and infinity are explained by Aquinas in a similar way: as being outside of limits and as non-received acts of being. In a last section of my chapter I then proposed that a third way between temporalism and eternalism cannot be ruled out too easily, for it can be argued (1) that talking about 'before' the beginning of time refers to an ordering relation that is not necessarily time, and (2) that the connection between change and duration is not a conceptual one.

Chapter 7

The Difference Creation Makes:
Relative Timelessness Reconsidered

Alan G. Padgett

The relationship between God and time may seem an obscure subject to some. Yet the more one studies it, the more convinced one becomes that this doctrine plays a key role in our grasp of the relationship between God and the world. I personally have been fascinated by this subject for several decades of my life, involving as it does physics, philosophy, and theology. How we understand God's relationship to the world, in turn, is a central part of any theistic worldview. So despite the seeming obscurity of the topic to some Christian thinkers, the doctrine of divine eternity is an important part of any fully developed doctrine of God.

In this chapter I will consider the difference the act of creation and continuing creating makes to our understanding of God's eternity. We begin by looking again at the idea that God's eternity is relatively timeless, borrowing the term 'relative' from modern physics, especially relativity theory. I will also set forth the ways in which my thinking has changed since 1989 when I finished my doctoral work at Oxford which I later published as *God, Eternity and the Nature of Time*.[1] Because this third viewpoint of relative timelessness is still new to many philosophers and theologians, even those who work on the topic of time and eternity, I will take a few moments to review the evidence and arguments that led me to this conclusion and sketch out the basic viewpoint.

7.1 What Is Relative Timelessness?

Normally scholars distinguish between two views of the relationship between God and time, the everlasting model (sometimes called 'sempiternal') and the absolute timelessness or atemporal model. As we know, the debate has been framed historically between these two views, with problems being pointed out for each position by its opponent. For some time now I have been promoting an alternative model: God is timeless *relative* to the created spacetime cosmos, but also in some ways temporal. With respect for the great doctors of the church in the past, I have found neither

---

[1] Padgett, *God, Eternity, and the Nature of Time* [1992].

the everlasting nor the atemporal models finally satisfactory. I have promoted a third alternative which one hopes preserves key insights from both of the traditional views.

The basic picture of relative timelessness is this:

(1)   God's time is infinite and immeasurable. Because they are involved in created frames of reference and depend upon stable laws of nature, measured time words like 'day' or 'week' do not properly apply to eternity. All points of our created time are simultaneous with some points of God's eternity, but our spacetime universe does not *measure* God's infinite temporality.

(2)   God's life is in no way defective or undermined by the passage of time. God is the Lord of time, not its prisoner.

(3)   Because God is a dynamic and changing being, God is still temporal in some sense: God is immutable in essence, but changing in inter-relationship with the world and with us. Because God is a changing being, God has to be temporal to some degree. For this reason there are intervals within God's life, but those intervals have no specific or intrinsic temporal measure.

This viewpoint has recently been adopted and modified by Gary DeWeese[2] under the name 'omnitemporality'. I'm happy to accept that as another way of talking about this third model. Having introduced this third perspective, we turn to alternative viewpoints on divine eternity and survey some of their problems.

7.2 The Biblical Witness

Over recent decades I have moved more fully into the discipline of Christian doctrine (i. e., systematic and moral theology). I have come to appreciate more than I did before the importance of allowing biblical theology and the biblical narrative of God, creation, Israel, Jesus, and the early church to give a decisive shape to the doctrine of God. What is important here is not only the words used for eternity in the Bible, or even the isolated sayings about God and time, but also the character of God in the biblical story. When we put together all of these kinds of sources, it becomes quite clear that the Christian Bible presents us with a view of God in which God is not absolutely timeless but rather eternal in the sense of everlasting. Psalm 90:2 is a good example: 'Before the mountains were born, and You gave birth to the earth and world, from eternity to eternity You are God.' The Hebrew word for 'eternity' here (*olam*) means a long period of time (not a timeless eternity) and is often translated as 'everlasting.' This is consistent with the narratives concerning God and Israel or the Church. For example, the prophet Isaiah (speaking for God) proclaims: 'I the LORD, the first and the last, I am He' (Is 41:4). A God who exists from the first to the last is an everlasting Lord, not a timeless one. This is the viewpoint of the vast majority of biblical scholarship, especially since Oscar Cullmann's important monograph, *Christ and Time* [1950]. For this reason as a Christian

---

2   DEWEESE, *God and the Nature of Time* [2004].

theologian I believe that the everlasting model is the one we should begin with in thinking about God and time in the discipline of systematic theology. We need reasons to modify this view. The classical tradition has long provided such reasons, of course, but they did not always begin with the priority of the Scriptures and historical reality of Jesus Christ for the doctrine of God, the way many contemporary theologians (I among them) think we should.

My friend and esteemed colleague William Lane Craig, one of the world's great experts on time, eternity, and the nature of God, has recently argued that the Bible is more ambiguous on this topic than one might think at first glance.[3] He sees the biblical teaching of *creatio ex nihilo* as setting up or implying an absolute beginning to time. I do agree with Craig that creation out of nothing *is* a biblical doctrine. There is good support for the doctrine of creation out of nothing in passages like 2 Macc 7:25, Rom 4:7 and Heb 11:3 (cf. 2 En 24:2). What I cannot agree with is that creation out of nothing is taught in Gen 1. Even if we read the opening sentence of the Bible as an independent sentence which makes a kind of title for the whole section, and not as a temporal clause as some Bible translations have it, Gen 1 does not itself teach creation out of nothing.[4] The presence of a formless waste and the waters of the deep lead to the conclusion that this chapter is teaching a creation out of chaos, as almost all academic exegetes will agree. Old Testament scholar Terry Fretheim writes, 'The word beginning probably does not refer to the absolute beginning of all things, but to the beginning of the ordered creation, including the temporal order.'[5] The evidence for a creation out of *nothing* in Gen 1 is too weak to support Craig's conclusions. What we might find in the text of Gen 1, and its seven-day creation, is the beginning of ordered time or measured time. As John Edward Wright puts this, 'with Gen 1 cosmic time and historical time begin.'[6] That Gen 1 implies an absolute beginning to time itself, i. e., to metaphysical time or pure duration, is a conclusion which goes beyond the biblical data. This point about Gen 1 which we must press against Craig does introduce an important distinction: the difference between (1) measured time, that is cosmic or physical time, the time of science, clocks, and calendars, which does begin with the origin of the spacetime cosmos; and (2) metaphysical time or pure duration, which may not have any beginning at all.

The Bible does unambiguously point to a God who is temporal but also eternal (everlasting). The burden of proof for theologians should be on the side of a timeless God. So what are the problems with the everlasting viewpoint? We do seem to have some sense of the transcendence of God, requiring that She be outside of any merely created category. For example, we hold that God is beyond space or spaceless, and is infinite in being while all other things are finite. The main problem with the everlasting model is not logical consistency but theological inadequacy. Given our notion of God as an infinite, personal creator, we would expect God to transcend

---

3   CRAIG, *Time and Eternity* [2001], pp. 14–20.
4   Contra COPAN AND CRAIG, *Creation Out of Nothing* [2004].
5   FRETHEIM, *Genesis* [1994], p. 342.
6   WRIGHT, *Cosmogony, Cosmology* [2006], p. 755.

time in some way. Merely knowing the future, and living forever, is not enough to satisfy this demand. Another important point is pressed by recent developments in physics. We would join with St Augustine and many others to insist that time in some sense is a created category, which came into existence with the physical universe. Space and time – or we had better say spacetime – has a beginning, but God does not. Spacetime is warped by the presence of matter; but God is not. Thus God must be beyond time as we know it in science, at least in some way. This is a continuing problem for an everlasting view of eternity. I will argue that what we will call in general 'physical time' began with the creation of the universe, and distinguish this from a 'metaphysical time': a time which can go by without change, without material things, and without laws of nature. This allows us to affirm that spacetime had a beginning in time without thinking that metaphysical time had a beginning.

7.3 Problems with Timeless Eternity

What, then, of an absolutely timeless God, that is, what about the classical tradition of divine eternity as *totum simul*? Logically, one problem with the classical view that keeps appearing is the attempt to write temporality back onto the being of the One who is utterly timeless. This often happens when thinking of eternity as if all of time could actually be *at* one time. In the actual world both the reality of temporality and the process of becoming between things and events enters into the core being of created reality. When we abstract from this dynamic reality in mathematics and physics or in theology and philosophy, we can discover important truths but are leaving behind an essential part of the actual world. The standard classical model of all of time being "at once" before a timeless God leaves behind something important about the world God has created, namely, the dynamic character of time and history.

Recent philosophers, including our esteemed colleagues Eleonore Stump and Brian Leftow, have attempted to create a model of eternity that is consistent with the A-theory or dynamic theory of time. I do agree that the classical model of a timeless creator and sustainer of the world is internally coherent, but only when we reject or abandon the dynamic theory of time for a stasis or B-theory. Some philosophers are willing to embrace this conclusion. As Katherin Rogers recently wrote, '[C]riticisms of the tenseless view of time are not powerful enough to necessitate abandoning the venerable tradition of an eternal God.'[7] Unlike some critics, I believe that the atemporal model is logically consistent, but only when one adopts a stasis theory of time can such a God interact with creation.[8]

---

[7]   ROGERS, *Omniscience, Eternity, and Freedom* [1996], p. 408. This is also found in her new book, *The Anselmian Approach* [1997].

[8]   PADGETT, *God, Eternity, and the Nature of Time* [1992], pp. 76–81.

Because a timeless God is alive, God's life will have a timeless, 'atemporal extensive mode of existence'.[9] As was argued by John Duns Scotus in the Middle Ages,
God's being has 'succession' only in a conceptual sense, not in a temporal one.[10] But
such a God will not be able to change in order to interact with a created, contingent
world that comes into being and passes out of being, wich the process or dynamic
theory of time demands. The main difference between process and stasis (or A- and
B-) theories has to do with temporal passage. Imagine a time T, in the far future, and
an event E which (let us say) will certainly happen at T. If we take the combination,
E-at-T, we can get a sense of the difference between the process and stasis views.
For the stasis view, E-at-T is real always. Of course, E is not real now, but then
neither view thinks it is. Rather, the stasis view believes that E is always real at T
(and only at T). The process theory, however, denies that E is always real at T. E is
only fully real when T is *now*, when T is the present moment. Nothing is real-at-T
unless T is present. Of course, on the process theory, you can contrast the abstract
set of all things past, present, and future that will ever be real with illusions, myths,
and other non-real things. But within that set, for the process view, only present
things are fully real. Past things used to be real, and future things will be real. If
this view of time is correct, then either a timeless God does the same thing forever,
and cannot interact with time; or God must change somehow over time not merely
in appearance but in reality. For the action of God sustains all things in their very
being-in-becoming.

Some esteemed and learned philosophers, whose work deserves more careful
analysis than I can give it here, have sought to avoid this conclusion. I am thinking
especially of Eleonore Stump and Brian Leftow. They have sought to make coherent
a timeless model of divine eternity with a dynamic theory of temporal passage. They
want to press the point that God co-exists with every moment of time while not
becoming temporal himself. What we need, however, is not mere co-existence but
a theory of direct divine action in which God acts upon and interacts with temporal
things at moments which do not and *cannot* all exist at once. By thinking that past,
present and future things can somehow exist all at once, we do violence to the idea
that reality is fully temporal. Only present things are fully real; past things used to

---

[9]   STUMP AND KRETZMANN, *Atemporal Duration* [1987], p. 215. Stump and Kretzmann later
insist that their language of a 'timeless now', a 'timeless simultaneity' and a 'timeless duration'
are meant to be analogies, in STUMP AND KRETZMANN, *Eternity, Awareness, and Action*
[1992], pp. 463–82, esp. 464–5. Stump and Kretzmann use terms like timeless 'duration',
timeless 'now', and timeless 'simultaneity' because they wish to retain some aspects of
the ordinary predicates. But why not use ordinary words when possible? Especially in
specialist publications (like theirs), it is better to use ordinary terms in univocal predication, to avoid confusion and hasty conclusions. For example, if they had used 'timeless
co-existence' instead of 'ET-simultaneity' in the publications, a great deal of confusion (and
a few errors on their part) could have been avoided.
[10]   DUNS SCOTUS, *Ordinatio I* [1950], I, d. 9 & d. 43. This work is sometimes entitled *Opus
Oxoniense*, but is called *Ordinatio* in the beautiful modern critical edition of DUNS SCOTUS,
Opera Omnia [1950].

be real and future things will be real. Past and future are not fully real, and to think they are is to abstract from and leave behind a key element of created existence in the actual world.

What I am saying is that the very idea that all times co-exist timelessly with God in eternity is incoherent. First of all, things which exist in time cannot co-exist timelessly. Nothing that is temporal can also be timeless. In the second place, all times cannot and do not co-exist in any sense – and certainly not 'timelessly' or 'in eternity'. Different times are not all present, and only present things are fully real (on the process view). Therefore, they cannot co-exist with present things.

The Special Theory of Relativity does not change this logical fact, but forces us to say, 'present according to what system of measurement?' An event may be present in one system of measurement, but past in another. However, a timeless God does not have a system of measurement. God co-exists with the true present, that is, the real moment of becoming, in the life of everything in the universe. If the physical universe as a whole is in the process of becoming (as the process theory demands), then so is each object (really existing thing) in it. Even a timeless God must await the future of any and all objects in the universe, in order to act directly upon future (non-existent) episodes of that object. Thus a timeless God must do exactly the same thing forever, and cannot change to interact with a changing reality. This argument, of course, presupposes a process theory of time.

Defenders of God's timeless being are often captured by a picture. This is a picture of God, high and lifted up, seeing all of time at once, in the way an observer on a high hill can see the whole of a road at once. The problem here is that only one step of the road exists, even for the observer. The typical abstraction of thinking about all events forever in spacetime is just that: an abstraction. In reality, on the process theory, time is not like space. I have elsewhere given fuller time to a consideration and critique of their theories, and cannot repeat all of that here.[11] Interestingly, John Duns Scotus considered similar ideas in his *Lectura* centuries ago, and rejected them, making the following comment: 'If all future beings were present to God according to their actual existence, it would be impossible for God to cause them to exist anew.'[12] Since timeless existence is so very different from temporal being, even if every event existed in God's timeless "frame of reference" then God would have to re-create all events within the flow of temporal passage – which is absurd.

Just what is so bad with the stasis theory, then? If we have a strong attachment to atemporal eternity, can we not choose to hold on to a stasis theory of time? Here my only comment would be that we should allow philosophy of science and metaphysics to put forward the best theory. It is inappropriate for doctrinal theology or philosophy of religion to dictate in advance the conclusion that other

---

[11] PADGETT, *Eternity* [1993], pp. 219–23. Some of these same criticisms can be found in CRAIG, *The Special Theory of Relativity* [1994], pp. 19–37.

[12] '*Si omnia futura essent praesentia Deo secundum eorum actualem existentiam, impossibile esset Deo causare aliquid de novo.*' (DUNS SCOTUS, *Lectura I* [1950], d. 39, q. 5, sec. 28) There is an English translation and commentary on this Distinction, entitled *Contingency and Freedom* [1994].

sciences or disciplines must embrace. Coherence with other truths is an important criterion for any theory, including our theology of eternity. My own work in the philosophy of time has convinced me that the process theory of time is correct. Thus I cannot embrace the traditional model of timeless eternity. Of course I respect those who come to different conclusions, but I would argue with their metaphysical understanding of temporal reality.

7.4 Timelessness sans Creation

Recently Craig has come up with an interesting twist on the traditional view that takes seriously the dynamic character of creation. His new view is that God is timelessly eternal before the first moment of creation and the first change (and here 'before' must be a logical or causal before, not a temporal one). God then *becomes* a temporal being with the creation of time itself. I have a problem with this model, but thinking through Craig's arguments has also forced me to change my mind in one respect which I will spell out later.

The problem I have with Craig's model has to do with the necessary connections between time and change. Bringing all of the cosmos into existence at or soon after the first change is a decisive event in the history of God and of all existence. In order for this to happen, something has to change. For all eternity past, even before all creation, God is at least capable of changing in order to make reality *be* in the first place. This change cannot be attributed to the world, for the world did not yet exist back then. I have argued for some time that there is a necessary relationship between time and change. It is a principle that goes like this: necessarily, if change is possible for something then that thing is temporal in some way. Earlier I spelled out this relationship in a long argument involving modal counterfactual logic. I have since then come upon a much shorter argument which I would like to present here for the first time.

First, I will propose as a principle of reason confirmed by experience the following proposition: without time nothing can change. Time and change are not the same thing, and time can possibly go by without any change happening. But when we imagine an infinitely thin slice of some event, in which no duration, no temporal extension occurs at all, then change simply cannot happen at that instant. Change takes time to happen, and in fact some philosophers have gone so far as to define change as an entity having different properties at different times.

Yet we have not gone far enough. Where there is no duration, that is, no temporal extension of any kind, then change is not even possible. It is not just that as a matter of fact no change can happen in a durationless instant. It is metaphysically impossible for any change to take place. Imagine such an instantaneous time slice of a colloquium. In that snap-shot of time, nothing can change simply because change takes time. In that durationless instant change is not even possible.

One more modal point needs to be made. The principle I am speaking of does not just apply in the actual world. It is a necessary truth, flowing from the very idea of change itself. It applies in all possible worlds of necessity. This gets us to our first proposition. If we let X range across things or events, then:

1. Necessarily, if a duration does not occur for X then change is not possible for X. In symbols this would be:

   (1) $\Box[\neg D(x) \rightarrow \neg \Diamond C(x)]$

   Where D is a symbol for duration, and C for change. Now in a short logical step or two we can reach the principle we want:

2. Necessarily, if change is possible for X then a duration occurs for X. Again, in symbols:

   (2) $\Box[\Diamond C(x) \rightarrow D(x)]$

Applying principle (2) to the case of God before the first change, that is, before creation, we get this truth: If God is even capable of change at all, then God is in some way temporal. When we reflect upon the very first change in the life of God, the momentous change of bringing about the physical spacetime universe in the beginning, that change belongs to God alone. So God must be capable of change for Craig, even without or before creation. Yet principle (2) means that God must still be temporal in some way even apart from creation, if it is even possible for God to change. Principle (2) is also the reason that I define metaphysical time as the dimension of the possibility of change.

While we should not accept Craig's viewpoint because of the problem I have just outlined, we can go pretty far along with him. I now think that we should restrict the term 'relative timelessness' to the non-finite eternity of God *before creation and before all change*. Before creation, although time does go by there was no change, i. e., no alteration in the infinite being and blessed rest of the triune God. There were no true intervals or metrics to mark off the passage of time: just pure duration, pure being without change. God only changes to bring about the first moment of physical time and of all creation with it. Once God does bring about a world, then things change for God as well as for creatures. What about God's eternity after creation? I would now accept the term 'omnitemporal' from Gary DeWeese, in which God's time or eternity transcends physical time by being infinite and immeasurable. So I would change Craig's model only in this respect: before the first change, God is *relatively* timeless, and also contingently without change (but still capable of changing). With creation God becomes omnitemporal, entering into a relative change with us, while still being immutable in those essential properties which set off God as fully divine.

I have argued in this chapter that both of the traditional notions of eternity have their problems. In dialogue with Craig I have proposed a modified version of relative timelessness for divine eternity. Prior to creation, God is changeless and free of temporal measure or temporal decay, that is, *before creation God is relatively timeless*. After creation, God is essentially immutable but changes in relationship with a dynamic world of time. In other words, after creation God is *omnitemporal*. For all eternity God is in some ways temporal, yet is never bound by time. Thus in dialogue with my colleagues and critics I have learned to alter my earlier position, and so develop and strengthen the notion of *relative* timelessness.

Chapter 8

Timeless Action?
Temporality and/or Eternity in God's Being and Acting

Reinhold Bernhardt

8.1 God and Time

In his book *Divine Action and Modern Science* (2002), Nicholas Saunders reviews the contemporary discussion of divine action and concludes that 'the prospects for supporting anything like the "traditional understanding" of God's activity in the world are extremely bleak ... we simply do not have anything other than bold assertions and a belief that SDA [special divine action, R. B.] takes place'.[1] The only comfort he offers to his readers is taken from the hope that perhaps an understanding 'of God's role in guiding and directing nature' might be possible in the future.[2] It is a cold comfort.

Saunders develops the question of divine action from the perspective of the sciences. But already within the doctrine of God any attempt to conceptualize the belief in God's active engagement in creation leads to difficulties, involving assumptions about the relationship between God, whose nature is assumed to be time-transcending, and the time-space continuum of the cosmic process. The notion of timelessness obviously contradicts both the concept of action and the concept of causality, which are the main models for conceiving God's activity in creation.

- The concept of action is anthropomorphic, derived from the experience and the logic of human action. It is tied to the ideas of subjectivity and intentionality, and thus to the theistic view of God as a divine person, who intervenes teleologically in natural and historical processes.
- The concept of causality is technomorphic, modelled in terms of the experience and logic of the connection between cause and effect. It is tied to the idea of substance and power, and thus to a deistic or pantheistic view of God as primary cause which, in the case of a pantheistic understanding, empowers the secondary causes and directs the development of natural and historical processes.

---

[1] SAUNDERS, *Divine Action and Modern Science* [2002], p. 215.
[2] SAUNDERS, *Divine Action and Modern Science* [2002], p. 216.

These two basic ideal-typical models need not be clearly separated from one another, since action can be conceived as the intentional causation of events ('agent-causality'). That approach made it possible for Thomas Aquinas and others to combine a theistic view of God with the notion of the prime cause. On the other hand it is also possible to combine a rather non-personal view of God's effectiveness as spiritual power with the concept of action as it appears in the mind-body analogy. God as the logos or the soul or the spirit of the world "acts" in the world like the human soul "acts" in and through the human body.[3] Thus the language of action can be applied to an understanding of divine activity which tends to be causational in its logic and, conversely, the language of cause-and-effect can be applied to the action-model.

Especially the model of personal action is inextricably linked to time and thus comes into conflict with the neo-Platonic idea of divine timelessness – an idea which exerted a powerful influence on Augustine. If God is atemporal, as Augustine maintains in the 11th book of his *Confessions*[4] and as 'eternalists' such as Brian Leftow,[5] Eleonore Stump[6] or Paul Helm[7] hold, then one must make a clear distinction between God's eternal being and his action in time. It is the predicament of action-in-time which must be made intelligible. If, on the other hand, God is related to nature and history not only in his activity but even in his very being – as the 'temporalists' hold – then the predicament of eternity as time-transcendence (including omniscience/foreknowledge, omnipotence and omnipresence) must be made intelligible. For Nicholas Wolterstorff as a representative of the temporalist position the 'temporality of the event that God acts on infects his own action with temporality'.[8] God has a temporal existence within the very same time-continuum as contains the universe, but enduring without beginning or end.[9] William Lane Craig also places God in worldly time, but insists that he also transcends this time.[10] God is beyond time but participates actively in the flux of time and affects creation.[11]

The debate appears to me largely as a piece of what Luther called '*theologia gloriae*', a speculative philosophy or theo-ontology or metaphysics, based on an epistemological realism which deals with the very nature of God and of creatural reality as if we could grasp these objectively without the hermeneutics of tradition. God is assumed to be a perfect rational super-person who 'knows', 'wills' and 'acts'. His being and acting are then subjected to the dissecting instruments of

---

[3]   JANTZEN, *God's World, God's Body* [1984]; McFAGUE, *The Body of God* [1993], chs. 5 and 6.

[4]   See FISCHER AND HATTRUP, *Schöpfung, Zeit und Ewigkeit* [2006].

[5]   LEFTOW, *Time and Eternity* [1991].

[6]   STUMP AND KRETZMANN, *Eternity* [1981]; STUMP AND KRETZMANN, *Eternity, Awareness, and Action* [1992].

[7]   HELM, *Eternal God* [1988]; HELM, *Divine Timeless Eternity* [2001].

[8]   WOLTERSTORFF, *God Everlasting* [1975], p. 197.

[9]   WOLTERSTORFF, *Unqualified Divine Temporality* [2001].

[10]   CRAIG, *God, Time, and Eternity* [2001]; CRAIG, *Time and Eternity* [2001]; CRAIG, *Timelessness and Omnitemporality* [2001].

[11]   See also the contributions to: GANSSLE AND WOODRUFF, *God and Time* [2002].

analytical philosophy.[12] 'Creation' is taken to signify the starting point of the metric time-line, instead of being considered a theological qualification of all reality as a whole in the face of God. 'Eternity' is placed in opposition to time as if it were a divine realm "above" the realm of the creational time-space continuum as the sphere of movement and change, whereas in most strands of biblical literature 'eternity' is a predicate of God.[13] Thus Aquinas states succinctly: 'aeternitas non est aliud quam ipse deus' ('eternity is nothing else but God in His very being[14]). 'Eternity' needs to be complemented by 'life'. The meaning of the term 'eternity' is not to be elaborated primarily in opposition to time, movement and change (as in philosophy where, since Parmenides, 'eternity' functions as the ideal contrast-term to all the deficiencies of temporal events and where, according to Kant, it is a negative term),[15] but rather elaborated in opposition to 'death' – which is to say, in opposition to perishability and to the experience of the broken wholeness of the creaturely life.[16] It qualifies God as the bearer and source of the enduring power of life persisting in the flux of time. Not time ('Zeit') is the counterpart to eternity but timeliness ('Zeitlichkeit') and finiteness ('Endlichkeit') as indications of the condition of creaturely life. Thus it is ultimately 'creatureliness' ('Geschöpflichkeit') which can be said to constitute the antonym to 'eternity'.

To a large extent, the way in which the eternalist-temporalist debate discusses the question rests upon the Greek philosophical understanding of eternity as time-lessness or 'sempiternity' as opposed to metric time. The Platonic conception of eternity is defined precisely in its *unrelatedness* to time. According to Boethius,

---

[12]   See William Alston's discussion on the univocity of speaking about human action and divine action, facing the insight: '[W]e can hardly pretend to any such insight into what it is like to be God, or even to have purposes, intentions, and the like in the way God does. Thomas Nagel has gained fame … by pointing out we don't have much idea of what it is to be a bat. How much less are we in a position to know what it is like to be God' (ALSTON, *Divine and Human Action* [1988], p. 277). That is not to deny the necessity of a philosophical analysis of talk about God's being and acting but reminds philosophers that they sail on 'seas of the figurative and symbolic' (ALSTON, *Divine and Human Action* [1988], p. 280).

[13]   'Der Gesichtspunkt der Zeitlosigkeit spielt nur eine untergeordnete Rolle. Als Attribut Gottes kennzeichnet Ewigkeit den Aspekt der intensiven Wirksamkeit und beständigen Dauer.' (ERNST, *Ewigkeit* [1995], col. 1083. 'The aspect of timelessness only plays a subordinate role. As an attribute of God eternity indicates the aspect of the intense effectiveness and constant duration'; my translation).

[14]   AQUINAS, *Summa theologiae* [2006], 1 q. 10, a. 2 ad 3.

[15]   BARTH claims to liberate the term 'eternity' from the Babylonian captivity of an abstract opposition to time (BARTH, *Kirchliche Dogmatik*, II/1 [1987], p. 689).

[16]   'Als Vollzugsform trinitarischer Existenz ist E. der Raum und Zeit in sich einschließende ereignisreiche Beziehungsreichtum und weist damit als ihr Gegenteil die Sterilität der Ereignis-losigkeit und Beziehungslosigkeit des Todes aus.' (JÜNGEL, *Ewigkeit* [1999], col. 1775. 'As the performance of the trinitarian existence, eternity is the abundance of active relations which includes space and time and hence contradicts the sterility of the *uneventfulness* (*Ereignislosigkeit*) and the *unrelatedness* (*Beziehungslosigkeit*) of death.'; my translation).

eternity is the fullness, the plenitude, the all-at-once-ness (*totum simul*) of time.[17] Thus from the outset the very formulation of the issue of eternity follows a primarily philosophical and not a biblical agenda. Timelessness is part of an abstract philosophical portrayal of God which stresses God's immutability (and impassibility).[18] As a predicate of God, timelessness comes into tension with the testimony of both the Old and the New Testaments, wherein eternity is understood as the divine quality of deathlessness, of abundance and wholeness of life. If one is to avoid a theological Platonism, Docetism or Deism, then that understanding has to be kept in mind.

When the doctrine of God is developed within a framework of historicity – as was characteristic of theology in the twentieth-century, especially in the second half of the century – then 'eternity' comes to be interpreted with reference to history.[19] Generally speaking, the major strands of twentieth-century theology moved away from the assumption that God in his very essence is atemporal. It was emphasized that God was and is actively present and thus involved in history – without being subjected to time. Only a few voices in the present choir of theology and philosophy stick to the Augustinian view. Let me take Timothy N. Sansbury as an example. In his Princeton dissertation, entitled *Divine Temporal Transcendence. A Defense of the Traditional Theological Position in Science, Philosophy and Theology*, he attempts to revive that view.[20] His intention is to avoid all limitations on the being of God. According to his position, omniscience and omnipotence are conceivable only together with the presupposition of God's temporal transcendence. Thus, Sansbury wants to show that temporal transcendence is not contrary to becoming or emergence, does not entail fatalism or determinism, and is not contrary to God's activity, knowledge, or personhood.[21] Only the attribution of atemporality guarantees – in his view – that God in his action is neither subjected to time (which would make the future inaccessible to him) nor dependent upon history.

Yet in his insistence on the temporal transcendence of God, Sansbury fails to make the notion of divine action intelligible. He distinguishes between the atempo-

---

[17] '*Aeternitas igitur est indeterminabilis vitae tota simul et a possesio.*' (BOETHIUS, *De consolatione philosophiae* [2005], p. 262). See MÜHLING, *Ewigkeitsauffassungen* [2005], p. 158 ff.; MÜHLING, *Grundinformation Eschatologie* [2007], p. 84 ff.

[18] '[T]here is a conceptual connection between divine immutability and divine eternity in that an individual who is immutable in the strong sense must be eternal, and vice versa.' (HELM, *Eternal God* [1988], p. 94).

[19] As in PANNENBERG's approach. Following Boethius, Pannenberg holds that the idea of eternity '*der Zeit nicht nur entgegengesetzt, sondern zugleich positiv auf sie bezogen ist und sie in ihrer Totalität umfasst ... Die Ewigkeit als in sich vollendete Ganzheit des Lebens erscheint ... in der Perspektive der Zeit im Zeichen der von der Zukunft erstrebten Vollendung.*' (PANNENBERG, *Systematische Theologie I* [1988], p. 441. '... is not just opposed to time, but at the same time positively related to it and embracing it in its totality... Eternity as in itself perfect wholeness of life appears ... in the perspective of time in the light of the perfection to which the future aims at.'; my translation).

[20] SANSBURY, *Divine Temporal Transcendence* [2006].

[21] SANSBURY, *Divine Temporal Transcendence* [2006], ch. 3.

ral actor and the temporal action, but he is not able to develop a convincing model for relating both. He attempts to achieve shape and cogency for his atemporal actor by developing the implications of the ideas of limitlessness and absolute perfection – which, however, remain a philosophical fiction.

In the following considerations I would like to present a view of God's action which I claim to be compatible with the notion of eternity as God's 'non-timeliness' ('Nicht-Zeitlichkeit'). In my opinion this view is in accordance both with the biblical testimonies and with major strands of the theological tradition. I believe that it is consistent and intelligible in itself and helpful for the dialogue with modern sciences and for the interpretation of existential experiences in the perspective of Christian faith.

The basic idea of my approach is to delineate the relation between God and the time-bound cosmic reality not in simplex, one-dimensional terms, but in a three-fold way – a threefold way corresponding to the Trinitarian nature of God. Thus, the term 'eternity' has not one but three different meanings, which belong together like the "persons" of the trinity.[22] Should the intellectual consistency of this concept of eternity be questioned, I will reply: it is no less consistent than the doctrine of the trinity.

(a) The notion of the 'First Person' of the trinity indicates the creation-transcending primordial nature of God *per se*, God in his aseity, radically beyond timeliness and spatiality, beyond finitude and perishability. As developed by Augustine, in that dimension God as creator is atemporal and aspatial;[23] eternity has then to be understood in opposition to timeliness and as an expression of divine transcendence. But it bears the potential to create time in it.

(b) The notion of the 'Second Person' of the trinity, the *Logos*, symbolizes God's self-communication. In his non-timeliness he is not timeless – which is to say, he is not to be conceived as unrelated to temporal reality (reality in its *Zeitlichkeit*) – but rather constitutes and encompasses created reality, including both space and time. In that dimension God is God *quod nos*. As distinct from

---

[22]   Cf. BARTH: '*Man kann und muß hier wie in der Trinitätslehre selbst von einer Perichorese, einem Ineinandersein und Ineinanderwirken der drei Gestalten der Ewigkeit reden.*' '*Vorzeitlichkeit, Überzeitlichkeit und Nachzeitlichkeit*' (BARTH, *Kirchliche Dogmatik, II/1* [1987], pp. 721, 720. 'At this point, as in the doctrine of the trinity itself, we can and must speak of a perichoresis, a mutual indwelling and interworking of the three forms of eternity:' '[p]re-temporality, supra-temporality and post-temporality'; BARTH, *Church Dogmatics, II/1* [1957], pp. 640, 638). – '*Die wahre Ewigkeit schließt … die Potentialität zur Zeit in sich.*' (BARTH, *Kirchliche Dogmatik, II/1* [1987], p. 696. 'True eternity includes … the potentiality of time'; BARTH, *Church Dogmatics, II/1* [1957], p. 617) Sie ist, '*ohne selbst Zeit zu sein, als schlechthinniger Grund der Zeit zugleich die schlechthinnige Bereitschaft für sie.*' (BARTH, *Kirchliche Dogmatik, II/1* [1987], p. 696. And '… we cannot deny that although God's eternity is not itself time it is as such the absolute basis of time, and therefore absolute readiness for it'; BARTH, *Church Dogmatics, II/1* [1957], p. 618).

[23]   Cf. DALFERTH, *Gedeutete Gegenwart* [1997], p. 264: '*Gott ist als Schöpfer zeitlos ewig*' ('As creator, God is timelessly eternal'; my translation).

the Creator the creation bears the signum of timeliness and finitude; as such it is related to God.

According to the Prologue of the Gospel of John the *Logos* is ἐν ἀρχῇ. That is not to be understood temporally, in the sense of the starting point of the time-line, but qualitatively. In his *Logos* God calls the reality in its timeliness into being. That is expressed in the symbol of the *Logos* as the mediator of creation. In this view eternity has to be understood as the womb from which the time-space continuum is (continuously!) born, without ever having left it. The whole process is encompassed by eternity. Thus, eternity is not to be placed over against time but is related to it as its transcendent ground of being, its horizon of wholeness ('*Ganzheitshorizont*') and its promise of fulfillment. Eternity is a divine predicate which indeed transcends the timeliness of creation – while including time. As the ever-presence of the wholeness of life it is the condition of the possibility and of the reality of temporal life.

According to that understanding, 'eternity' means that God in His non-time-liness stands in an utterly immediate relation to all moments of the reality in its timeliness; He creates at all times and through all times; every moment of time is in God – not in a temporal sequence but simultaneously, in one undivided present. This is, in the main, the position of Boethius, Kierkegaard ('fullness of time'[24]) and Karl Barth. Here, eternity is neither the antithesis to time nor its extension to infinity. It is related to time but qualitatively different from time and blasts open its categories.

In the incarnation of the *Logos* in Jesus the Christ, the divine reality which encompasses and constitutes the reality in its timeliness becomes present in one historical moment of time. That breakthrough of eternity into time makes this particular event a *kairos*.

(c) The non-timely God, who transcends, encompasses and constitutes temporal reality and who has revealed Himself in the *kairos* of the Christ-event, is also actively present in nature and history, interacting with creation and affected by natural events, historical incidents and human deeds. The notion of the 'Third Person' of the trinity, the Spirit, focuses on this power of God's presence within time (*cum tempore*). While the second dimension of the divine reality – God in His *Logos*, in the mode of His self-communication which constitutes the created reality – can be summarized in the formula 'time is in God', the third dimension – God in His spirit, in the mode of His self-representation – makes it possible to say that 'God is in time' – meaning in the flux of time as we experience it (according to the A-theory of time).

The third dimension allows us to emphasize the conviction (a conviction pre-supposed and expressed throughout the scriptures) that the non-temporal infi-nite God is immanent in creation, in finite space and time. In that view, eternity means omnipresence: God is actively present at every moment of the cosmic process, co-present with every moment, wandering with his people through all

---

[24]   KIERKEGAARD, *Der Begriff Angst* [1952], p. 92.

times as the biblical narratives portray it. Transcending time, God encounters his people from the future so as to lead his people into the future. Within time, the future, as the sphere of unrealized possibilities, is the privileged time of God. God is the power of the future. According to the understanding of the biblical authors, events are generally not determined by time, but rather time is determined by events. Where God represents himself, he sets time-markers. Thus God is not subjected to linear metric time but rather constitutes the very structure of time. Time is not homogeneous but occurs only in the plural, as "times". Each event has its own "time" and God stands in relation to these times. Every manifestation of his self-representation is a *kairos*, a breakthrough of the eschatological plenitude of time into history, an intensification of time.

The Trinitarian approach to eternity opens up an understanding of the three dimensions outlined above as aspects of the one reality of God. On the other hand it also calls for making a distinction between God in relation to Godself (in his very being); God in relation to the whole time-space continuum (as called into being by His *Logos*, the revelation of His self-communication which breaks through at one *kairos*-point of history); and God in relation to each and every single event (His omnipresence). Eternity appears first as the non-timeliness of God's primordial nature; second as the "ground of being" of the created reality, the constituting horizon encompassing all finite processes and relating them back to the wholeness of infinity; and third as God's active presence throughout reality in its timeliness. The three dimensions with their three distinct relations between God and created reality are bound up with one another in a perichoretic interpenetration.[25]

Within this conception of the threefold relation between Creator and creation it is the third dimension of God's nature – God's presence in the power of His spirit – to which His activity in history can be attributed. And thus pneumatology is the starting point for the development of a theology of God's activity in creation.

8.2 God's Activity as Spiritual Self-Representation

What kind of analogy might prove to be apt for conceptualizing divine activity? Obviously, the model of human action is problematic if spelled out in terms of immediate, particular, purposive interventions in natural processes and historical developments. 'Action' implicates the intentional changing of (or the preventing of change in) specific states of affairs by a personal agent. It consists of a sequence of intention, decision and performance under specific given conditions in the time-space-continuum. Thus, if divine activity is conceptualized within the frame of that model then the portrayal of God as an agent among agents and causes can hardly be avoided.

---

[25] Cf. DALFERTH, *Gedeutete Gegenwart* [1997], p. 263, who depicts eternity as '*Einheit von Zeitlosigkeit und Vielzeitigkeit*' ('unity of timelessness and multi-temporality'; my translation).

Of course, in the biblical testimony as well as in the main strands of theological tradition God is indeed portrayed as a personal agent. But one should take into account the fact that the scriptures do not give a plain and univocal description of God's being and acting, and that what has been handed down to us are *interpreted* human experiences with God. To take them as factual reports is to deliver the view of God to anthropomorphism.

Thus, I follow theologians like Moltmann, Pannenberg, Process-thinkers and Peter Hodgson who seek alternative analogies for describing God's active relation to creation. I propose that we opt for the analogy of a force-field – not a physically-conceived force-field (such as a magnetic field for instance) but a spiritual one. Employing this model I will try to reconstruct the notion of divine activity within pneumatology.[26] Like an energy field, God's spiritual presence is laid over the whole of the creational process, permeating it and influencing all actualizations and transformations in the spheres of nature, history and consciousness.

This spiritual force-field is not to be identified with God in the fullness of His reality.[27] It is rather the mode of His immanence, the mode of His creative, soteriological and eschatological activity. In the power of His spirit God is present in creation – but He is "more" than that. Thus, to view God's active presence in terms of a force-field does not by any means lead to a non-personal understanding of God, for God transcends any distinction between personal and non-personal features. Both personal and non-personal metaphors can be employed when talking about God and with God. The personal dimension safeguards the concept of God from falling into pantheism. The approach I advocate comes closer to a panentheism, according to which the whole of creation exists within – and human beings *act* within – the activity of God, in the force-field of God's spirit and all are, to a greater or lesser extent, affected by it. As Paul puts it in Acts 17,28: 'In him we live and move and have our being.'

Let me make two further comments on my understanding of the efficacy of the spiritual force-field. Firstly, this effectiveness is not to be seen as the product of some mechanical impact but instead as a "personal" impulse which requires a response. The individual can resist its influence or comport him- or herself in relation to it in very different ways. There is interaction between the pneuma-field and the individual person or entity. God's operative presence cannot be considered in terms of a deterministic causality. The presence of God "acts" not in an instrumental but in a communicative way, by means of 'word' and 'spirit'. 'Word' is the symbol for a relatively clear and unambiguous perception of the spiritual power.

---

[26] For a more detailed outline of my argument, see BERNHARDT, *Was heißt 'Handeln Gottes'?* [1999].

[27] In his article *The Eternal Act* [1998] DON LODZINSKI suggests that an identification of God's timeless will with the creation itself offers a solution to the problem of how eternity relates to time and how God acts in time. That solution leads into pantheism, as he admits. The force-field model, however, avoids that consequence by insisting that the created reality is "in" the power of God's presence which transcends it. God's spirit as the mode of his active presence has to be distinguished from God's very being.

Second, the field itself need not be understood as a uniform general energy, spraying its influence about in some undifferentiated, automatic way. On the contrary, the powerful presence of the living God may be more or less dense and concentrated. Biblical witness presents abundant testimonies to that unequal distribution (and perception) of the power of God's spirit.[28]

To enhance the plausibility of this model I would cite three experiences drawn from the personal and interpersonal arena, and relate them to theological conceptions of divine action.

(a) First, I would call attention to the energy of pure presence. Without performing any specific actions at all, a person can alter a situation simply by being there. This can be experienced particularly in situations marked by suffering, mourning, and grief, or alternatively in situations wherein love, compassion and caring predominate. Not only external actions, but also enacted relationships have an effect on those who are affected by the situation. Though *being present* is not a specific act, it can nevertheless be understood as the result of an intention and thus as an act in a broader sense. In that broader sense it becomes possible to employ *being present* as an analogy when speaking of divine 'action'.

Schleiermacher takes this path. He adamantly rejects the notion of special divine action, pleading instead for an understanding of God's activity as *one indivisible act* of ongoing creation and power over the world. This one act is performed by means of God's self-representation and self-radiation in His spirit.[29] God acts by inspiration.

(b) Second, I would call attention to the inter- and transpersonal "ambience" which prevails in a given community and influences the individual persons. Indeed, there is a certain spirit which transcends the motivations and deeds of those who are exposed to that force-field. In this respect it is not so much a person who alters a situation by her sheer presence but the situation which alters the person. The situation with its specific "atmosphere" necessarily affects the persons present, and thus has an effect on their *self*-understanding. Action cannot be ascribed to an atmosphere of course – and it is here that the model of causation comes into play.

A highly fruitful approach to the conceptualization of divine activity stems from Johann Friedrich König (1619–1664), a German scholar who taught that

---

[28] Cf. Krötke, *Gottes Klarheiten* [2001], pp. 265–6: '*Wo immer Gott ist, ereignet sich die Klarheit seiner Ewigkeit als ... ursprüngliche Konzentration von Zeit. Das ist die Grunderfahrung des christlichen Glaubens ... Im Kommen der Ewigkeit Gottes in die Zeit, wie sie der Glaube erfährt, wird ... die konzentrierte Zeit der Ewigkeit als Grund und Quelle unserer irdischen Zeitlichkeit erlebbar und verstehbar.*' ('Wherever God is, the clarity of his eternity occurs as ... original concentration of time. This is the fundamental experience of Christian faith... In the advent of the eternity of God into time, as it is experienced in faith, ... the concentrated time of eternity becomes experienced and comprehensible as the ground and source of our earthly temporality'; my translation).

[29] Schleiermacher, *Der christliche Glaube (1830/31)* [1960], §§ 36–9, 46–9, 164–9.

God's activity in the world is not to be conceived as a series of personal acts but instead as an influence.[30] God 'gently influences' ('*suaviter influit*') the actions of the creatures by an 'inflowing' (an '*influxus*') of his operative presence. This presence adapts to the condition of each creature and each occasion, such that there is no competition on the same level between God's activity, human action and natural causality. It is God's spiritual power generating that '*influxus*', that indwelling, that immediate divine '*praesentia operosa*'. The creatures do not act conjointly *with* God's action. Rather, they perform their free actions within a spiritual force-field – which nonetheless has an influence upon them. The Holy Spirit comes to be 'the agent of providence' ('*effector providentiae*'), as Calvin had put it. God's activity is *intrinsically* involved in human action, it does not simply accompany it. The relationship between the two is not one of cooperation but rather of *participation* in the (inner-trinitarian) divine life.[31] God's activity has to be spelled out in terms of relationship, not in terms of these or those specific deeds. 'Grace', for example, does not primarily signify an act, but rather a relationship of unconditional acceptance which attracts the creature as the unconditionally accepted one – as the beloved. God "acts" by the power of attraction.

(c) Third, I would point to the experience of 'transpersonal energies' – the elusive 'power of love', for instance, which cannot be reduced to the emotional affection between individuals, nor to a particular quality of the relation between them. Love is, moreover, experienced as a power that goes beyond human powers, so that one is inclined to say: 'I am in love' – infused by the power of love. This means: Not 'I' am the subject of being in love, but love is the subject transforming me. I am subjected to an experience of participation, of being *full-of*, of being affected by a super-personal reality. The distinction between subject and object is effectively overcome. The transpersonal power does exercise its activity not in specific deeds (as in the action-model) but in its operative presence, by creating and sustaining a force-field which inevitably touches those who participate in it. As Arthur Peacocke would put it, it "acts" as a whole to the parts.

Again I shall refer to a classical theological approach in order to relate that experience to the notion of divine action. Bonaventure (1217–1274) understands God's effectiveness as powerful presence and representation. God's love is not a self-enclosing but rather a self-circulating, all-pervading, radiating love. It is, in the first instance, the love between Father and Son within their inner-trinitarian relationship which calls creation into being. More precisely: in loving the Son = Word, the Father's inherently self-radiating and all-embracing goodness becomes creative. The Word as the expression of the Father's love is thus the ground and mediator of creation. By loving the Word the Father loves

---

[30]   König, *Theologia positiva acroamatica* [2006], § 265.
[31]   Cf. Mühling, *Ewigkeitsauffassungen* [2005], pp. 168–72; Mühling, *Grundinformation Eschatologie* [2007], pp. 99–100.

all things in and through the Word. As the 'free overflow of God's necessary, inner-divine fruitfulness,'[32] creation is filled with God's representations – the traces not of this and that and the other particular deed but of his very being. These traces can be distinguished according to the clarity with which they represent God's being. The creation is "in" the love of God. 'God's being is God's action and God's being is love, God's action is an eternal-temporal act of love.'[33]

The patristic doctrine of divine energies as developed by Gregor Palamas, with precedents in the Cappadocians, can also be employed in elaborating the effectiveness of transpersonal powers. According to Palamas, God does not create in the way a craftsman fabricates an object. In other words, God's action is not an external action. God does, however, communicate energies, uncreated energies which are constituent in His very Trinitarian essence while not identical with that essence. The dissemination of these spiritual energies is in fact the mode of God's self-representation. Indeed, creaturely being means participating in the energy of God's being.[34]

These three experiences are as different as the theological approaches are. But as such they can be seen as counterbalancing one another and highlighting different aspects of the model of God's activity which I would like to propose. The first aspect to be considered stresses that God's activity is to be understood as spiritual self-representation. He is present in the power of his spirit – or to use the Jewish term: in his *Shekinah*. The second aspect offers an analogy for understanding the mode of activity of that presence. It influences created reality as a spiritual force-field necessarily exerts its influence upon all the entities and processes of reality. The third aspect presents an analogy for the type of power at work in divine activity: the transpersonal power of love. It is an *analogia entis* inasmuch as the power of God is the divine power of love. This third aspect is important because it underscores the idea that the spiritual force-field is not a mere indeterminate numinous power, but is rather qualified materially by a salvific *telos* rooted in the communicative, creative and salvific ground of being. According to the scriptural testimonies to the effects brought about by the spirit of God, the divine presence is the power of love which calls into being, promotes life itself as well as life-promoting social systems, it supports liberation and justice, leads to a communicative freedom striving for peace, reconciliation and intercultural understanding, and summons creation to an eschatological vision.

Within the pneumatological framework divine activity can be differentiated according to a Trinitarian scheme: first as creative activity constitutive of being,

---

[32]   HAYES, *Incarnation and Creation* [1976], p. 315. See also: CULLEN, *Bonaventure* [2006], ch. XII.

[33]   KEANE, *Why Creation?* [1975], pp. 117–9.

[34]   YANNARAS, *The Distincion Between Essence and Energies* [1975]; WENDEBOURG, *Geist oder Energie* [1980]; FLOGAUS, *Theosis bei Palamas und Luther* [1997], p. 77ff.; TORRANCE, *Precedents for Palamas' Essence-Energies Theology* [2009].

summarized by the formula 'creatio ex nihilo'; second as salvific activity in which the power of grace reveals its ultimate prevalence over the powers of self-centeredness, as symbolized in the polarity of cross and resurrection; and third as consummating activity, attracting the process of creation towards the provided goal (by God's providence), symbolized by the imagery of the kingdom of God.

8.3 Operative Presence – Action – Causation

The model of operative presence which understands God's activity primarily as the radiation of his self-representation does not completely rule out the models of action and of causation, but tries to integrate their intentions.

(a) The notion of action becomes seen in a wider sense which goes beyond particular acts. God's activity is to be envisioned not in terms of discrete serial actions but as a teleological enactment *of* the created agents: not as an external cooperation with them but as the internal empowering and guidance of them. Insights derived from human-action theory can be employed to open up the action-model beyond the notion of particular acts. Not only the performing of specific deeds but also the presenting of oneself can be understood as *act*. Not only individual sub-acts but also large-scale master-acts like building Solomon's temple can be seen as an act. There are not only instrumental acts but also communicative and representational acts motivated by the intention, whether conscious or unconscious, to express oneself, as seen in the "action" of a poet or an actor or an artist. These acts are no less efficacious than are physical interventions. Such an expanded understanding of the meaning of 'action' is most helpful in the attempt to reconstruct the notion of divine activity within the action-model.

(b) The notion of causation is also viewed in a wider sense which goes beyond effective causality. The mode in which the spiritual force-field works is better understood in terms of two other forms of causality as described by Aristotle: formative causality and teleological or final causality.

Under the conditions of history the divine force-field can realize its teleological dynamics only in a fragmentary way – in exemplary manifestations which Hodgson calls 'shapes of freedom'.[35] In the context of his theology of the sacraments, Karl Rahner spoke of 'formations of grace' ('*Gestalten der Gnade*'). Following Hodgson's line of thought (influenced by Hegel's philosophy of the spirit) those shapes are counterfactual breakthroughs of the promised 'new being' (to use Tillich's expression). In an analogy of formation ('*analogia formationis*'), shapes of grace, love, freedom and justice appear as representations of the all-encompassing grace, love, freedom and justice which God provides for creation.

These fragmentary shapes can be attributed to God's activity and experienced and signified as special divine acts. But such an interpretation of natural, historical

---

[35]   HODGSON, *God in History* [1989]; HODGSON, *Winds of Spirit* [1994].

or existential appearances cannot claim to refer to a real specific act – that is, to the realization of some 'special divine purpose' in the particular event. The concept of *special* divine action is a pattern of *seeing-as*, seeing creatural events and acts having been called forth via concentrations of the spiritual force-field *as* special acts of God. To speak of particular actions of God is therefore a *modus loquendi* for identifying certain events as shaped by God's spirit. According to that understanding the distinction between general and special divine action is overcome.

This approach goes beyond Maurice Wiles' conception of God's action as the call to follow an initial, general and overall purpose. Shapes of freedom and grace are more than prehensions of the 'universal and uniform action' which Wiles refers to. According to Wiles, God's activity endows creatures with the potential for their own activity, but He does not act in concert with them. Thus Wiles dismisses the concept of divine concurrence which constituted an essential element in classical doctrines of providence. God's creational activity consists in the creation of 'regular patterns according to which the physical world operates'[36] and in granting freedom to human beings.

Wiles suggests the model of an improvised drama for understanding God's activity: God as the author of the drama presents the actors with

> the basic character of the person he or she is to represent and the general setting, in which their interaction is to be worked out, but in which they are left free to determine experimentally how the drama is to develop. In the process of getting deeper into their parts and discovering their reactions to one another in the given situation, they may be led on to enact the kind of drama which the author had always intended and already envisaged in principle though not in detail. The resultant drama would be both his and theirs, a true case of double agency, even though one would be hesitant to speak of the author as the agent of any of the particular happenings within the drama.[37]

The approach I favour allows us to assume that the pneumatic morphogenetic field exerts a real influence on the diverse levels of created reality. First and foremost, it has transforming effects on the awareness of people and communities, on their attitudes and on their behaviour. On this personal and interpersonal level it shapes formations of consciousness, opens the minds of individuals and groups for the purposes of God and creates new relations inspired by the power of *agape*. But the pneumatic morphogenetic field exerts its influence on the levels of history and even of natural processes as well. It draws the various threads of evolution, history and individual life-stories together into patterns of meaning that represent "shapes" of God's salvation.

The assertion that the spiritual force-field is effective not only in creating patterns of consciousness but also in influencing natural processes leads to the question of a 'causal joint' as Austin Farrer termed it. Farrer rightly rejected the model of effective causality as an explication of divine action. He translated the classic

---

[36] WILES, *'God Acts in History'?* [1989], p. 193.
[37] WILES, *Continuing the Discussion* [1982], pp. 12–3.

concept of primary and secondary causality, as elaborated by Aquinas, into the model of personal action, interpreting divine action in predominantly *intentional* terms, and developed a theory of double action: God and the creatures act together on different levels of agency. The problem here: it remains unclear as to how we are to conceive of double agency and of God's contribution to it.

Unlike the models of action and of causality, the force-field model is neither centred on the notion of an immediate nexus of cause and effect nor on the assumption of double agency. The spiritual force-field is effective not in terms of efficient causality but rather in terms of calling forth, of evoking, "inducing" or inspiring. The search for a causal nexus between the force of the field and its effects is in vain, in the same way as it is useless to search for a causal nexus between the power of love and the loving person. We only can state that the spiritual field exerts its spiritual power in interaction with the circumstances of the entities affected by it. It creates a setting in which natural and historical processes organize themselves, influenced by the *telos* which the field holds out and energized by its spiritual power. It works by teleological attraction and formative influence. Arthur Peacocke's concept of a top-down causality is useful for an appreciation of its cogency.[38]

According to Gen 1:11 and 1:24, God does not intervene directly in physical and biological processes but calls forth the *self-creation* of natural systems. He calls for ever-higher levels of organization and complexity, for conditions and structures which foster the generation of life and are life-sustaining and life-promoting. The biblical tradition uses the term 'benediction' for God's gift of life – life not primarily in its biological facticity but in its quality of fullness and abundance. A theology of benediction seems to me to be the appropriate frame for a theology of nature.

There is no scientific evidence for formative and teleological divine impulses, and due to their spiritual nature there can be no such evidence. It requires what Calvin called the '*testimonium spiritus sancti internum*', the inspiration of the perceiving subject, so as to be able to perceive natural processes as the results of God's activity. It is a meta-empirical predication which is to be juxtaposed over other layers of perception and interpretation of reality such as physical causality or intentional human action. The birth of a child, for instance, can be seen as the result of a biological process of the fusion of ovum and sperm (first layer of interpretation: natural causality); as the result of an intentional act of the parents (second layer of interpretation: human action); and as the benediction of God (third layer of interpretation: divine action). These three layers of '*seeing-as*' do not contradict each other but can be integrally combined.

To state this is not at all to reduce divine action to a mere category of human perception. The perception is not an *arbitrary subjective* seeing-as but is based on a disclosure-experience, as described by Ian Ramsey.[39] The division of divine action into *either* subjective *or* objective needs to be overcome: It is indeed objective, and

---

[38] PEACOCKE, *Theology for a Scientific Age* [1993], pp. 53–4. See also CLAYTON, *God and Contemporary Science* [1997], p. 227.

[39] See BERNHARDT, *Offenbarung als Erschliessungsgeschehen* [2002].

yet at the same time can be perceived only in the perspective of faith, and as such lies beyond the scope of empirical scientific investigation. This epistemological and hermeneutical consciousness should constitute the framework of any reflection upon God's action as well as upon God's eternity.

God's activity is not evident in a third-person perspective but only in the faith-perspective of the first person – in the mode of 'Credo': 'I am certain.' However, this should by no means be used as a justification for dismissing it as a 'projection'. Why should the faith-perspective of the first person be any less capable of recognizing this kind of truth than is the general and supposedly objective third-person perspective?

Ultimately, theology is tied to the first-person perspective. Thus, I am hesitant to develop an ontological theory of divine action based on the theory of special relativity and other scientific theories, because this would tend to objectify God's activity. That, however, does not rule out the use of scientific theories as models for the elaboration of a conception of divine action. Indeed, they can and should be applied – with the full awareness, of course, that they have been *trans-lated* into another context or sphere of meaning and thus are to be understood as *models*.

8.4 The "Power of Weakness"

A spiritual power of love must, by its very nature, be self-limited. It would be a performative self-contradiction if that power were to be understood as operating by means of irresistible causal determination or even predetermination. God is active in the world by spiritual means, by 'inspiration'. The power of spirit is not a 'strong' power, like that of a mechanically-operating tool, but its power is the 'power of weakness', to which Paul referred in 1. Cor 1:25: 'The weakness of God is stronger than man's strength' (see also 2. Cor 12:9). That power cannot force anything or anybody irresistibly in terms of effective causality.

Due to its own self-determination and self-restriction, the divine activity does not cancel out the autonomy of creation in general nor the freedom of human beings in particular. God's active presence has to be assumed to be directly, and not inversely, proportional to created causality. It does not cut back contingency, non-determinism or human freedom but realizes and promotes these, precisely because they are essential elements of God's purpose. Omnipotence does not mean omnideterminism (whereby God would be causing all the events in nature and history) but rather that his power-of-being is present at all times.

Although this force-field transcends the powers of nature and history, it is in a permanent struggle with them insofar as they are shaped by the self-centredness of humans, by the autonomous dynamics of history and the momentum of nature with its play of chance and necessity. In view of such overlapping impulses and forces, I follow process-theological approaches with their distinction of other-creation, self-creation and God-creation, as Marjorie Suchocki formulates it.[40]

---

[40] SUCHOCKI, *The Fall to Violence* [1994], p. 54 ff.

As a non-coercive, spiritual power-of-love without the physical force of causal mechanisms, the divine force-field does not have the power to prevent all evil. Temporarily it can be overridden by opposing powers. The biblical scriptures amply witness to the fact that to a large extent finite reality is not in accordance with God's vision, with his pro-vision, his providence. Omnipotence is not to be understood as a physical and metaphysical super-power which has the created reality completely under its control. Such an abstract philosophical notion of omnipotence stands in contradiction to the prophetic view, which sees God not primarily as the sovereign author but more as the critic of history. Those who are being elected and mandated to be his representatives will be persecuted and in some cases – as in the case of Jesus of Nazareth – tortured and killed. The Christian answer to the question of divine action must take the theology of the cross into account. It cannot be a piece of *theologia gloriae*, but must be an expression of *theologia crucis*.

The power of weakness however is not powerless. The pneumatological model, as I propose it, depicts God's operative presence as an effective *power* and not only as a purposively attracting summons, as some Process Theologians tend to teach. Even if it can be defeated by opposing powers in the short run it carries the promise of prevailing in the plenitude of "eternity". The promise is certified by God who is in time but not subjected to time, who transcends time, encompasses all times and is atemporal. The spiritual force-field is pre-, super-, and post-temporal but as such pervasive and effective in time.

Part IV

In Defence of Divine Temporalism, or: In Debate With Science

Chapter 9

Divine Eternity and Einstein's
Special Theory of Relativity

William Lane Craig

9.1 Special Relativity and Divine Timelessness

A popular argument for divine timelessness arises from the concept of time in Albert Einstein's Special Theory of Relativity (STR). According to Einstein's theory, there is no unique, universal time and so no unique, worldwide "now". Each inertial frame has its own time and its own present moment, and there is no overarching, absolute time in which all these diverse times are integrated into one. So if God is in time, then, the obvious question raised by STR is: *Whose time is He in?*

The defender of divine timelessness maintains that there is no acceptable answer to this question. We cannot plausibly pick out some inertial frame and identify its time as God's time because God is not a physical object in uniform motion, and so the choice of any such frame would be wholly arbitrary. Moreover, it is difficult to see how God, confined to the time of one inertial frame, could be causally sustaining events which are real relative to other inertial frames but are future or past relative to God's frame. Similarly, God's knowledge of what is happening now would be restricted to the temporal perspective of His frame, leaving Him ignorant of what is actually going on in other frames. In any case, if God were to be associated with a particular inertial frame, then surely, as God's time, the time of that frame would be privileged. It would be the equivalent of the privileged ether frame in classical physics. So long as we maintain, with Einstein, that no frame is privileged, then we cannot identify the time of any inertial frame as God's time.

Neither can we say that God exists in the "now" associated with the time of every inertial frame, for this would obliterate the unity of God's consciousness. In order to preserve God's personal consciousness, it must not be fragmented and scattered among the inertial frames in the universe. But if God's time cannot be identified with the time of a single frame or of a plurality of frames, then God must not be in time at all, that is to say, He exists timelessly.

We can summarize this reasoning as follows:

(1)   STR is correct in its description of time.

(2)   If STR is correct in its description of time, then if God is temporal, He exists in either the time associated with a single inertial frame or the times associated with a plurality of inertial frames.

(3)   Therefore, if God is temporal, He exists in either the time associated with a single inertial frame or the times associated with a plurality of inertial frames.

(4)   God does not exist in either the time associated with a single inertial frame or the times associated with a plurality of inertial frames.

(5)   Therefore, God is not temporal.

What can be said in response to this argument?

9.2 Assessment

9.2.1 Premise (2)

Premise (2) is at best misleading in that it fails to take into account the fact that STR is a *restricted* theory of relativity and therefore is correct only within pre-scribed limits. It is a theory which deals with uniform motion only. The analysis of non-uniform motion, such as acceleration and rotation, is provided by the General Theory of Relativity (GTR). STR cannot therefore be expected to give us the final word about the nature of time and space; indeed, within the context of GTR a new and important conception of time emerges. For GTR serves to introduce into Relativity Theory a cosmic perspective, enabling us to draft cosmological models of the universe governed by the gravitational field equations of GTR. Within the context of such cosmological models, the issue of time resurfaces dramatically. All contemporary cosmological models derive from Russian mathematician Alexander Friedman's 1922 model of an expanding, material universe characterized by ideal homogeneity and isotropy. Although GTR does not itself mandate any formula for how to slice spacetime into a temporally ordered foliation, nevertheless certain models of spacetime, like the Friedman model, have a dynamic, evolving spatial geometry whose natural symmetries guide the construction of a cosmic time; in order to ensure a smooth development of this geometry, it will be necessary to construct a time parameter based on a preferred slicing of spacetime. Now as a parameter independent of spatial co-ordinates, cosmic time measures the duration of the universe as a whole in an observer-independent way; that is to say, the lapse of cosmic time is the same for all observers. Nevertheless, cosmic time is related to the local times of a special group of observers called 'fundamental observers'. These are hypothetical observers who are at rest with respect to the expansion of space itself. Cosmic time relates to these observers in that their local times all coincide with cosmic time in their vicinity. Because of their mutual recession, the class of fundamental observers does not serve to define a global inertial frame, technically speaking, even though all of them are at rest. But since each fundamental observer is at rest with respect to space, the events which he calculates to be simultaneous will coincide locally with the events which are simultaneous in cosmic time. What this implies is that, contrary to premise (2), it does not follow from the correctness of STR that, if God is in time, then He is in the time of one or more inertial frames.[1] For if God exists in cosmic time, there is no universal inertial frame with which He can be associated.

9.2.2 Premise (1)

But let that pass. Although it may come as something of a shock to many, it seems to me that the most dubious premise of the above argument is premise (1). In order to understand why I say this, let us take a backward glance at Isaac Newton's classical doctrine of absolute time (and space).

9.2.3 The Classical Concept of Time

The *locus classicus* of Newton's exposition of his concepts of time and space is the *Scholium* to his Definitions in the *Principia*. In order to overcome 'common prejudices' concerning such quantities as time, space, place, and motion, Newton draws a dichotomy with respect to these quantities between 'absolute and relative, true and apparent, mathematical and common'. With regard to time he asserts:

> Absolute, true, and mathematical time, of itself, and from its own nature, flows equably without relation to anything external, and by another name is called duration: relative, apparent, and common time, is some sensible and external (whether accurate or unequable) measure of duration by the means of motion, which is commonly used instead of true time; such as an hour, a day, a month, a year.[2]

The most evident feature of this distinction is the independence of absolute time from the relative measures thereof. Absolute time, or simple duration, exists regardless of the sensible and external measurements which we try, more or less successfully, to make of it. Newtonian time is thus first of all absolute in the sense that time itself is distinct from our measures of time.

But Newton also conceived of time as absolute in a yet more profound sense, namely, he held that time exists independently of any physical objects whatsoever. Usually, this is interpreted to mean that time would exist even if nothing else existed, that we can conceive of a logically possible world that is completely empty except for the container of absolute space and the flow of absolute time.

But here we must be very careful. Modern secular scholars tend frequently to forget how ardent a theist Newton was and how central a role this theism played in his metaphysical outlook. In fact, Newton makes quite clear in the *General Scholium*

---

[1]   In the sense that God exists in the time of the inertial frame of each fundamental observer, there is no objection, since all their local times fuse into one cosmic time.

[2]   NEWTON, *Mathematical Principles/System of the World* [1966], 1: p. 6.

to the *Principia*, which he added in 1713, that absolute time and space are constituted by the divine attributes of eternity and omnipresence. He writes,

> He is eternal and infinite...; that is, his duration reaches from eternity to eternity; his presence from infinity to infinity... He is not eternity and infinity, but eternal and infinite; he is not duration or space, but he endures and is present. He endures forever, and is everywhere present; and, by existing always and everywhere, he constitutes duration and space. Since every particle of space is *always*, and every indivisible moment of duration is *everywhere*, certainly the Maker and Lord of all things cannot be *never* and *nowhere*.[3]

Because God is eternal, there exists an everlasting duration, and because He is omnipresent, there exists an infinite space. Absolute time and space are therefore relational in that they are contingent upon the existence of God.

In Newton's view God's "now" is thus the present moment of absolute time. Since God is not "a dwarf-god" located at a particular place in space,[4] but is omnipresent, there is a worldwide moment which is absolutely present. Newton's temporal theism thus provides the foundation for absolute simultaneity. The absolute present and absolute simultaneity are features first and foremost of God's time, absolute time, and derivatively of measured or relative time.

Thus, the classical, Newtonian concept of time is firmly rooted in a theistic worldview. What Newton did not realize, nor could he have suspected, is that physical time is not only *relative*, but also *relativistic*, that the approximation of physical time to absolute time depends not merely upon the regularity of one's clock, but also upon its motion. Unless a clock were at absolute rest, it would not accurately register the passage of absolute time. Moving clocks run slowly. This truth, unknown to Newton, was finally grasped by scientists only with the advent of Relativity Theory.[5]

What Einstein did, in effect, was simply to remove God from the picture and to substitute in His place a finite observer. 'Thus', according to historian of science Gerald Holton, 'the *RT* [Relativity Theory] merely shifted the focus of spacetime from the sensorium of Newton's God to the sensorium of Einstein's abstract *Gedanken* experimenter – as it were, the final secularization of physics'.[6]

---

[3] NEWTON, *Mathematical Principles/System of the World* [1966], 2: p. 545.

[4] NEWTON, *Place, Time, and God* [1978], p. 123.

[5] Where Newton fell short, then, was not in his analysis of absolute or metaphysical time – he had theological grounds for positing such a time – but in his incomplete understanding of relative or physical time. He assumed too readily that an ideal clock would give an accurate measure of time independently of its motion. If confronted with relativistic evidence, Newton would no doubt have welcomed this correction and seen therein no threat at all to his doctrine of absolute time. In short, relativity corrects Newton's concept of physical time, not his concept of absolute time.

[6] HOLTON, *Special Theory of Relativity* [1973], p. 171. The sensorium was conceived to be that aspect of the mind in which mental images of physical objects are formed. Newton said that because physical objects exist in space and God is omnipresent, they literally exist in God and thus are immediately present to Him. Absolute space is, as it were, God's sensorium in the sense that He has no need of mental images of things, since the things themselves are

By eliminating Newton's absolute time and space, and along with them the ether, Relativity Theory left behind only their empirical measures. Since these are relativized to inertial frames, one ends up with the relativity of simultaneity and of length.

9.2.4 Einstein's Critique of the Classical Concept

What justification did Einstein have for so radical a move? How did he know that absolute time and space do not exist? The answer, in a word, is verificationism. Historians of science have demonstrated convincingly that at the philosophical roots of Einstein's theory lies a verificationist epistemology, mediated to the young Einstein chiefly through the influence of Ernst Mach, which comes to expression in Einstein's analysis of the concepts of time and space.[7]

In 1905, when Einstein published his paper on the electrodynamics of moving bodies, and for several years thereafter, he was a self-confessed epistemological pupil of Mach, and the epistemological analysis of space and time given in the opening section of that paper clearly displays this influence. Mach's positivism manifests itself most clearly in Einstein's *a priori* rejection of absolute time and reliance on operational definitions of crucial concepts. Absolute space or a privileged frame is presumed not to exist because 'to the concept of absolute rest there correspond no properties of the phenomena.'[8] It is taken for granted that '*all* our judgments in which time plays a role' must have a 'physical meaning'.[9] When it comes to judgments concerning the simultaneity of distant events, the concern is to find a 'practical arrangement' to compare clock times.[10] In order to 'define' a common time for spatially separated clocks, we assume that the time light takes to travel from A to B equals the time it takes to travel from B to A – a definition which *presupposes* that absolute space does not exist. Thus, time is reduced to physical time (clock readings) and space to physical space (readings of measuring rods) and both of these are relativized to local frames. Simultaneity is defined in terms of clock synchronization via light signals. All of this is done by mere stipulation. Through Einstein's operational definitions of time and space, Mach's positivism triumphs in the Special Theory of Relativity. Reality is reduced to what our measurements read; Newton's metaphysical time and space, which transcend operational definitions, are implied to be mere figments of our imagination.

---

present to Him. Einstein's *Gedankenexperimenter* (thought experimenter) is the hypothetical observer associated with any inertial frame, for whom time and space are purely relative quantities.

[7] See especially HOLTON, *Mach, Einstein and the Search for Reality* [1970], pp. 165–99; id., *Where Is Reality?* [1971], pp. 45–69; and the essays collected together in *idem, Scientific Thought* [1973].

[8] EINSTEIN, *Electrodynamics of Moving Bodies* [1981], p. 392.

[9] EINSTEIN, *Electrodynamics of Moving Bodies* [1981], p. 393 (my italics).

[10] EINSTEIN, *Electrodynamics of Moving Bodies* [1981], p. 393.

In Einstein's other early papers on relativity, his verificationist theory of meaning comes even more explicitly to the fore. Concepts which cannot be given empirical content, and assertions which cannot be empirically verified in principle, are discarded as meaningless. In his article in the *Jahrbuch der Radioaktivität und Elektronik* of 1907, after giving his operational definitions for time and simultaneity, he asserts that to refer to the time of an event without reference to its inertial frame has no sense (*Sinn*).[11] In his piece in the *Physikalische Zeitschrift* of 1909, he asserts that statements about the time of an event have no meaning (*Bedeutung*) unless one refers to clocks at rest in the relevant inertial system.[12] In his summary paper, *Die Relativitäts-Theorie*, published in 1911, Einstein expresses himself more at length concerning the meaning of statements about time and space. He states that 'in order to arrive at time specifications of a very precise sense' we use a prescription that relates to clocks which are relative to a certain coordinate system *k*. We have not gained simply a time, but a time relative to a coordinate system. 'It is not said that time has an absolute ... meaning. That is an arbitrary element which was contained in our kinematics.'[13] We then come, Einstein proceeds, to the second arbitrary element in kinematics: the absolute length of a body. 'We now ask: how long is this rod? This question can have only the meaning: what experiments must we carry out in order to discover how long the rod is?'[14] Einstein then proceeds to describe length measurement of a moving rod by means of synchronized clocks. By abandoning the presuppositions of absolute time and space and substituting in their stead operational definitions, Einstein reduces time and space to our measurements of them. He concludes, 'Since we have in a precise way physically defined coordinates and time, every relation between spatial and temporal entities will have a very precise physical content.'[15] Statements about spatial or temporal relations which are metaphysical in character, that is, are independent of clocks, rods, or reference frames, are nonsense.

It is frequently asserted that as Einstein laboured on the General Theory, he came to see the bankruptcy of Mach's positivism. But this claim needs to be carefully qualified. What Einstein's work on GTR in fact revealed to him was the inadequacy of Mach's phenomenalism. Scientific theorizing is not the mere linking of observation statements, but involves a creative exercise of the mind, which is free to postulate theoretical entities not directly given in observation. Nevertheless, even after GTR he continued to regard such theoretical terms as meaningless unless they could be somehow linked to observation statements. In 1920, for example, he wrote,

> We thus require a definition of simultaneity such that this definition supplies us with the means by which, in the present case, he [the hypothetical observer, W. L. C.] can decide by experiment whether both lightning strokes occurred simultaneously. As long as this requirement is not satisfied, I allow myself to be deceived as a physicist

[11] EINSTEIN, *Über das Relativitätsprinzip* [1907], p. 417.
[12] EINSTEIN, *Über die Entwicklung unserer Anschauungen* [1909], p. 819.
[13] EINSTEIN, *Relativitäts-Theorie* [1911], p. 9 (my translation).
[14] EINSTEIN, *Relativitäts-Theorie* [1911], p. 9.
[15] EINSTEIN, *Relativitäts-Theorie* [1911], p. 11.

(and of course the same applies if I am not a physicist) when I imagine that I am able to attach a meaning to the statement of simultaneity.[16]

For physicist and non-physicist alike the statement that two events occur simultaneously is meaningless unless an operational definition can be given for that concept. Thus, he continued to cling to his rejection of metaphysical time and space:

> The only justification for our concepts and system of concepts is that they serve to represent the complex of our experiences; beyond this they have no legitimacy. I am convinced that the philosophers have had a harmful effect upon the progress of scientific thinking in removing certain fundamental concepts from the domain of empiricism, where they are under our control, to the intangible heights of the *a priori*. For even if it should appear that the universe of ideas cannot be deduced from experience by logical means, but is, in a sense, a creation of the human mind, without which no science is possible, nevertheless this universe of ideas is just as little independent of the nature of our experiences as clothes are of the form of the human body. This is particularly true of our concepts of time and space, which physicists have been obliged by the facts to bring down from the Olympus of the *a priori* in order to adjust them and put them in a serviceable condition.[17]

Einstein's theory, far from disproving the existence of absolute space, actually presupposes its non-existence. All of this is done by mere stipulation. Reality is reduced to what our measurements read; Newton's metaphysical time and space, which transcend operational definitions, are implied to be mere figments of our imagination.

9.2.5 Failure of Einstein's Critique

How, then, shall we assess the claim that STR has eliminated absolute time and space? The first thing to be said is that the verificationism which characterized Einstein's original formulation of STR belongs essentially to the philosophical foundations of the theory. The whole theory rests upon Einstein's re-definition of simultaneity in terms of clock synchronization by light signals. But that re-definition assumes necessarily that the time which light takes to travel between two relatively stationary observers *A* and *B* is the same from *A* to *B* as from *B* to *A* in a round-trip journey. That assumption presupposes that *A* and *B* are not both in absolute motion, or in other words that neither absolute space nor a privileged inertial frame exists. The only justification for that assumption is that it is empirically impossible to distinguish uniform motion from rest relative to such a frame, and if absolute space and absolute motion or rest are undetectable empirically, therefore they do not exist (and may even be said to be meaningless).

---

[16]   EINSTEIN, *Relativity, the Special and the General Theory* [1920], p. 26.

[17]   EINSTEIN, *The Meaning of Relativity* [1967], p. 2. Cf. his *Fundamental Ideas and Problems* [1967], pp. 479–90, where he lays down a postulate called 'the stipulation of meaning', which requires that concepts and distinctions are only admissible to the extent that observable facts can be assigned to them without ambiguity. He considers this postulate to be of 'fundamental importance' epistemologically.

But if verificationism belongs essentially to the foundations of STR, the next thing to be said is that verificationism has proved to be completely untenable and is now outmoded. The untenability of verificationism is so universally acknowledged that it will not be necessary to rehearse the objections against it here.[18] Verificationism provides no justification for thinking that Newton erred, for example, in holding that God exists in a time which exists independently of our physical measures of it and which may or may not be accurately registered by them. It matters not a whit whether we finite creatures know what time it is in God's absolute time; God knows, and that is enough.

Now let me be very clear that I am not here endorsing Newton's view on divine eternity; but I am saying that the philosophical theologian who, like Newton, believes God to be temporal need not feel threatened by STR because STR's claim that absolute time does not exist is founded essentially upon a defunct and untenable epistemology.

9.2.6 Divine Temporality and Lorentzian Relativity

If we do suppose that God is in time, how then should we understand STR? Henri Poincaré, the great French mathematician and precursor of STR, helped to point the way. In a fascinating passage in his essay *The Measure of Time,* Poincaré briefly entertains the hypothesis of 'an infinite intelligence' (*une intelligence infinie*) and considers the implications of such a hypothesis. Poincaré is reflecting on the problem of how we can apply one and the same measure of time to spatially distant events. What does it mean, for example, to say that two thoughts in two people's minds occur simultaneously? Or what does it mean to say that a supernova occurred before Columbus saw the New World? Like a good verificationist, Poincaré says, 'All these affirmations have by themselves no meaning.'[19] Then he remarks,

> We should first ask ourselves how one could have had the idea of putting into the same frame so many worlds impenetrable to one another. We should like to represent to ourselves the external universe, and only by so doing could we feel that we understood it. We know we can never attain this representation: our weakness is too great. But at least we desire the ability to conceive an infinite intelligence for which this representation could be possible, a sort of great consciousness which should see all, and which should classify all *in its time,* as we classify, *in our time,* the little we see.

---

[18] See the excellent survey in Suppe, *Search for Philosophical Understanding* [1977], pp. 3–118. Verificationism was far too restrictive a theory of meaning to be plausible, for it would force us to dismiss as meaningless vast tracts of human discourse, including not just metaphysical and theological statements, but also aesthetic and ethical statements, as well as many scientific statements (e. g., the postulate of the constancy of the one-way velocity of light, an unprovable assumption which lies at the heart of STR). Worse, verificationism turned out to be self-refuting. For the statement 'Only sentences which can in principle be empirically verified are meaningful' is itself not an empirically verifiable sentence and so is by its own standard meaningless!

[19] Poincaré, *Measure of Time* [1982], p. 228.

This hypothesis is indeed crude and incomplete, because this supreme intelligence would be only a demigod; infinite in one sense, it would be limited in another, since it would have only an imperfect recollection of the past; it could have no other, since otherwise all recollections would be equally present to it and for it there would be no time. And yet when we speak of time, for all which happens outside of us, do we not unconsciously adopt this hypothesis; do we not put ourselves in the place of this imperfect God; and do not even the atheists put themselves in the place where God would be if he existed?

What I have just said shows us, perhaps, why we have tried to put all physical phenomena into the same frame. But that cannot pass for a definition of simultaneity, since this hypothetical intelligence, even if it existed, would be for us impenetrable. It is therefore necessary to seek something else.[20]

Poincaré here suggests that, in considering the notion of simultaneity, we instinctively put ourselves in the place of God and classify events as past, present, or future according to His time. Poincaré does not deny that from God's perspective there would exist relations of absolute simultaneity. But he rejects the hypothesis as yielding a definition of simultaneity because we could not know such relations; such knowledge would remain the exclusive possession of God Himself.

Clearly, Poincaré's misgivings are relevant to a definition of simultaneity only if one is presupposing some sort of verificationist theory of meaning, as he undoubtedly was. The fact remains that God knows the absolute simultaneity of events even if we grope in total darkness.[21] Poincaré's hypothesis suggests, therefore, that if God is temporal, His present is constitutive of relations of absolute simultaneity.[22] On this view, the philosopher Findlay was wrong when he said, 'the influence which harmonizes and connects all the world-lines is not God, not any featureless, inert, medium, but that living, active interchange called ... Light, offspring of Heaven firstborn'.[23] On the contrary, the use of light signals to establish clock synchrony

---

[20]   POINCARÉ, *Measure of Time* [1982], pp. 228–9.

[21]   Nor need we be concerned with Poincaré's argument that such an infinite intelligence would be a mere demigod, since there is no reason to think that a temporal being cannot have a perfect recollection of the past. There is no conceptual difficulty in the idea of a being which knows all past tense truths. His knowledge would be constantly changing, as more and more events become past. But at each successive moment he could know every past-tense truth that there is at that moment. Hence, it does not follow that if God is temporal, He cannot have perfect recollection of the past.

[22]   Cf. Lorentz's illustration in a letter to Einstein in January of 1915 in response to the latter's paper *The Formal Foundations of the General Theory of Relativity*. In a passage redolent of the *General Scholium* and *Opticks* of Newton, Lorentz broached considerations whereby 'I cross the borderland of physics': 'A "World Spirit" [*Weltgeist*] who, not being bound to a specific place, permeated the entire system under consideration or "in whom" this system existed and who could "feel" immediately all events would naturally distinguish at once one of the systems U, U', etc. above the others' (H. A. Lorentz to A. Einstein, January, 1915, Boerhaave Museum, cited in ILLY, *Einstein Teaches Lorentz* [1989], p. 274). Such a being, says Lorentz, could 'directly verify simultaneity'.

[23]   FINDLAY, *Time and Eternity* [1978], pp. 6–7.

would be a convention which finite and ignorant creatures have been obliged to adopt, but the living and active God, who knows all, would not be so dependent. In God's temporal experience, there would be a moment which would be present in absolute time, whether or not it were registered by any clock time. He would know, without any dependence on clock synchronization procedures or any physical operations at all, which events were simultaneously present in absolute time. He would know this simply in virtue of His knowing at every such moment the unique class of present tense truths at that moment, without any need of physical observation of the universe.

So what would become of STR if God is in time? From what has been said, God's existence in time would imply that Hendrik Antoon Lorentz, rather than Einstein, had the correct interpretation of Relativity Theory. That is to say, Einstein's clock synchronization procedure would be valid only in the preferred (absolute) reference frame, and measuring rods would contract and clocks slow down in the customary special relativistic way when in motion with respect to the preferred frame. Such an interpretation would be implied by divine temporality, for God in the "now" of absolute time would know which events in the universe are now being created by Him and are therefore absolutely simultaneous with each other and with His "now". This startling conclusion shows that Newton's theistic hypothesis is not some idle speculation but has important implications for our understanding of how the world is and for the assessment of rival scientific theories.

Lorentzian relativity is admitted on all sides to be empirically equivalent to Einsteinian relativity, and there are even indications on the cutting edge of science today that a Lorentzian view may be preferable in light of recent discoveries. In fact, due to developments in quantum physics, there has been what one participant in the debate has called 'a sea change' in the attitude of the physics community toward Lorentzian relativity.[24]

Again, none of this proves that Newton was right in thinking that God is in time; but it does undercut the claim that STR has proven Newton to be wrong. The defender of divine temporality can plausibly reject the first premise of the argument for divine timelessness based on the Special Theory of Relativity.

9.2.7 Conclusion

In conclusion, Relativity Theory does not provide good grounds for thinking that God is timeless. The Einsteinian interpretation of STR is based essentially upon an untenable and obsolete verificationist epistemology and so cannot force abandonment of the classical concept of time which is constituted by God's duration. Moreover, GTR in its cosmological application furnishes us with a cosmic time

---

[24]   John Kennedy in a paper delivered to the American Philosophical Association, Central Division Meeting, Pittsburgh, Penn., April 23–26, 1997. Compare the passing remark of BALASHOV, 'the idea of restoring absolute simultaneity no longer has a distinctively pseudoscientific flavor it has had until very recently' (BALASHOV, *Enduring and Perduring Objects* [2000], p. 159).

parameter which may be plausibly interpreted as the appropriate measure of God's time since the moment of creation.

Chapter 10

Eternity in Process Philosophies

Hans Kraml

10.1 Introduction

Although I have always taken the process character of reality for granted, I have never worried very much about the intricacies of process philosophy and its different branches. But in my sinful youth I had written a small thesis on process theology. This sin I could not hide from Christian Tapp, and so he proposed that I present something from this point of view. Unfortunately, I have no view from nowhere, neither have I managed – although I tried hard – to achieve a stance outside space and time which undoubtedly would be necessary in order to find the ultimate truth about God, time, and eternity. From within, every endeavour remains completely fragmentary, which will be the only thing that can be proved by this paper.

10.2 Part of the Problem: God, Time and Foreknowledge

Reflections on the possibility of God's knowledge of the whole of all the events and things occurring in the universe in its totality lead to the idea that from God's point of view all the movements and changes in the world are present at once. Change and movement in the world are due to a time-bound being's, like a human person's, view of the whole of the universe. For such a time-bound being, the world is constituted as a sequence of events and the acquisition of knowledge takes place step by step, whereas from the point of view of eternity there are no sequences and processes, but only one great whole of all the events together. For an eternal being all the events and occurrences are present simultaneously and thus known in simultaneous presence.

10.3 The Four-Dimensional Worm of Four-Dimensional Worms

This is the idea underlying the solution of the problem of God's foreknowledge of future contingents proposed prominently by Boethius and followers of his idea, as, for example, Thomas Aquinas. It is an old idea in philosophy and theology that things and events that occur in time for us, are simultaneous for God. There is, for instance, the idea of simultaneous creation as opposed to the way in which the process of creation is reported in the Bible as a sequence of actions in the course of six days. According to Saint Augustine, human beings not concerned with philosophical reflections cannot easily grasp the idea that different things in change and motion could come into being all at once, and that all the things and events were created together with the time in which they occur. In order to describe the whole wealth of things created by God at once, the Bible tells a story of successive divine actions. The creation of matter is prior to that of form, though not temporally.[1] Matter, he explains, is at the roots of every substantial being and in this sense comes first of all individual things and events, but it is not temporally prior, because there is no such thing as mere unformed matter. Possibility is prior to actuality in some sense, but possibility is not temporally prior because this would mean that there was actually a time where there was such a possibility actually, which is just confused. In addition, the way in which God's creation of the world is narrated in the Bible has, according to Augustine, a pedagogical and mystagogical purpose, too. I do not want to go into historical details here, but I think this type of consideration is closely connected with Neoplatonic theories, perhaps directly with Plotinus, but I am far from being an expert in this. Of course, the famous conception of Boethius is notoriously influenced by neoplatonism, too.

A picture of the world that is similar to the world-view of antiquity is presently current even among modern philosophers. According to this view, the world is a four-dimensional whole that is perceived by beings that are capable of developing knowledge of their existence and of the conditions they are existing in. These beings are themselves bound to act step by step and thus to develop measures for the coordination and comparison of their respective activities. They perceive their surroundings as a three-dimensional configuration of objects that change in a constant flux. In other words: the world is a large whole of which beings, acting within it, receive knowledge in the form of series of slices that consist of three-dimensional things changing over time. Change and temporality are due to the structure of the observers within this world, but they are not real attributes of the world itself.[2]

A picture of this kind has been extensively developed by Rucker's, *The Fourth Dimension*,[3] which in turn makes use of a famous little novel, *Flatland*, by Abbott.[4] In this essay is described how a two-dimensional being, a square actually, makes the acquaintance of a three-dimensional being. Although the three-dimensional being is a complete whole in itself, a sphere indeed, to a two-dimensional being it is only accessible as a surface, actually a slice through the sphere, constantly changing in time. This is meant to give an illustration of the situation in which we as three-dimensional human beings gain our knowledge with respect to the four-dimensional world we are bound to live in without being able to look at it from

---

[1] See AUGUSTINE, *De Genesi ad litteram* [1894], 1, c. 15.
[2] See, for example, KLEINKNECHT, *Phänomenale und wirkliche Zeit* [1996].
[3] RUCKER, *The Fourth Dimension* [1984].
[4] ABBOTT, *Flatland* [1998].

outside. Our problem is that we usually are convinced to live in a world that is just the way it looks like to us. It has always been the endeavour of philosophers to show how it is possible that the world is really the way we see it and think to know it, at least according to the best kind of knowledge we have, namely especially scientific knowledge. Even if we assume that there is no such correspondence, and even if we develop sophisticated theories to show that we are confined to the possibilities of our mental and intellectual capacities without being able to judge reality independently from the outside, we nevertheless constantly act as if reality was just what it looked like.

But our confidence in reality as it seems to be is, at best, half the truth. Usually, we also constantly act as if reality was quite different from what it looks like. We do not see, and indeed we do not hear or taste or feel or whatever, that the ground we are standing on will remain solid, that behind the white surface in front of us there is really a wall and that behind that wall there is an apartment and that behind the fluffy and coloured shape in front of us there is a human being, and that this human being is a person and so on. But we take all that for granted, and we have to do so in order to behave reasonably. Almost all our activities rest on knowledge that is gained over a long period of learning, that has brought us far beyond everything we can have access to immediately. We rely completely on things that are only very weakly grounded in immediate sensual perception. So we take reality as very different from what we really perceive of it.

We have to rely on our perceptions and on what we take as reality on the basis of these perceptions, but we can also assume that many things are very different from what we take for granted under certain circumstances. 'There are more things between heaven and earth than are dreamt of in your everyday-wisdom!' We have to stick to our everyday wisdom, but we can, and indeed should be convinced of the fact that everything is also completely different. So what?

To use a little bit of philosophical jargon, I would say that we constantly use two types of metaphysics, descriptive metaphysics and revisionary metaphysics. Here I allude to a distinction made by Peter Strawson.[5] Descriptive metaphysics is preferred by Aristotelians, for example by Edmund Runggaldier. It is concerned with most fundamental aspects of the objects of our everyday-life. We have to do with things and their properties, with particulars and universals. Revisionary metaphysics is envisaged by people who are interested in the ontology of scientific theories. Its main trait is that it assumes a different type or different types of fundamental entities. Peter Simons[6] counts process metaphysics among revisionary types of metaphysics.

Descriptive metaphysics in Peter Strawson's sense is widely presupposed and used in our language acquisition. This is of course the background for Strawson's arguments in favour of this type of metaphysics against different sorts of revisionary metaphysics including process philosophy. We use proper names, definite descrip-

---

5   STRAWSON, *Individuals* [1987].
6   SIMONS, *Metaphysical Systematics* [1998].

tions and indexicals of all kinds because we want to direct the attention of our community members and audiences in everyday life at certain things and circumstances in our surroundings, and because we want to trace our friends as exactly this very individual through different circumstances changing in time, and we cannot learn common linguistic devices without being made aware of particular cases of such generally important sorts of things. As a matter of fact we use such devices and several others, and in everyday life we make use of the fact that certain individual things have properties that make them useful in a general way that does not depend on their individuality. But we also know that we cannot have properties without things that have those properties. We use bricks to build walls, because bricks have certain properties of stability, and they are formed in a certain way that makes work with them easier. But we know for sure that we cannot have the stability and impermeability and intransparency of bricks without using individual bricks. But of course, we are not really interested in the particular bricks we use, and although we perhaps may count them, we surely do not dub them.

On the other hand, we have names for people in our world, for our parents and siblings, friends and pets. And we are convinced that the bearers of the names are individuals that are identical over time. This is not just a strange attitude without further importance, but it is rather essential for our life in a certain type of community. I am legally married to my present wife only if she is identical with the woman I married at the beginning of our marriage. She may have changed in many aspects, but if she is a different woman, I may be suspected of just pretending to be married or of having committed a crime. Undoubtedly, we have here a case where we apply a substance – attribute and/or relation ontology without much hesitation. Nevertheless, we can be aware of several difficulties in this case without dismissing the Aristotelian attitude. We might be quite aware of the fact that those persons whom we think our children to be identical with, have changed very much. My son for instance became 15 cm taller within a few months last winter, so there are aspects under which he is not identical with the lad of the winter before. Is this a reason to give up substance ontology all together? What is the alternative?

I think there could be several alternatives, but one among them is at any rate a process ontology and metaphysics. We are used to applying an ontology that includes processes without much hesitation, but perhaps also without much philosophical reflection. We know that we need food quite regularly, that our shoes get worn out and that our car needs gas and lubricant every now and then. Although certainly most of us are convinced that they are identical over time with the person they remember to have been all the time, we surely do not deny that we are in constant change even with respect to aspects we are not aware of. I myself have no qualms about thinking of myself as an ongoing process of blood circulation, nutrition, energy exchange, changing brain and nerve states and cognitional activities. And even with material objects and artifacts we take it for granted that they are changeless and stable things only under superficial considerations, but in reality in constant change and at least molecular motion.

10.4 A World of Changes and Processes

However this may be, what I am concerned with is the fact that we usually apply different ontologies, and I think we can state this not only for our everyday life, but also for science. Should we accept this situation and be content with it? Well, I think we should, for several reasons and under some constraints.

First I would like to make some remarks in favour of an ontology that is close to a substance-property ontology. In order to establish the meaning of some of the most important elements of language, for example proper names and predicates, we use the very things for which these linguistic devices are to be introduced as means in order to learn the correct usage of the words. Later on, we of course use the words in order to direct the attention of other people to circumstances in our world, but in order to be able to do that we have to learn the words and their meanings. The things to be used to introduce our linguistic devices and to fix their standard usage are sometimes detachable from their surrounding, they can be passed around and handled by all those who use or learn to use a language. Sometimes it is not the things as such that we are interested in, but effects of these things on ourselves or on other things. These effects cannot be detached from the things, although a comparable effect might be achieved by a different thing. Thus, the special case of a thing is not of importance, any similar thing might do what we want to have. In order to build a wall, I am not interested in the individual bricks I need, every whole brick with the properties that bricks generally have might do. But of course in the case of a wall I am primarily interested in the properties of the bricks, yet I know that I cannot have the properties as such.

Thus, we learn to handle two different types of linguistic devices, names and predicates, on the one hand, and, on the other hand, we make use of the properties of things that we take as constant and stable enough for the purposes at hand. Our linguistic institutions are closely connected with the idea of things and their properties. This is why Peter Strawson, for example, took the idea of substances as basic. In addition, we constantly need things for their substantial properties, as we would be inclined to say, and our ability to get along in our life depends on our capability to sort out the right, durable if needed, things for the different purposes we have. We have to assume persistent, even enduring substances in order to learn our language on the one hand, and to be successful in a vast field of enterprises we undertake on the other hand.

Yet we have to accept and we constantly assume an underlying resistance to persistence in almost all our activities. We are in many cases interested in the universality of the properties of many objects we use. But alas! Contrary to a widespread type of ontology, properties are no universals, they are individuals. Each thing has certain properties, and comparable things may have properties that are very much alike. Nevertheless, each thing has its own properties, and that is the reason why we often examine comparable things whether they have a certain property to an extent required by our aims. In many cases we use the things because they have those properties, and we are not interested in the individual object, if only the object at hand has the required properties to an extent that conforms to our purposes. But we know that the properties change, and they change individually in many cases. Some cars even of the same series are more reliable as to certain properties than others, each single car may have its very special individual properties, although they may be in margins within which the differences are negligible for our special activities. The properties of the things we are dealing with are in more or less constant change. In virtue of their properties the things influence other things and their properties and vice versa. We take this into account when we avoid putting our large luggage trunk on the notebook and so on.

10.5 Process Philosophies

It is therefore not surprising that many philosophers think that the basis of reality are not things, but processes and occurrences that, however, sometimes result in something that should best be treated as a thing, and perhaps as a thing of a certain sort, too. All the different processes influence each other and are influenced by other such processes, influences that can result in very different outcomes, in modifications for example, but also in convergences and complexifications which result, from the point of view of other types of influence, in wholes that can be distinguished from other wholes or from environments. Although there are several different types of process metaphysics and cosmologies, the most elaborate and complicated one is almost undoubtedly that of Alfred North Whitehead. According to him, the basic real entities constituting our cosmos are actual entities or actual occasions constituting phases in the process of the existence of the whole cosmos. These phases are influenced by their predecessors and by parallel phases which thus are "prehended" by the actual entity or occurrence. This fact of prehension of other occurrences or entities by actual entities is fundamental in that it serves to understand the possibility of apprehension of entities by special sorts of entities at later stages. In this way, it is Whitehead's achievement to give an illuminating account of the fact that some beings in the world, for example human beings, are able to take notice of their environment and attain knowledge of it. The idea of substances, that plays an important role in our everyday life, is a product of abstraction. Thus, entities which are according to our everyday-ontology concrete things or substances are abstract entities in the sense of Whitehead. There is nothing wrong with our assumption of such substances for special purposes, but it is a mistake to think of these substances as of the most concrete elements of the furniture of our world. This mistake is called 'the fallacy of misplaced concreteness'. Substances and things and so on are the result of processes that grow together and go on for a certain time. Concrete, actual entities are the stages of these processes at a given moment. As the processes go on, different actual entities appear. From an everyday perspective, a substance may thus go on to be the bearer of certain properties, although the actual entities give way to new entities, and the substances may disappear, although the processes go on to pass into new actual entities. The processes that constitute human persons are influenced by other processes in such a way as to apprehend those processes as unities in place and time. This is due to the special way in which processes in a human being prehend other processes, thus making cognition and knowledge possible.

Within the process of the change of actual entities or occasions there are recurrent structures that are prehended by an intelligent being as more or less stable units. These structures that appear only for the intellectual cognition are, I think, the eternal objects that determine special aspects of the entities within the ongoing process, similar to forms actualizing matter in an Aristotelian outlook. These eternal objects might be comparable to the 'strange attractors' of chaos theory, where processes show the same structure for some time, as for example in the case of a hurricane, but I do not know how helpful such comparisons may be. Further details of Whitehead's theory cannot be given here, for lack of time and competence. But I would like to say a few words about Whitehead's concept of God. God, according to Whitehead, is an actual entity, though not an actual occasion because He is outside the scheme of time. As there is a reason for the appearance of actual entities within the process only if there is an actual entity that initiates the following actual entities, there must be an actual entity that sets forth the whole process of creativity that brings new actual entities into being. This is God in His so called 'primordial nature'. The evolving states of the whole realm of actual entities are again prehended by God, thus forming His consequent nature. 'God is the infinite ground of all mentality, the unity of vision seeking physical multiplicity. The world is the multiplicity of finities, actualities seeking a perfected unity.'[7] God is not something like an unmoved mover but rather the act of all the potentialities that are conceived by Him. And He is finally the consumption of all the actualities. Whatever this exactly means, it seems clear to me that there is in principle something at work like a process-variant of Neoplatonic theology. This is nothing new about Whitehead and I want to leave things at this stage for the moment. The question now is, instead: what about time in a process-philosophy, about timelessness, endless time, and eternity?

10.6 Time and Process

Generally speaking and without direct relation to the differences between process-views and other ontological or metaphysical conceptions, time must be considered as an abstract entity similar to straight lines, plane surfaces and Euclidean space and the like. Arguments for this attitude can be derived from several occasions. In order to explain to a person what time is, I could not point at some special process within which all the other processes take place, although time has to do with such

---

[7] WHITEHEAD, *Process and Reality* [1969], p. 411. Quoted from: WOLF-GAZO, *Whitehead* [1980], p. 131. Where Wolf-Gazo quotes 'finities', the edition of 1969 has 'finites'.

processes.[8] I think time is a device introduced by us on the basis of equality relations between processes in order to be able to compare processes and to coordinate our activities. Processes take time, but they are not in time, although to say this is on a metaphorical level innocuous. They are not in time because time is neither a container nor a stream in which things drift, in addition to the things drifting. Time is invoked for two quite different types of problems.

First, there is the problem of coordinating the activities of people. The task is to make the activities coincide at certain occasions. The different processes constituting the activities must be directed in a way that makes cooperation possible because people effectively meet. This has been done by the use of processes that are accessible to all the participants and that are suitably structured. Clearly the rhythm of day and night, the annually recurrent seasons, lend themselves for such purposes. The processes are useful for the "timing" of activities. Thus, times are fixed and used for the coordination of activities. The devices and institutions that allow for the coordination of activities in this sense are not founded on time, but constitute it.

Second, there is the problem that activities of all sorts, processes and so on, "take time", which means that as long as I do something, some other possible activities are excluded. This could make it desirable to have a possibility to compare activities, and if the relevant activities cannot be done in parallel, one must find a means to compare the activities. A very obvious way to do this is to produce a repeatable process parallel to the process that has to be compared to the other process, and to compare the repeatable process to this other process. Here, the famous axiom of Euclides can be used,[9] or, to put it correctly, Euclides's axiom is the explicit formulation of a practice that had been widespread long before him.

But neither the processes to be measured nor the process used to measure other processes are time. Time as such is the equivalence between all these different processes. And this of course is a version of Frege's classical principle of abstraction. It is important to notice that such an abstraction does not create a new sort of entities in a strict sense, but mainly a way to treat entities of a quite different kind. This is just the same with numbers. Numbers, too, are not things in addition to the things counted, but just things counted without regarding the counted things. 'A number is the exponent of an operation.'[10] And time is the number of movement – or change – according to what comes first and what comes later.[11] That means that we create an ordinality over processes and events, and this ordinality we call time.

---

[8]   WITTGENSTEIN, *Tractatus* [1960], 6.3611: 'We cannot compare a process with 'the passage of time' – there is no such thing – but only with another process (such as the working of a chronometer).'

[9]   EUCLIDES, *Elementa* [1883], *Communes animi conceptiones* I.

[10] WITTGENSTEIN, *Tractatus* [1960], 6.021.

[11] ARISTOTLE, *Physics* IV.11 (219b1–2).

This creation of an ordinality over processes is, I think, a procedure of abstraction in a sense in which abstraction is introduced by Frege.[12]

The idea of time indicated here is close to that of Aristotle, which I think is not very far from many descriptions of time in contemporary philosophy. I think even that in this sense it is common to a substance metaphysics and a process theory of time. Aristotle's theory of time is compatible with a process theory of reality. It is – so I would say – much less compatible with a so-called Aristotelian metaphysics or ontology that takes substances – again under a special description or definition of 'substance' – as basic. Instead of seeing reality as blocks of substances and asking ourselves how there can be continuous change when there is an infinity of steps from every point within the process to the infinitely near next point,[13] we should take the processual character of reality seriously and see that a given stage of the process is due to a cut made by observers. If the time-slice is considered in itself, there is no way to restart the process, according to the argument of Zeno just mentioned, because we have to pass infinitely many points in order to arrive at the infinitely near next point for every point in the series. But if we realize that the slice is an abstract artifact, the question of how the process in reality can continue disappears. The process has been continuing in reality all the time.

The main difference between a process theory of the universe and a classical theory can be seen in the fact that, according to classical theory, God can know the course of the universe and even the future activities of human beings because they are in principle realized. Human beings do not know the future because they can take notice of the four-dimensional totality of the world only by exploring it step by step. But for a being of higher dimensions the whole world is one great closed unity. *Flatland* is a good model for that, which shows that a situation of that kind can well be imagined.

A process theory by contrast takes novelty seriously and rejects the idea that the universe could be conceived as a closed totality even from the point of view of alleged higher dimensions. The only totality that there is is the co-presence of a certain stage of all the processes at a certain moment. What is past is past, but remembered and kept present as an influencing phase that is prehended by the following phases, thus being taken over into the present stage of process that is the only actual reality. But as such and as a stage in a process, it is the starting point of the next actual entity by the concrescence of the different actualities constituting the actual world.

As a stage in the actual process, what is prehended in the present phase is past, but present in its effects, so to speak. And the present phase of actual entities will be prehended by future states, thus influencing those further stages. In this sense, future has memory and is thus foreseen by the present, because the present is

---

[12]   I think this is in line with KÜNNE, *Abstrakte Gegenstände* [1987]. At any rate, it is indebted to him. It is directly dependent on Paul Lorenzen, for example, LORENZEN, *Konstruktive Wissenschaftstheorie* [1987], pp. 161–9.

[13]   WHITEHEAD, *Process and Reality* [1969], pp. 84–5.

something that will be remembered by the future.[14] This memory can be a positive conservation of the past. In this sense God can know what happens in the future from what He set into development without the presupposition of a world as a static whole. This is so because God Himself sustains the productive activities of the real events and occasions to make them produce their results. God is invariably and unchangingly the aim of every activity of any kind of His creatures. This is according to Whitehead His primordial, but abstract, nature. On the other hand, He is with this nature present to every occasion and every entity in its concrete situation, thus offering different concrete goals for the occurrences in different stages of the process. In this so-called consequent nature He presents Himself differently to His creatures in different situations. God's eternity consists in His invariable and invariably different presence to His creatures throughout the whole process of the universe.

It is characteristic for Whitehead and for many other typical process philosophers, of whom I personally most appreciate the one analytical process philosopher I know, namely Nicholas Rescher, that they do not insist on dichotomies and mutual exclusions.[15] It is therefore not surprising that one can find the central issues of historical developments in their theories. The idea of an essentially evaluative, ordering, and attracting nature of God is not far from Aristotle's prime mover who moves 'sicut amatum et desideratum'.[16] It is also common to medieval philosophy and theology and can be found in Thomas Aquinas as well as in those who otherwise are critics of Aquinas. The idea that God is 'actus purus' can be understood in a process view as well as in a classical substance-metaphysics.

A concluding remark on the possibility of several ontologies: if we look at the relationship between the assumptions and suppositions of our everyday life and the different scientific enterprises, we can realize that quite often the events, processes and objects described and used or presupposed by the sciences are taken to be basic for all that can be known in our world, whereas the assumptions of our usual life are considered to be either erroneous or superstitious or at least and at best something like supervenient on these allegedly hard facts. But at a closer look we must inevitably admit that all that we can understand of the scientific results depends on the fact that we are in possession of a language that has its roots and functioning in everyday life. All our terms ultimately rest on linguistic or, in a broader sense, semiotic devices that gain their meaning out of the coordination of human activities among human beings. Within this social and communicative frame of coordinative activities there are those that lead to the execution of long-termed plans and projects. The formulation of such projects again presupposes the usual language of our daily life. But within the frame of such planned activities we need knowledge of the self-induced, so to say "natural", processes that lead from sets of states of affairs to different sets of states of affairs. In order to get systematic

---

[14] HARTSHORNE, *Das metaphysische System Whiteheads* [1980], p. 38.

[15] RESCHER, *Process Metaphysics* [1996].

[16] ARISTOTLE, *Metaphysics*, 12, c. 7 (1072b3s.). AVICENNA, *Liber de philosophia prima* [1977], 9, c. 3. 1980, 475.

knowledge of these processes and occurrences, we can and must develop languages that can serve to describe the changes of states of affair independently of human desires and goals as precisely as possible from a pure observer's point of view. These processes can then be taken into account for the procedures that are necessary in order to achieve the goals envisaged. On the basis of our everyday language we can understand the results of such researches and use them. But there is no way back from a purely observational language to the language of our everyday life, except by tacitly using precisely that language that is considered to rest on erroneous and superstitious assumptions. The point of view of physicalism cannot be formulated in a physicalistic language, and the uses to which the knowledge of physical and other facts can be brought and through which the scientific enterprise usually is justified, cannot be described in physical or physicist language. The neglect of this fact is due to the idea that languages and, as refinements, theories consist in syntactic structures that contain positions at which semantically interpreted elements can be introduced that allow consequently for some use to be introduced into the usual life of human or other beings. But the description as well as the construction of a syntax demands cooperation among theoreticians using meaningful advices and devices. Meaningful language starts with efforts to coordinate activities among living beings, giving hints to addressees as to what they are expected to do or what they should be aware of. Thus, utterances or other activities gain the value of signs with special content, which provides the activities with a semantic. The occurrences used as signs must be produced according to the constraints of the material, sounds for example must be produced in a series. This may lead to habits of production which at a certain level may be collected and described as a grammar or syntax for the signs.[17] The coordination of activities with other active people provides the pragmatic basis for semantically relevant devices, and these underlie standardization by habit, thus creating something like a normative grammar, which contains the paradigm for syntax.

The interesting task is, so it seems to me, to construct theories that show the relations between the different types of ontology and their relative merits.

---

[17] SCHNEIDER, *Pragmatik als Basis* [1975].

Bibliography

ABBOTT, EDWIN A. [1998]: *Flatland. A Romance of Many Dimensions*. Ed. A. Square. With ill. by the author and an introduction by Alan Lightman. Republ. of the 2nd, rev. edn 1884. New York: Penguin Books 1998.

ALBERT OF SAXONY [1999]: *Expositio et questiones in Aristotelis physicam ad Albertum de Saxonia attributae*. Ed. Benoît Patar. 3 vols (Philosophes médiévaux, vols 39–41). Louvain-la-Neuve: Peeters 1999.

ALSTON, WILLIAM P. [1988]: 'Divine and Human Action'. In Thomas V. Morris (ed.): *Divine and Human Action. Essays in the Metaphysics of Theism*. Ithaca: Cornell Univ. Press 1988, pp. 257–80.

ANSELM OF CANTERBURY [1968]: *De concordia praescientiae et praedestinationis et gratiae dei cum libero arbitrio*. In ANSELM, *Opera Omnia* [1968], vol. 2, pp. 243–88.

— [1968]: *Monologion*. In ANSELM, *Opera Omnia* [1968], vol. 1, pp. 1–87.

— [1968]: *Opera Omnia*. Ed. Franciscus Salesius Schmidt. 6 in 2 vols. Stuttgart: F. Frommann 1968.

— [1968]: *Proslogion*. In ANSELM, *Opera Omnia* [1968], vol. 1, pp. 89–122.

AQUINAS, THOMAS [1882]: *Sancti Thomae Aquinatis Opera Omnia iussu impensaque Leonis XIII P. M. edita*. Rome: Typographia Polyglotta 1882 ff.

— [1888]: *Summa theologiae*. In AQUINAS, *Opera Omnia* [1882], vols 4–12.

— [1918]: *Summa contra gentiles*. In AQUINAS, *Opera Omnia* [1882], vols 13–15.

— [1929]: *Scriptum super IV libros Sententiarum*. Vols I–II, ed. Pierre Mandonnet. Paris: Lethielleux 1929.

— [1952]: *Summa theologiae*. Ed. Pietro Cramello. 3 vols. Taurini: Marietti 1952–1962.

— [1954]: *In octo libros physicorum Aristotelis expositio*. Ed. Mariano Maggiòlo. Taurini: Marietti 1954.

— [1959]: *In Aristotelis librum de anima commentarium*. Ed. Angelo M. Pirotta. Taurini: Marietti 1959.

— [1964]: *Quaestiones disputatae de veritate*. In Thomas Aquinas: *Quaestiones disputatae*, vol. 1. Ed. Mariano Maggiòlo. Taurini: Marietti 1964.

AQUINAS, THOMAS [1965]: *Quaestiones disputatae de potentia*. In Thomas Aquinas: *Quaestiones disputatae*, vol. 2. Ed. Mariano Maggiòlo. Taurini: Marietti 1965.

— [1966]: *Commentary on Saint Paul's Epistle to the Galatians*. Trans. Fabian R. Larcher and introduction Richard Murphy (Aquinas Scripture Series, vol. 1). Albany: Magi Books 1966.

— [1980]: *Commentary on the Gospel of St. John. Part I*. Ed. James A. Weisheipl et al. Albany: Magi Books 1980.

— [2006]: *Summa theologiae*. Latin text and English trans., introductions, notes, appendices and glossaries. Ed. Thomas Gilby. Cambridge: Cambridge Univ. Press 2006.

ARISTOTLE [1987]: *Physik*. Greek text and German trans. Ed., trans., introduction, and notes Hans Günther Zekl. 2 vols. Hamburg: Meiner Verlag 1987–1988.

— [1989]: *Metaphysik*. Greek text and German trans. Trans. Hermann Bonitz. Ed., rev. trans., introduction, and commentary Horst Seidl. 2 vols. Hamburg: Meiner Verlag (3rd edn) 1989–1991.

AUGUSTINE OF HIPPO [1861]: *De genesi ad litteram*. Ed. Jacques-Paul Migne. (Patrologia Latina, vol. 34) Paris: Migne 1861.

— [1894]: *De genesi ad litteram*. Ed. Joseph Zycha. (Corpus Scriptorum Ecclesiasticorum Latinorum, vol. 28.1) Wien: Hoelder-Pichler-Tempsky 1894.

— [1968]: *De trinitate libri XV*. Ed. William J. Mountain. (Corpus Christianorum Series Latina, vol. 50a = Augustinus: *Opera*, vol. XVI,2) Turnhout: Brepols 1968.

— [1992]: *Confessiones*. Ed. and trans. Henry Chadwick. Oxford: Oxford Univ. Press 1992.

AVERROES [1961]: *Destructio destructionum philosophiae Algazelis. In the Latin version of Calo Calonymos*. Ed. Beatrice H. Zedler. Milwaukee: Marquette Univ. Press 1961.

AVICENNA [1977]: *Liber de philosophia prima sive scientia divina*. Ed. Simone van Riet. Leiden: Brill 1977–1983.

BALASHOV, YURI [2000]: 'Enduring and Perduring Objects in Minkowski Space-Time'. In *Philosophical Studies* 99 (2000), pp. 129–66.

BARTH, KARL [1957]: *Church Dogmatics. Vol. II/1, The Doctrine of God 1*. Eds Geoffrey W. Bromiley and Thomas F. Torrance. Edinburgh: T&T Clark 1957.

— [1987]: *Die kirchliche Dogmatik. Vol. II/1 Die Lehre von Gott 1*. Zürich: Theologischer Verlag 1987.

BERNHARDT, REINHOLD [1999]: *Was heißt 'Handeln Gottes'? Eine Rekonstruktion der Lehre von der Vorsehung Gottes*. Gütersloh: Gütersloher Verlagshaus 1999.

— [2002]: 'Offenbarung als Erschliessungsgeschehen'. In *Theologische Zeitschrift* 58 (2002), pp. 61–80.

BLOOM, HAROLD [1997]: *The Anxiety of Influence. A Theory of Poetry.* New York: Oxford Univ. Press (2nd edn) 1997.

BOETHIUS [1949]: *Consolationis philosophiae libri quinque / Trost der Philosophie.* Ed. Eberhard Gothein. Latin and German. Zürich: Artemis 1949.

— [1957]: *Philosophiae consolatio.* Ed. Ludwig Bieler. (Corpus Christianorum Series Latina, vol. 94) Turnhout: Brepols 1957.

— [1988]: *Quomodo trinitas unus deus ac non tres dii.* In Boethius: *Die theologischen Traktate.* Ed. Michael Elsässer. Hamburg: Meiner 1988, pp. 2–27.

— [2005]: *De consolatione philosophiae. Opuscula theologica.* Ed. Claudio Moreschini. München: K. G. Saur 2005.

BRUECKNER, ANTHONY [1985]: 'Skepticism and Epistemic Closure'. In *Philosophical Topics* 13 (1985), pp. 89–117.

— [1994]: 'The Structure of the Skeptical Argument'. In *Philosophy and Phenomenological Research* 45 (1994), pp. 827–35.

BURRELL, DAVID B. [1992]: 'Review of HUGHES, *Complex Theory* [1989]'. In *The Journal of Religion* 72 (1992), pp. 120–21.

CANTOR, GEORG [1932]: *Gesammelte Abhandlungen mathematischen und philosophischen Inhalts.* Ed. Ernst Zermelo. Berlin: Springer 1932.

CAROTI, STEFANO (ED.) [1994]: 'La position de Nicole Oresme sur la nature du mouvement (Questiones super physicam III, 1–8): Problèmes gnoséologiques, ontologiques et sémantiques'. In *Archives d'histoire doctrinale et littéraire du Moyen-âge* 61 (1994), pp. 303–85.

CLAGETT, MARSHALL (ED.) [1968]: *Nicole Oresme and the Medieval Geometry of Qualities and Motions. A Treatise on the Uniformity and Difformity of Intensities Known as Tractatus de configurationibus qualitatum et motuum.* Trans. Marshall Clagett (Publications in Medieval Science, vol. 12). Madison: Univ. of Wisconsin Press 1968.

CLAYTON, PHILIP D. [1997]: *God and Contemporary Science.* Grand Rapids: Eerdmans 1997.

COPAN, PAUL AND CRAIG, WILLIAM L. [2004]: *Creation Out of Nothing. A Biblical, Philosophical, and Scientific Exploration.* Grand Rapids: Baker Academic 2004.

CRAIG, WILLIAM L. [1994]: 'The Special Theory of Relativity and Theories of Divine Eternity'. In *Faith and Philosophy* 11 (1993), pp. 19–37.

— [1998]: 'The Tensed vs. the Tenseless Theory of Time. A Watershed for the Conception of Divine Eternity'. In Robin Le Poidevin (ed.): *Questions of Time and Tense.* Oxford: Oxford Univ. Press: 1998, pp. 221–50.

— [2001]: 'Timelessness and Omnitemporality'. In GANSSLE, *God & Time* [2001], pp. 129–60.

CRAIG, WILLIAM L. [2001]: *God, Time, and Eternity.* Dordrecht: Kluwer 2001.

— [2001]: *Time and Eternity. Exploring God's Relationship to Time.* Wheaton: Crossway Books 2001.

— [2009]: *Divine Eternity* In FLINT AND REA, *Oxford Handbook of Philosophical Theology* [2009], pp. 145–66.

CULLEN, CHRISTOPHER M. [2006]: *Bonaventure.* New York: Oxford Univ. Press 2006.

CULLMANN, OSCAR [1950]: *Christ and Time. The Primitive Christian Conception of Time and History.* Trans. Floyd Vivian Filson. Philadelphia: Westminster Press 1950.

DALFERTH, INGOLF ULRICH [1997]: *Gedeutete Gegenwart. Zur Wahrnehmung Gottes in den Erfahrungen der Zeit.* Tübingen: Mohr Siebeck 1997.

DAVIES, BRIAN [1993]: *An Introduction to the Philosophy of Religion.* Oxford: Oxford Univ. Press 1993.

— [1998]: *Philosophy of Religion. A Guide to the Subject.* Washington: Georgetown Univ. Press 1998.

— [2000]: *Philosophy of Religion. A Guide and Anthology.* Oxford: Oxford Univ. Press 2000.

DESCARTES, RENÉ [1897]: *Oeuvres de Descartes.* Eds Charles Adam and Paul Tannery. Paris: Cerf 1897–1913.

DEWEESE, GARRETT J. [2004]: *God and the Nature of Time.* Aldershot: Ashgate 2004.

DOOLAN, GREGORY T. (ED.) [2011]: *The Science of Being as Being. Metaphysical Investigations.* Washington: Catholic University Press 2011.

DUMMETT, MICHAEL [2006]: *Truth and the Past.* New York: Columbia University Press 2006.

DUNS SCOTUS, JOHN [1950]: *Lectura in librum primum sententiarum.* In DUNS SCOTUS, *Opera Omnia* [1950], vols 16–17.

— [1950]: *Opera Omnia.* Eds Carolo Balic et al. Civitas Vaticana: Typis Polyglottis Vaticanis 1950 ff.

— [1950]: *Ordinatio. Liber primus.* In DUNS SCOTUS, *Opera Omnia* [1950], vols 2–6.

— [1994]: *Contingency and Freedom.* Introduction, trans. and commentary by Antonie Vos. Dordrecht: Kluwer 1994.

EINSTEIN, ALBERT [1907]: 'Über das Relativitätsprinzip und die aus demselben gezogenen Folgerungen'. In *Jahrbuch der Radioaktivität und Elektronik* 4 (1907), pp. 411–62.

— [1909]: 'Über die Entwicklung unserer Anschauungen über das Wesen und die Konstitution der Strahlung'. In *Physikalische Zeitschrift* 10,22 (1909), pp. 817–25.

EINSTEIN, ALBERT [1911]: 'Die Relativitäts-Theorie'. In *Vierteljahrsschrift der naturforschenden Gesellschaft in Zürich* 56 (1911), pp. 1–14.

— [1920]: *Relativity, the Special and the General Theory.* Trans. Robert William Lawson. London: Methuen 1920.

— [1967]: 'Fundamental Ideas and Problems of the Theory of Relativity'. In *Nobel Lectures, Physics: 1901–1921.* New York: Elsevier 1967.

— [1967]: *The Meaning of Relativity.* 1922 rep. ed. London: Chapman and Hall (6th edn) 1967.

— [1981]: 'On the Electrodynamics of Moving Bodies'. Trans. Arthur I. Miller. Appendix to Arthur I. Miller: *Albert Einstein's Special Theory of Relativity* Reading: Addison-Wesley 1981.

ELDERS, LEO [1990]: *The Philosophical Theology of St. Thomas Aquinas.* Leiden: Brill 1990.

ERNST, JOSEF [1995]: 'Ewigkeit II. Im Verständnis der Schrift'. In *Lexikon für Theologie und Kirche.* Freiburg: Herder (3rd edn) 1995, vol. 3, col. 1083.

EUCLIDES [1883]: *Elementa I.* Ed. Johann L. Heiberg. Leipzig: Teubner 1883.

FALES, EVAN [2009]: *Divine Intervention – Metaphysical and Epistemological Puzzles.* New York: Routledge 2009.

— [forthcoming]: *Is Middle Knowledge Possible?* Manuscript (2010), forthcoming.

FINDLAY, JOHN N. [1978]: 'Time and Eternity'. In *Review of Metaphysics* 32 (1978), pp. 3–14.

FISCHER, JOHN M. [1994]: *The Metaphysics of Free Will An Essay on Control.* Oxford: Blackwell 1994.

— [2008]: 'Molinism'. In KVANVIG, *Philosophy of Religion* [2008], pp. 18–43.

FISCHER, JOHN M. AND RAVIZZA, MARK [1998]: *Responsibility and Control. A Theory of Moral Responsibility.* Cambridge: Cambridge Univ. Press 1998.

FISCHER, NORBERT AND HATTRUP, DIETER (EDS) [2006]: *Schöpfung, Zeit und Ewigkeit. Augustinus* Confessiones *11–13.* Paderborn: Schöningh 2006.

FLINT, THOMAS P. AND REA, MICHAEL C. (EDS) [2009]: *Oxford Handbook of Philosophical Theology* Oxford: Oxford Univ. Press 2009.

FLOGAUS, REINHARD [1997]: *Theosis bei Palamas und Luther. Ein Beitrag zum ökumenischen Gespräch.* (Forschungen zur systematischen und ökumenischen Theologie, vol. 78.) Göttingen: Vandenhoeck und Ruprecht 1997.

FREDDOSO, ALFRED [1988]: 'Introduction'. In FREDDOSO, *Molina: On Divine Foreknowledge* [1988], pp. 1–81.

FREDDOSO, ALFRED (ED.) [1983]: *The Existence and Nature of God.* Notre Dame: Univ. of Notre Dame Press 1983.

— [1988]: *Luis de Molina: On Divine Foreknowledge. Part IV of the Concordia.* Ithaca: Cornell Univ. Press 1988.

FRETHEIM, TERENCE [1994]: 'Genesis'. In Leander E. Keck et al. (eds): *The New Interpreter's Bible.* Vol. 1. Nashville: Abingdon 1994.

GANSSLE, GREGORY E. (ED.) [2001]: *God & Time. Four Views.* Downers Grove: InterVarsity Press 2001.

GANSSLE, GREGORY E. AND WOODRUFF, DAVID M. (EDS) [2002]: *God and Time. Essays on the Divine Nature.* Oxford: Oxford Univ. Press 2002.

GEACH, PETER T. [1969]: *God and the Soul.* London: Routledge 1969.

GOODMAN, NELSON [1976]: *Languages of Art. An Approach to a Theory of Symbols.* Indianapolis: Hackett (2nd edn) 1976.

HAIGHT, ROGER [1999]: *Jesus. Symbol of God.* Maryknoll: Orbis 1999.

HALES, STEPHEN [1995]: 'Epistemic Closure Principles'. In *The Southern Journal of Philosophy* 33 (1995), pp. 185–201.

HARTSHORNE, CHARLES [1980]: 'Das metaphysische System Whiteheads'. In WOLF-GAZO, *Whitehead* [1980], pp. 28–44.

HASKER, WILLIAM [1989]: *God, Time, and Knowledge.* Ithaca: Cornell Univ. Press 1989.

— [2002]: *The Absence of a Timeless God.* In GANSSLE AND WOODRUFF, *God and Time* [2002], pp. 182–206.

HAYES, ZACHARY [1976]: 'Incarnation and Creation in the Theology of St. Bonaventure'. In Romano S. Almagno et al. (eds): *Studies Honoring Ignatius Charles Brady, Friar Minor, St. Bonaventure.* New York: The Franciscan Institute 1976, pp. 309–30.

HEGEL, GEORG WILHELM FRIEDRICH [1995]: *Vorlesungen über die Philosophie der Religion. Vol. 3: Die vollendete Religion.* Ed. Walter Jaeschke. Hamburg: Meiner 1995.

HEIDEGGER, MARTIN [1989]: *Beiträge zur Philosophie. Vom Ereignis.* In Martin Heidegger: *Gesamtausgabe.* Vol. 65. Ed. Friedrich-Wilhelm von Hermann. Frankfurt a. M.: Vittorio Klostermann 1989.

HELM, PAUL [1988]: *Eternal God. A Study of God without Time.* Oxford: Clarendon Press 1988.

— [1998]: 'Eternality'. In DAVIES, *Philosophy of Religion* [1998], pp. 75–9.

— [2000]: 'A different modern defence of divine eternity'. In DAVIES, *Philosophy of Religion* [2000], pp. 519–31.

HELM, PAUL [2001]: 'Divine Timeless Eternity'. In GANSSLE, *God & Time* [2001], pp. 28–60.

HODGSON, PETER C. [1989]: *God in History. Shapes of Freedom.* Nashville: Abingdon Press 1989.

— [1994]: *Winds of Spirit. A Constructive Christian Theology.* Louisville: Westminster/Knox 1994.

HOLTON, GERALD J. [1970]: 'Mach, Einstein and the Search for Reality'. In Robert S. Cohen et al. (eds): *Ernst Mach. Physicist and Philosopher* (Boston Studies in the Philosophy of Science, vol. 6). Dordrecht: Reidel 1970, pp. 165–99.

— [1971]: 'Where Is Reality? The Answers of Einstein'. In *Science and Synthesis.* Ed. UNESCO. New York: Springer 1971, pp. 45–69.

— [1973]: 'On the Origins of the Special Theory of Relativity'. In HOLTON, *Scientific Thought* [1973], pp. 165–83.

— [1973]: *Thematic Origins of Scientific Thought. Kepler to Einstein.* Cambridge: Harvard Univ. Press 1973.

HUGHES, CHRISTOPHER [1989]: *On a Complex Theory of a Simple God. An Investigation in Aquinas' Philosophical Theology.* Ithaca: Cornell Univ. Press 1989.

ILLY, JOZSEF [1989]: 'Einstein Teaches Lorentz, Lorentz Teaches Einstein. Their Collaboration in General Relativity, 1913–1920'. In *Archive for History of Exact Sciences* 39 (1989), pp. 247–89.

JANTZEN, GRACE M. [1984]: *God's World, God's Body.* Philadelphia: Westminster Press 1984.

JENSON, ROBERT W. [1982]: *The Triune Identity. God According to the Gospel.* Philadelphia: Fortress Press 1982.

JOHN DAMASCENE [1955]: *De fide orthodoxa.* Ed. Eligius M. Buytaert. St Bonaventure: Franciscan Institute 1955.

JOHN WYCLIF [1891]: *De ente praedicamentali.* Ed. Rudolf Beer. London: Trubner 1891.

JORDAN, MARK D. [1983]: 'The Names of God and the Being of Names'. In FREDDOSO, *Existence and Nature of God* [1983], pp. 161–90.

JÜNGEL, EBERHARD [1999]: 'Ewigkeit III. Dogmatisch'. In *Religion in Geschichte und Gegenwart. Handwörterbuch für Theologie und Religionswissenschaft.* Tübingen: Mohr-Siebeck (4th edn) 1999, vol. 2, cols 1774–6.

KANT, IMMANUEL [1996]: *Writings on Religion and Rational Theology.* Trans. and ed. Allan W. Wood et al. Cambridge: Cambridge Univ. Press 1996.

KASPER, WALTER [2005]: *The God of Jesus Christ.* New York: Herder and Herder 1984 (reprint 2005).

KEANE, KEVIN P. [1975]: 'Why Creation? Bonaventure and Thomas Aquinas on God as Creative Good'. In *Downside Review* 93 (1975), pp. 100–121.

KIERKEGAARD, SØREN [1952]: *Der Begriff Angst*. In Søren Kierkegaard: *Gesammelte Werke*. Ed. and trans. Emanuel Hirsch. Vol. 11/12. Düsseldorf: Diederichs 1952.

KLEINKNECHT, REINHARD [1996]: 'Phänomenale und wirkliche Zeit'. In Alfred Schramm (ed.): *Philosophie in Österreich*. Wien: Hölder-Pichler-Tempsky 1996, pp. 77–90.

KÖNIG, JOHANN FRIEDRICH [2006]: *Theologia positiva acroamatica*. Ed. and trans. Andreas Stegmann based on the 17th edn 1775. (Beiträge zur historischen Theologie, vol. 137) Tübingen: Mohr Siebeck 2006..

KREINER, ARMIN [2006]: *Das wahre Antlitz Gottes. Oder was wir meinen, wenn wir Gott sagen*. Freiburg: Herder 2006.

KRÖTKE, WOLF [2001]: *Gottes Klarheiten. Eine Neuinterpretation der Lehre von Gottes "Eigenschaften"*. Tübingen: Mohr Siebeck 2001.

KÜNNE, WOLFGANG [1987]: *Abstrakte Gegenstände: Semantik und Ontologie*. Frankfurt a. M.: Suhrkamp 1987.

KVANVIG, JONATHAN L. (ED.) [2008]: *Oxford Studies in Philosophy of Religion*. Vol. 1. Oxford: Oxford University Press 2008.

LEFTOW, BRIAN [1991]: *Time and Eternity*. Ithaca: Cornell Univ. Press 1991.

— [2001]: 'Parts, Wholes, and Eternity'. In Nathan L. Oaklander (ed.): *The Importance of Time. Proceedings of the Philosophy of Time Society, 1995-2000*. Dordrecht: Kluwer 2001, pp. 199–206.

— [2002]: 'The Eternal Present'. In GANSSLE AND WOODRUFF, *God and Time* [2002], pp. 21–48.

— [2003]: 'Eternity'. In TALIAFERRO AND GRIFFITHS, *Philosophy of Religion* [2003], pp. 73–77.

— [2005]: 'Eternity and Immutability'. In MANN, *Blackwell guide to philosophy of religion* [2005], pp. 48–77.

— [2010]: 'Eternity'. In TALIAFERRO ET AL., *Companion to Philosophy of Religion* [2010], pp. 278–84.

LEIBNIZ, GOTTFRIED WILHELM [1956]: *The Leibniz-Clarke Correspondence*. Ed. Henry G. Alexander. Manchester: Manchester Univ. Press 1956.

LEWIS, DAVID K. [1981]: 'Are We Free to Break the Laws?'. In *Theoria* 47 (1981), pp. 113–21, repr. in David K. Lewis: *Philosophical Papers*. Vol. 2, New York: Oxford Univ. Press 1986, pp. 291–9.

— [1986]: 'Extrinsic Properties'. In *Philosophical Studies* 44 (1983), pp. 197–200.

LEWIS, DAVID K. [1986]: *On the Plurality of Worlds.* London: Blackwell 1986.

LEWIS, DELMAS [1988]: 'Eternity, Time and Tenselessness'. In *Faith and Philosophy* 5 (1988), pp. 72–86.

LODZINSKI, DON [1998]: 'The Eternal Act'. In *Religious Studies* 34 (1998), pp. 325–52.

LOMBARD, PETER [1971]: *Sententiae in IV libris distinctae.* Grottaferrata: Collegium S. Bonaventurae 1971–1981.

LORENZEN, PAUL [1987]: *Lehrbuch der konstruktiven Wissenschaftstheorie.* Mannheim: BI-Wissenschaftsverlag 1987.

LOUX, MICHAEL J. [2002]: *Metaphysics. A Contemporary Introduction.* London: Routledge (2nd edn) 2002.

LOWE, E. JONATHAN [2009]: *A Survey of Metaphysics.* Oxford: Oxford University Press 2002 (reprint 2009).

LUDLOW, PETER / NAGASAWA, YUJIN / STOLJAR, DANIEL (EDS) [2004]: *There's Something About Mary. Essays on Phenomenal Consciousness and Frank Jackson's Knowledge Argument.* Cambridge: MIT Press 2004.

MANN, WILLIAM E. [2005]: *The Blackwell Guide to the Philosophy of Religion.* Malden: Blackwell 2005.

MARKOSIAN, NED [2004]: 'A Defense of Presentism'. In Dean W. Zimmerman (ed.): *Oxford Studies in Metaphysics.* Vol. 1. Oxford: Clarendon Press 2004, pp. 47–82.

MCFAGUE, SALLIE [1993]: *The Body of God. An Ecological Theology.* Minneapolis: Fortress Press 1993.

MCKENNA, MICHAEL [2001]: 'Source Incompatibilism, Ultimacy, and the Transfer of Non-Responsibility'. In *American Philosophical Quarterly* 38 (2001), pp. 37–51.

— [2008]: 'Saying Goodbye to the Direct Argument the Right Way'. In *Philosophical Review* 117 (2008), pp. 349–83.

MOLINA, LUIS DE [1953]: *Liberi arbitrii cum gratiae donis, divina praescientia, providentia, praedestinatione et reprobatione concordia.* Critical edn of the second edn from 1595. Ed. Johann Rabeneck. Oña & Madrid: Collegium Maximum 1953.

— [1988]: *Concordia. Part IV.* In FREDDOSO, *Molina: On Divine Foreknowledge* [1988].

MOORE, DEREK / HOBSON, PETER / LEE, ANTHONY [1997]: 'Components of Person Perception. An Investigation With Autistic, Non-autistic Retarded and Typically Developing Children and Adolescents'. In *British Journal of Developmental Psychology* 15 (1997), pp. 401–23.

MORE, HENRY [1671]: *Enchiridion metaphysicum. Sive, de rebus incorporeis succincta et luculenta dissertatio.* London 1671.

MORRIS, THOMAS V. [1986]: *The Logic of God Incarnate*. Ithaca: Cornell Univ. Press 1986.

MÜHLING, MARKUS [2005]: 'Ewigkeitsauffassungen. Die Aporien der exemplarischen Ver-hältnisbestimmungen von Zeit und Ewigkeit bei Augustin, Boethius und Swinburne und trinitarische Lösungswege'. In *Neue Zeitschrift für systematische Theologie und Religions-philosophie* 47 (2005), pp. 154–72.

— [2007]: *Grundinformation Eschatologie. Systematische Theologie aus der Perspektive der Hoffnung.* Göttingen: Vandenhoeck und Ruprecht 2007.

NEWTON, ISAAC [1966]: *Sir Isaac Newton's Mathematical Principles of Natural Philosophy and his System of the World.* Trans. Andrew Motte, rev. edn with an appendix by Florian Cajori. 2 vols. Los Angeles: Univ. of California Press (6th edn) 1966.

— [1978]: 'Place, Time, and God'. In James E. McGuire: 'Newton on Place, Time, and God. An Unpublished Source' *British Journal for the History of Science* 11 (1978), pp. 114–29.

OAKLANDER, L. NATHAN (ED.) [2001]: *The Importance of Time. Proceedings to the Philosophy of Time Society, 1995–2000.* Dordrecht: Kluwer 2001.

O'CONNOR, TIMOTHY [2002]: *Persons and Causes. The Metaphysics of Free Will.* New York: Oxford Univ. Press 2002.

NICOLE ORESME [1968]: *Tractatus de configurationibus qualitatum et motuum.* In CLAGETT, *Nicole Oresme and the Medieval Geometry* [1968].

— [1994]: *Questiones super physicam. III, 1–8.* In CAROTI, *La position de Nicole Oresme* [1994].

PADGETT, ALAN G. [1992]: *God, Eternity and the Nature of Time.* New York: St. Martin's Press 1992.

— [1993]: 'Eternity and the Special Theory of Relativity'. In *International Philosophical Quarterly* 33 (1993), pp. 219–23.

— [2007]: 'Eternity'. In Chad Meister et al. (eds): *The Routledge Companion to Philosophy of Religion.* London: Routledge 2007, pp. 287–95.

PANNENBERG, WOLFHART [1988]: *Systematische Theologie I.* Göttingen: Vandenhoeck & Ruprecht 1988.

— [1991]: *Systematic Theology.* Vol. 1. Trans. Geoffrey W. Bromiley. Grand Rapids: Eerd-mans 1991.

— [2001]: 'Unendlichkeit'. In *Historisches Wörterbuch der Philosophie.* Vol. 11. Basel: Schwabe 2001, cols 140–46.

PASNAU, ROBERT [2011]: *Metaphysical Themes 1274–1671.* Oxford: Clarendon Press 2011.

PEACOCKE, ARTHUR [1993]: *Theology for a Scientific Age. Being and Becoming-Natural, Divine, and Human.* Minneapolis: Fortress Press 1993.

PIKE, NELSON [1970]: *God and Timelessness*. London: Routledge & Kegan Paul 1970.

PINNOCK, CLARK / RICE, RICHARD / SANDERS, JOHN / HASKER, WILLIAM / BASINGER, DAVID [1994]: *The Openness of God. A Biblical Challenge to the Traditional Understanding of God*. Downers Grove: InterVarsity Press 1994.

PLANTINGA, ALVIN [1986]: 'On Ockham's Way Out'. In *Faith and Philosophy* 3 (1986), pp. 235–69.

— [2000]: *Warranted Christian Belief*. New York: Oxford Univ. Press 2000.

PLOTINUS [1951]: *Enneades*. In Plotinus: *Opera*. Eds Paul Henry et al. Paris: Desclée de Brouwer 1951–1973, vols 1–3.

POINCARÉ, HENRI [1982]: 'The Measure of Time'. In Henri Poincaré: *The Foundations of Science*. Ed. and trans. George B. Halstead. Washington, D.C.: Univ. Press of America 1982, pp. 235–69.

QUINE, WILLARD VAN ORMAN [1970]: *Philosophy of Logic*. Englewood Cliffs: Prentice-Hall 1970.

QUINN, PHILIP L. AND TALIAFERRO, CHARLES [2004]: *A Companion to Philosophy of Religion*. Oxford 1997 (reprint 2004).

RAHNER, KARL [1967]: 'Zur Theologie des Symbols'. In Karl Rahner: *Schriften zur Theologie*. Vol. 4. Einsiedeln: Benzinger (5th edn) 1967, pp. 275–311.

— [1970]: *The Trinity*. London: Burnes and Oates 1970.

RAVIZZA, MARK [1994]: 'Semi-Compatibilism and the Transfer of Nonresponsibility'. In *Philosophical Studies* 75 (1994), pp. 61–93.

RESCHER, NICHOLAS [1996]: *Process Metaphysics. An Introduction to Process Philosophy*. New York: State Univ. of New York Press 1996.

ROGERS, KATHERIN A. [1996]: 'Omniscience, Eternity, and Freedom'. In *International Philosophical Quarterly* 36 (1996), pp. 399–412.

— [1997]: *The Anselmian Approach to God and Creation*. Lewiston: Edwin Mellen Press 1997.

— [2006]: 'Anselm on Eternity as the Fifth Dimension'. In *Saint Anselm Journal* 3 (2006), pp. 1–8.

ROZEMOND, MARLEEN [2003]: 'Descartes on Mind-Body Union and Holenmerism'. In *Philosophical Topics* 31 (2003), pp. 343–67.

RUCKER, RUDY [1984]: *The Fourth Dimension. A Guided Tour of the Higher Universes*. Boston: Houghton Mifflin 1984.

RUSSELL, ROBERT J. [2002]: 'Bodily Resurrection, Eschatology, and Scientific Cosmology'. In Ted Peters et al. (eds): *Resurrection. Theological and Scientific Assessments*. Cambridge: Eerdmans 2002, pp. 3–30.

SANSBURY, TIMOTHY N. [2006]: *Divine Temporal Transcendence. A Defense of the Traditional Theological Position in Science, Philosophy, and Theology*. PhD thesis. Princeton Theological Seminary 2006.

SAUNDERS, NICHOLAS [2002]: *Divine Action and Modern Science*. Cambridge: Cambridge Univ. Press 2002.

SCHÄRTL, THOMAS [2007]: 'Zeichen der Freundschaft mit Gott. Konturen einer christologischen Denkform'. In Thomas Fliethmann et al. (eds): *'Freunde habe ich Euch genannt'. Freundschaft als Leitbegriff systematischer Theologie*. Berlin: Lit-Verlag 2007, pp. 83–110.

SCHLEIERMACHER, DANIEL FRIEDRICH ERNST [1960]: *Der christliche Glaube. Nach den Grundsätzen der evangelischen Kirche im Zusammenhange dargestellt*. Ed. Martin Redeker. Berlin: Walter De Gruyter (7th edn) 1960.

SCHNEIDER, HANS JULIUS [1975]: *Pragmatik als Basis von Semantik und Syntax*. Frankfurt a. M.: Suhrkamp 1975.

SCHÖNBERGER, ROLF AND NICKL, PETER (EDS) [2000]: *Bonaventura, Thomas von Aquin, Boethius von Dacien. Über die Ewigkeit der Welt*. Introduction Rolf Schönberger. Trans. Peter Nickl. Frankfurt a. M.: Vittorio Klostermann 2000.

SENOR, THOMAS D. [2009]: 'The Real Presence of an Eternal God'. In Kevin Timpe (ed.): *Metaphysics and God. Essays in Honor of Eleonore Stump*. New York: Routledge 2009, pp. 39–59.

SHANLEY, BRIAN J. [2002]: *The Thomist Tradition*. Dordrecht: Kluwer 2002.

SIMONS, PETER [1998]: 'Metaphysical Systematics. A Lesson from Whitehead'. In *Erkenntnis* 48 (1998), pp. 377–93.

SPAEMANN, ROBERT [2007]: *Der letzte Gottesbeweis. Mit einer Einführung in die großen Gottesbeweise und einem Kommentar zum Gottesbeweis Robert Spaemanns von Rolf Schönberger*. München: Pattloch 2007.

STRAWSON, PETER F. [1987]: *Individuals. An Essay in Descriptive Metaphysics*. London: Methuen 1965 (reprint 1987).

STUMP, ELEONORE [1993]: *Reasoned faith. Essays in philosophical theology in honor of Norman Kretzmann*. Ithaca: Cornell Univ. Press 1993.

— [2000]: 'The Direct Argument for Incompatibilism'. In *Philosophy and Phenomenological Research* 61 (2000), pp. 459–66.

— [2002]: 'Control and Causal Determinism'. In Sarah Buss et al. (eds): *Contours of Agency. Essays on Themes of Harry Frankfurt*. Cambridge: MIT Press 2002.

STUMP, ELEONORE [2003]: *Aquinas*. London: Routledge 2003.

— [2008]: 'Presence and Omnipresence'. In Paul Weithman (ed.): *Liberal Faith. Essays in Honor of Philip Quinn*. Notre Dame: Univ. of Notre Dame Press 2008, pp. 59–82.

STUMP, ELEONORE AND FISCHER, JOHN M. [2000]: 'Transfer Principles and Moral Responsibility'. In *Philosophical Perspectives* 14 (2000), pp. 47–55.

STUMP, ELEONORE AND KRETZMANN, NORMAN [1981]: 'Eternity'. In *The Journal of Philosophy* 78 (1981), pp. 429–58.

— [1987]: 'Atemporal Duration. A Reply to Fitzgerald'. In *Journal of Philosophy* 84 (1987), pp. 214–19.

— [1987]: 'Eternity'. In Thomas V. Morris (ed.): *The Concept of God*. Oxford: Oxford Univ. Press 1987, pp. 219–52.

— [1992]: 'Eternity, Awareness, and Action'. In *Faith and Philosophy* 9 (1992), pp. 463–82.

— [2000]: 'A Modern Defence of Divine Eternity'. In DAVIES, *Philosophy of Religion* [2000], pp. 505–18.

SUÁREZ, FRANCISCO [1866]: *Disputationes metaphysicae*. Paris: Vivès 1866.

SUCHOCKI, MARJORIE H. [1994]: *The Fall to Violence. Original Sin in Relational Theology*. New York: Continuum 1994.

SUPPE, FREDERICK [1977]: 'The Search for Philosophical Understanding of Scientific Theories'. In Frederick Suppe (ed.): *The Structure of Scientific Theories*. Urbana: Univ. of Illinois Press (2nd edn) 1977, pp. 1-241.

SWINBURNE, RICHARD [1993]: 'God and Time'. In STUMP, *Reasoned faith* [1993], pp. 204–22.

— [1993]: *The Coherence of Theism*. Oxford: Oxford Univ. Press (2nd edn) 1993.

— [1994]: *The Christian God*. Oxford: Oxford Univ. Press 1994.

TALIAFERRO, CHARLES [1998]: *Contemporary Philosophy of Religion. An Indroduction*. Malden: Blackwell 1998.

TALIAFERRO, CHARLES AND GRIFFITH, PAUL J. (EDS) [2003]: *Philosophy of Religion. An Anthology*. Malden: Blackwell 2003.

TALIAFERRO, CHARLES / DRAPER, PAUL / QUINN, PHILIP L. (EDS) [2010]: *A Companion to Philosophy of Religion*. Malden: Blackwell (2nd edn) 2010.

TAPP, CHRISTIAN [2005]: 'On Some Philosophical Aspects of the Background to Georg Cantor's Theory of Sets'. In *Philosophica Scientiae* special vol. no. 5 (2005), pp. 157–73.

— [2005]: *Kardinalität und Kardinäle*. (Boethius, vol. 53) Stuttgart: Steiner 2005.

Tapp, Christian [2010]: 'Joseph Ratzinger on Resurrection Identity'. In Georg Gasser (ed.): *Personal Identity and Resurrection. How Do We Survive Our Death?* Farnham: Ashgate 2010, pp. 207–24.

Torrance, Alexis [2009]: 'Precedents for Palamas' Essence-Energies Theology in the Cappadocian Fathers'. In *Vigiliae Christianae* 63 (2009), pp. 47–70.

van Inwagen, Peter [1983]: *An Essay on Free Will.* Oxford: Oxford Univ. Press 1983.

— [2008]: 'What Does an Omniscient Being Know About the Future?'. In Kvanvig, *Philosophy of Religion* [2008], pp. 216–30.

Warfield, Ted [1996]: 'Determinism and Moral Responsibility Are Incompatible'. In *Philosophical Topics* 24 (1996), pp. 215–26.

Weatherson, Brian [2006]: 'Intrinsic vs. Extrinsic Properties'. In *The Stanford Encyclopedia of Philosophy* (online resource). 2006.

Wendebourg, Dorothea [1980]: *Geist oder Energie. Zur Frage der innergöttlichen Verankerung des christlichen Lebens in der byzantinischen Theologie.* München: Chr. Kaiser 1980.

Westphal, Jonathan [2003]: 'A New Way With the Consequence Argument, and the Fixity of the Laws'. In *Analysis* 63 (2003), pp. 208–12.

Wettstein, Howard [2008]: 'Against Theology'. In Charles Manekin et al. (eds): *Philosophers and the Jewish Bible.* College Park: Univ. Press of Maryland 2008, pp. 218–245.

Whitehead, Alfred North [1969]: *Process and Reality. An Essay in Cosmology.* New York: Macmillan 1969.

Widerker, David [1987]: 'On an Argument for Incompatibilism'. In *Analysis* 47 (1987), pp. 37–41.

Wiles, Maurice [1982]: 'Continuing the Discussion'. In *Theology* 85 (1982), pp. 10–13.

— [1989]: 'In What Contexts Does It Make Sense to Say, "God Acts in History?"'. In Philip E. Devenish et al. (eds): *Witness and Existence. Essays in Honor of Schubert M. Ogden.* Chicago: Univ. of Chicago Press 1989, pp. 190–199.

William of Sherwood [1995]: *Introductiones in logicam.* Eds Hartmut Brands et al. Latin text and German trans. Hamburg: Meiner 1995.

Wittgenstein, Ludwig [1960]: *Tractatus logico-philosophicus.* London: Routledge & Kegan Paul (8th edn) 1960.

Wolf-Gazo, Ernest (ed.) [1980]: *Whitehead. Einführung in seine Kosmologie.* Freiburg: Alber 1980.

Wolterstorff, Nicholas [1975]: 'God Everlasting'. In Clifton Orlebeke et al. (eds): *God and the Good. Essays in Honor of Henry Stob.* Grand Rapids: Eerdmans 1975, pp. 181–203.

WOLTERSTORFF, NICHOLAS [2000]: 'God is "everlasting", not "eternal"'. In DAVIES, *Philosophy of Religion* [2000], pp. 485–504.

— [2001]: 'Unqualified Divine Temporality'. In GANSSLE, *God & Time* [2001], pp. 187–213.

WRIGHT, JOHN EDWARD [2006]: 'Cosmogony, Cosmology'. In Katharine D. Sakenfeld et al.: *New Interpreter's Dictionary of the Bible*. Vol. 1. Nashville: Abingdon 2006, pp. 755–63.

YANDELL, KEITH E. [1999]: *Philosophy of Religion. A Contemporary Introduction*. London: Routledge 1999.

YANNARAS, CHRISTOS [1975]: 'The Distincion Between Essence and Energies and its Importance for Theology'. In *St. Vladimir's Theological Quarterly* 19 (1975), pp. 232–45.

ZAGZEBSKI, LINDA [1991]: *The Dilemma of Freedom and Foreknowledge*. New York: Oxford Univ. Press 1991.

— [2002]: 'Recent Work on Divine Foreknowledge and Free Will'. In Robert Kane (ed.): *The Oxford Handbook of Free Will*. Oxford: Oxford Univ. Press 2002, pp. 45–64.

ZIMMERMAN, DEAN W. [2002]: 'God Inside Time and Before Creation'. In GANSSLE AND WOODRUFF, *God and Time* [2002], pp. 75–94.

Sigla

In DA	THOMAS AQUINAS: *Sentencia libri De anima*
In Gal.	THOMAS AQUINAS: *In/Super epistolam beati Pauli ad Galatas lectura*
In Sent.	THOMAS AQUINAS: *Scriptum super Sententiis*
QDP	THOMAS AQUINAS: *Quaestiones disputatae de potentia*
QDV	THOMAS AQUINAS: *Quaestiones disputatae de veritate*
SCG	THOMAS AQUINAS: *Summa contra gentiles*
STh	THOMAS AQUINAS: *Summa theologiae*

Index